**TO CONTEST WITH
ALL THE POWERS
OF DARKNESS**

TO CONTEST WITH ALL THE POWERS OF DARKNESS

NEW ENGLAND BAPTISTS,
RELIGIOUS LIBERTY, AND
NEW POLITICAL LANDSCAPES,
1740–1833

Jacob E. Hicks

America's Baptists
Keith Harper • Series Editor

THE UNIVERSITY OF TENNESSEE PRESS / KNOXVILLE

Copyright © 2024 by The University of Tennessee Press / Knoxville.
All Rights Reserved. Manufactured in the United States of America.
First Edition.

Library of Congress Cataloging-in-Publication Data

Names: Hicks, Jacob E., 1985- author.

Title: To contest with all the powers of darkness : New England Baptists, religious liberty, and new political landscapes, 1740-1833 / Jacob E. Hicks, Keith Harper.

Description: First edition. | Knoxville : The University of Tennessee Press, [2024] | Series: America's baptists | Includes bibliographical references and index. | Summary: "This book examines the ecclesiological and political networks that John Leland (1754-1833) and other Baptist leaders-among them, Jonathan Going, Luther Rice, Isaac Backus, and Samuel Stilman-created to attempt political disestablishment in Massachusetts during Leland's lifetime. The author contends that historiography that focuses narrowly on Leland tends to distort the very important role he played in the development of religious freedom in the revolutionary and Early Republic period"— Provided by publisher.

Identifiers: LCCN 2024021622 (print) | LCCN 2024021623 (ebook) | ISBN 9781621908289 (hardcover) | ISBN 9781621908296 (adobe pdf) | ISBN 9781621909118 (kindle edition)

Subjects: LCSH: Baptists—New England—History—17th century. | Church and state—New England—History—17th century. | Freedom of religion—New England—History—17th century.

Classification: LCC BX6239 .H42 2024 (print) | LCC BX6239 (ebook) | DDC 286.0974/09033--dc23/eng/20240628

LC record available at https://lccn.loc.gov/2024021622
LC ebook record available at https://lccn.loc.gov/2024021623

To Rachel,

High school and college sweetheart,
wife of sixteen years, best friend:

We did it!

In loving memory of

Kimberly Elaine Hicks Storey (1966–2015),
dear mother

Belle Dusseault Hambacher (1983–2016),
beloved cousin

Barbara Hicks (1946–2023),
my one-of-a-kind grandma

Larry Hicks (1944–2024),
my grandpa, my rock

CONTENTS

Foreword	xi
Acknowledgments	xiii
Introduction: A New Political History of Baptists	1
1. Young Baptist Men Acquiring Skills for Political Leadership	13
2. From "Tactics" to "Strategy": Becoming a Unified Political Movement	39
3. Baptist "Political Ecumenism" in the First Party Era	79
4. Reconciliation through Institutionalization	111
Conclusion: The Power of Preachers	139
Appendix: Statewide Clergy Exclusions from Political Office in the Revolutionary Era and the Early Republic	143
Notes	147
Selected Bibliography	195
Index	215

ILLUSTRATIONS

A Depiction of the Unfinished United States Capital Building, 1800	3
Rev. George Whitefield	25
Isaac Backus	28
Rev. Samuel Stillman, D.D.	33
Title Page of an Isaac Backus Pamphlet	60
View of the College in Providence	62
Cover Page to the *Minutes of the Warren Association*, 1771	65
John Leland	91
A Modern Monument to Leland and the Cheese Press	105
Andover Theological Seminary, Early 1800s	121
First Page of "Constitution of the Massachusetts Baptist Missionary Society," 1802	130
First Missionary Ordination	132
John Witherspoon (1723–1794)	145

TABLES

Table 1. Frequency of Writings and Advertisements for Writings of Key New England Baptist and Separate Leaders Found in Colonial/Early Republic Newspapers, 1745–1792   54

Table 2. Types of Writings and Advertisements for Writings of Key New England Baptist and Separate Leaders Found in Colonial/Early Republic Newspapers, 1745–1792   57

FOREWORD

Whoever coined the adage "religion and politics do not mix" never studied the history of Baptists in America. As a minority in Colonial America, Baptists were frequently involved in politics at all levels, and after the ratification of the Constitution they were especially keen to use the political process to secure their rights. Thus, it may be more accurate to say that in America religion and politics not only mix, they are inseparable.

The role Baptists played in shaping church-state relations are both complicated and open to inquiry. Jacob E. Hicks's *To Contest with All the Powers of Darkness: New England Baptists, Religious Liberty, and New Political Landscapes, 1740–1833* demonstrates precisely how complicated those contours were. By focusing on New England ministers, especially John Leland, Hicks offers a close look at one of the nation's most outspoken advocates for religious liberty. As Hicks points out, however, *To Contest with All the Powers of Darkness* is not a biography. Rather, Hicks uses Leland and his fellows as a lens into the political thought of certain New England Baptists in the late-eighteenth and early nineteenth centuries. Suffice it to say that established religion, or "the standing order," did not go quietly.

In many ways, John Leland might be an unlikely advocate for religious liberty in New England. Leland was an ardent Jeffersonian who had relocated to Massachusetts from Virginia in 1791. And, yes, the story about the cheese is true. Leland was so excited that Jefferson had been elected President of the United States that he delivered a 1,235-pound wheel of cheese to Washington along with the assurance that no Federalist cows were used in its production.

But what about Jefferson's declaration to the Danbury Association of Baptists (Connecticut) that a "wall of separation" existed between church and state? Defining what that meant and determining its limits, especially in New England, would be challenging. How it developed is the story that Hicks tells here.

The University of Tennessee Press is excited to offer *To Contest with All the Powers of Darkness*. There is much to consider in this work, and we hope it inspires others to explore the ways that religion and politics intersect in the fabric of American history. Ask Jacob Hicks and he will readily tell you; Baptists have a legacy of political engagement. That is a legacy well worth investigating.

Keith Harper
Southeastern Baptist Theological Seminary

ACKNOWLEDGMENTS

I would like to thank, first and foremost, Dr. Amanda Porterfield, my mentor and major professor of American religious history in the Florida State University (FSU) Department of Religion, for her support and guidance during the entire process of writing my dissertation, which is the foundation of my current work. Her comments and suggestions on how to improve the work helped me to avoid, as the famous hymn says, "many dangers, toils, and snares." I also thank her for her enthusiasm in my doing a dissertation centered on John Leland and Baptists in the Early Republic. Dr. John Corrigan and Dr. Michael McVicar were on my dissertation committee and deserve high praise as well. I would like to thank them for all of their helpful comments I received in colloquium and in chatting with them about my project over the years in their offices. I would like to thank Dr. Edward Gray from the Department of History for serving as the university representative for my dissertation.

This project originally would not have come into fruition without the fellowship, support, and critiques of my friends, fellow master's and Ph.D. students in the Department of Religion. I will not list them all for fear of leaving anyone out, but each one encouraged me, caused me to think more clearly about my topic, and helped me to take time away from work when the occasion called for it. Many of them even provided specific help by commenting on chapter 1 in a colloquium meeting. One graduate student does deserve special mention, however. John L. Crow, a fellow American religious history doctoral student, stayed in contact with me almost every week for the last year of the dissertation phase through email and the occasional lunch meeting. We each made sure that the other finished his dissertation, and we both completed them during the same semester.

I would also like to thank the Congregational Library and Archives in Boston, Massachusetts, for providing me with a research grant to do research in their beautiful facility on Beacon Street. The staff was immensely helpful in helping me to find just the right church books. Diana Yount at the Trask Library at the Andover Newton Theological School was instrumental in assisting me with The Backus Papers and various New England Baptist resources. The staff at the Massachusetts Historical Society in Boston, the Library of Virginia, the Virginia Baptist Historical Society, and the Virginia Historical Society, the last three in Richmond, Virginia, provided immeasurable help. At FSU, the staff at Strozier Library, particularly the interlibrary loan and u-borrow departments, was exceedingly helpful in procuring books for the project.

Many Ph.D. students write dissertations, but not all of them become books. Dr. Keith Harper, senior professor of Baptist Studies at Southeastern Baptist Theology Seminary, where I earned my M.Div., kept track of the progress of my dissertation in his mentoring of me from North Carolina while I was enrolled at FSU. He saw its potential as a book before perhaps anyone, including me! After my graduation from FSU, the dissertation morphed into a book that is broader in scope, yet deeper in analysis, than the original dissertation. I thank him for his patience and all of his advice over the years as my work went under extensive revision. I am beyond thankful to him for wanting my book to be a part of the America's Baptists series he edits for the University of Tennessee Press. Additionally, I would like to thank Scot Danforth, recently retired director of the University of Tennessee Press, and his staff for publishing my first book.

Since my graduation from FSU, I have found a home as a full-time online professor in the College of Theology at Grand Canyon University (GCU) and have been a part of a team—a close-knit family of professors—for six years. They have been intrigued about my work since I have been at GCU and have offered insightful feedback on some of my book revisions during a couple of our faculty colloquia.

Finally, as I mentioned in my dedication, my wife, Rachel, has always been there to love and support me. I have been working on some form of this project since 2014, for over half of our marriage. Finishing this book is as much her doing as it is mine. My grandparents who raised me, Larry and Barbara Hicks, never stopped believing that this day would come. They were behind me every step of the way as a first-generation college student and as the first person in my family to earn graduate degrees. Unfortunately, my grandparents passed away before the publishing of this book, but they did see an earlier completed version of it before they died.

Soli Deo Gloria

INTRODUCTION

A NEW POLITICAL HISTORY OF BAPTISTS

On New Year's Day in 1802, Baptist minister John Leland and a representative of the Committee of Cheshire delivered an unprecedented gift in Washington, DC: a "Mammoth Cheese" that the ladies of Cheshire made for President Thomas Jefferson. Cheshire was a small town located in the hills of Berkshire County in western Massachusetts that primarily consisted of Baptists who were devout Democratic-Republicans in a Federalist-controlled state. Their cheese measured "four feet in diameter . . . and seventeen inches in height" and weighed 1,235 pounds.[1] It took Leland and Darius Brown, the son of town committee chairman Daniel Brown, over a month to travel from Massachusetts to Washington, DC, to deliver their cargo. They carried the large wheel of cheese by sleigh, sloop, and horse cart. Popular excitement for the cheese came about partly because the Federalist and Democratic-Republican newspapers of the time had scorned and defended, respectively, the making and delivery of the cheese for months (the Cheshirites started making the cheese in July 1801). In every place along their route, which included New York City and Baltimore, a parade-like crowd formed to see the enormous and delicious gift. Never one to let a good-sized crowd go to waste, Leland also preached to the throngs as he travelled. For preaching and for his efforts in delivering the cheese, Federalist media outlets called him the "Mammoth Priest."[2]

Once Leland and Brown finally arrived at the White House, Thomas Jefferson came out to meet them. Surprised at the sight and size of the cheese, he gladly received the token of their esteem. The Committee of Cheshire expressed to Jefferson through a letter (probably written by Leland) accompanying the cheese the town's belief that God "has raised up a *Jefferson* at this critical day, to defend *Republicanism*, and the baffle the arts of *Aristocracy*" (i.e., Federalism). The committee then gushingly thanked him for his leadership over the nation.[3] According to local Cheshire tradition, "no Federalist cows were allowed to contribute milk" in the making of the cheese.[4] The citizens, and apparently the animals of Cheshire, too, were Republicans to the core.

In addition to marking the Cheshirites' delectable offering to Jefferson, New Year's Day 1802 was also significant because it was the day that Jefferson finished penning his famous "Letter to the Danbury Baptists." The Danbury Baptist Association of Connecticut was a collection of churches whose members experienced oppression at the hands of the Congregational religious establishment in Connecticut just as the Cheshire Baptists had in Massachusetts. They voiced their concerns about persecution to Jefferson in an October 1801 letter, and Jefferson responded that the religion clauses in the First Amendment required a "wall of separation between church and state" on the federal level. He expressed hope to the Danbury Baptists that the state of Connecticut would embrace religious disestablishment as well, but explained that the federal government did not have the legal authority to enforce disestablishment on the state level.[5]

Jefferson soon made his "Letter to the Danbury Baptists" public by allowing its printing in various newspapers throughout the country. He wanted people to know his official stance on church-state separation. While the letter theoretically may have encouraged his persecuted supporters in Connecticut and western Massachusetts, the Danbury letter did not assuage many Americans' fears that Jefferson was irreligious. In fact, Jefferson's lack of religious observance and his "heretical" beliefs were major charges that New England Federalists levelled at Jefferson during the contentious election of 1800. He did not proclaim days of fasting and thanksgiving like Washington and Adams had, and his wall of separation statement seemed to sever any meaningful relationship between church and state.

To counteract the public's perception of him, Jefferson asked Leland to preach at the House of Representatives on Sunday, January 3, two days after the cheese delivery, and Jefferson attended the service in person. To Jefferson's joy and Federalists' displeasure, Leland preached from Matthew 12:42 and Luke 11:31 that "a greater than Solomon is here." With this text, Leland not so subtly alluded to Jefferson being present at the service and equated him with Jesus. Jefferson knew that the media would notice his attendance at the service and print their accounts throughout the country. That way, Jefferson could demonstrate to Americans that he cared about religion. Leland, a strict separationist like Jefferson and one of the most popular Baptist preachers in America, endorsed Jefferson's presidency. Despite his stated views, Leland expressed no qualms about his endorsement or with preaching in a federal government building.[6]

One could conclude that Jefferson's and Leland's stated belief in the strict separation of church and state did not match their actions. However, as Monica Najar has argued in her work *Evangelizing the South: A Social History of Church and State in Early America*, scholars have reified the categories of "church and state" by "[suggesting] a coherence and stability of meaning that neither religious nor governmental bodies could claim in the 1770s and 1780s." For religious groups like Baptists

A Depiction of the Unfinished United States Capital [*sic*] Building in 1800. Library of Congress.

and Quakers, the word "church" reminded them of the "centralized institutional structures" that established churches used in denying equal status to the dissenting groups. Najar further contends that "'state,' too, is a rather grandiose term for the nascent governmental bodies still very much contested and rudimentary."[7] As the rest of her book makes clear, "church" and "state" remained fluid categories throughout the eighteenth century and into the nineteenth century in the South, and Baptists were involved in the process of defining each category in that region.

Like the efforts of Baptists in the South, the approach of New England Baptist leadership to participating in local, statewide, and national politics to overturn the Congregationalist establishment demonstrate how malleable the boundary between church and state was in between 1740 and 1833, as well as the crucial roles that these Baptists played in shoring up each category. Leland was one of the principal Baptist leaders in New England whose lifetime roughly corresponded to the late colonial era, the Early Republic, and Jacksonian America (1754–1841). An examination of Baptists' political labors during Leland's long lifespan thus provides a useful entryway into understanding the creation of these categories and their complex interplay.

However, this examination is not a full biography of John Leland's life.[8] Instead, the focus of this work will be on the ecclesiological and political networks that Baptist leaders formed to work for political disestablishment in New England. Leland's networking efforts will figure prominently in chapter 3 but less so in other portions of my analysis. Older contemporary Baptist leaders like Samuel Stillman and especially Isaac Backus in addition to Leland's younger contemporaries like Jonathan Going and Luther Rice will receive attention as well. My approach is analogous to an analysis of the American civil rights movement of the 1950s and 1960s. My analysis would give significant attention to the contributions of the Dr. Martin Luther King Jr., but it would also discuss Ralph Abernathy, Andrew Young, Fannie Lou Hamer, and John Lewis's relationships to one another and their roles in the movement.

The historiography as it currently exists has focused on whether individualism or communitarianism is the primary lens that historians and religious studies scholars should use in investigating New England Baptists' efforts to disestablish Congregationalism, and by extension, the boundary between church and state in that time. This unhelpful historiographic trajectory is shockingly apparent when it comes to scholars who study John Leland specifically. A brief overview of the historiography of Leland will illustrate this trend.

Most works comprising the historiography of Leland portray him as a radical individualist not strongly connected to church, creed, or anything else. In other words, he serves as the pure embodiment of Baptist individualism and a model for the "pro-individualism" party to emulate. Like the following scholars (although they do not quite express it as I do), I define individualism as a person being able to exercise autonomy in all aspects of life, especially in regard to religious matters. Creeds, governmental entities, and denominational bodies cannot and should not infringe upon one's rights of conscience and freedom to live (with only minimal legal constraints) the way that one wants. The ultimate authority one is accountable to is oneself.

The fountainhead for a lot of scholarship on the individualism of Leland is William G. McLoughlin's two-volume *New England Dissent*. Although this work is the most important and comprehensive work that exists on New England Baptists in the American colonies and the Early Republic, especially as it pertains to the Baptist fight for religious liberty, McLoughlin "mentions Leland on twenty-five pages of his 1294 page *New England Dissent* but limits substantive engagement to about ten pages."[9] Despite a relatively limited analysis of Leland's works, McLoughlin still had a strong opinion of him: "Leland's liberal pietism pointed directly toward the increasing disintegration of the corporate or organic social theory of the seventeenth century and the rising individualism, atomism, and secularism of the nineteenth century."[10] For McLoughlin, Leland was a creature and key example of a rapidly changing post-revolutionary society in which people cared mainly for their personal faith (if they had one) and the unhindered exercise of their own rights, both religious and political. McLoughlin was writing most of his opus during the rights revolution of the 1960s and was an activist himself. He was a member of the American Civil Liberties Union, fought for integration of public schools in 1967, and was an anti–Vietnam War and free speech advocate, among many other causes.[11] Like all historians, his life experiences and his context impacted how he viewed Leland and New England Baptists more generally.

Similar to McLoughlin, John Bradley Creed in his dissertation "John Leland: American Prophet of Religious Individualism" once declared that "as a Jeffersonian patriarch, he played a vital role in championing republican values, the heart of which was individualism."[12] Republicanism was an essential political philosophy in the founding of the United States, and Leland motivated others to fight against tyranny of all sorts, whether it was an overbearing centralized authority, like Leland perceived the Adams administration to be, or the established church in New England. Both had the potential to quell individual rights, and Creed's Leland could not endure the oppression of individual expression.

Creed's dissertation supervisor at Southwestern Baptist Theological Seminary, the renowned Baptist historian H. Leon McBeth, likely influenced Creed's views about Leland, Baptists, and their individualistic tendencies. In the introduction to the first unit of his popular Baptist history textbook, *The Baptist Heritage*, McBeth argues that "Clearly the Baptists fit the temperament of their times," specifically the seventeenth century. "Conditions were right for the emergence of more individualistic forms of religion," he contends, "and the spate of new religious groups in England show that they took full advantage of the day. Not only Baptists but also Levellers, Runners, Ranters, Quakers, Independents, and others rose during this unstable time."[13] These groups, most notably the Baptists, came to the American colonies in the 1600s and spread what McBeth saw as individualistic forms of Protestant Christianity in the New World in the centuries thereafter.

Following McLoughlin's path and agreeing with Creed, Nathan Hatch casts Leland as an archetypal individualist and purveyor of the religion of the "common man" in the Early Republic.[14] According to Hatch, Leland "believed that individuals had to make a studied effort to free themselves of natural authorities: church, state, college, seminary, even family. Leland's message carried the combined ideological leverage of evangelical urgency and Jeffersonian promise . . . This kind of liberal individualism could be easily embraced at the grass roots. Ordinary people gladly championed the promise of personal autonomy as a message they could understand and a cause to which they could subscribe—in God's name, no less."[15]

In Hatch's view, the gospel seed of Jeffersonian individualism that Leland widely scattered to the masses took fertile root in an Early Republic context in which people, without the aid of religious and political elites, could shape the destiny of their own lives and of the new nation by participating in popular evangelical Christian movements, particularly the Baptist and Methodist denominations.[16] Indeed, Hatch's interpretation of Leland's life and ministry dovetails perfectly with his book's thesis on the "democratization" of Christianity in the Early Republic.[17]

Two final major sources in the stream of Leland's historiography that emphasize individualism, though, in these instances, with important qualifications, are L. H. Butterfield's extended essay "Elder John Leland, Jeffersonian Itinerant" (1952) and Eric C. Smith's new biography *John Leland: A Jeffersonian Baptist in Early America*. In his essay, Butterfield draws significant attention to Leland's leadership of the Baptists of Cheshire, Massachusetts, in supporting Jefferson and the Democratic-Republican Party, as well as Leland's regional political influence, which he exerted by contributing to a partisan Republican newspaper, the nearby Pittsfield *Sun*.[18] Likewise, Smith details Leland's efforts as an active "party whip" for Jeffersonian Democratic-Republicans and, later, Jacksonian Democrats.[19] A "whip" is a clever and appropriate term to describe Leland's activities. In modern American politics, "party whips are members of either chamber of the Legislature who support the party leadership by acting as a two-way channel, communicating party positions to the rank-and-file membership and keeping leaders informed of member's views."[20] In Leland's day there were no official party whips, and Leland did not hold political office for most of his life, but he certainly served as a mediator between political leaders and their constituents like contemporary whips do within their own parties on Capitol Hill. So, Butterfield and Smith's Leland is not quite the radical individualist that is McLoughlin, Creed, and Hatch's Leland.

Nevertheless, using individualism as the primary lens to analyze Leland's life and ministry seduces Butterfield and Smith. Once Baptists began to form missions societies and national denominational structures in the early nineteenth century, Butterfield comments that Leland disagreed with these novel intrusions into Baptist life. According to Butterfield, these innovations "did not suit Leland's individualistic temperament."[21] After all, Leland was just "a lone and self-reliant saver of souls" who "found that the times were passing him by."[22] While Leland certainly differed with the majority of Baptists in America who became involved in denomination-building and establishing missions societies, to classify him merely as an individualist who pined after the "good ole days" of Baptist ministry does a disservice to the political sway and connections that he still possessed with Baptists and other Jeffersonian Republicans (as Butterfield himself points out) during that time.

In agreement with Butterfield, McLoughlin, and others, Smith argues that "Leland embodied the rise of liberal individualism that marked American society in the latter eighteenth century. As a thoroughgoing

Jeffersonian, he wished to unshackle himself from the tyranny of the past, as well as from the present control of the wealthy and educated, that he might think for himself."[23] In his first chapter, Smith highlights how Leland's individualism was "forged" in his childhood. He then sees him as a precursor to famous Transcendentalist Ralph Waldo Emerson's notion of "self-reliance" and the individualistic "trajectory of broader American religious life" as the nineteenth century progressed.[24] In focusing upon Leland being a trendsetter for individualism, he diminishes his valuable observation that Leland served as a party whip, a man closely interconnected with those "above" him and those "below" him, at least in partisan politics.[25]

To correct historians who have examined Leland and Baptists as individualists, a few scholars have argued that they had a strong sense of communitarian values that coincided well with the eighteenth-century American context. Political philosopher Barry Alan Shain, an antagonist to scholars of American Revolutionary-era politics who argue that the predominant political philosophy of the time was individualism, describes how eighteenth-century Americans instead practiced a communitarian ethic. According to Shain, "The vast majority of Americans lived voluntarily in morally demanding agricultural communities shaped by reformed-Protestant social and moral norms. These communities were defined by overlapping circles of family- and community-assisted self-regulation and even self-denial, rather than by individual autonomy or self-defining political activity."[26]

Christian ethicist and Shaw University professor Mikael Broadway sees Leland's life and ministry, and Baptists of that time in general, as exemplifying a Shainesque view of communitarianism. Broadway's project is to tear down the "myth of Baptist individualism and [offer] resources for a more communal ecclesiology based in the Baptist heritage."[27] Broadway draws upon several works by Leland discussing Leland's views of the relationship between the individual conscience and Baptist churches. Broadway notes Leland's belief that "the conscience must be rightly informed through training in the life of the community of faith as one studies the scriptures and discerns God's message." The conscience, without the aid of the church community, could not rightly "recognize God's leadership." Individuals also needed the discipline that Baptist churches offered to regulate the self, as Shain stated.[28] Another scholar who contributes to the minority opinion in Leland's historiography is lawyer-turned-Baptist historian Sammie

Pedlow Strange. Strange maintains that Leland had a robust if not systematically expressed theology and ecclesiology that centered on Christians voluntarily coming together in churches and associations to work to expand the kingdom of God and subordinating individual conscience to scriptural and congregational authority. Rather than Leland being an outlier in Baptist thought, Strange details how his ideas largely coincided with the views of early English Baptists in the seventeenth century and Isaac Backus.[29]

Historians who have chosen to examine Leland and the Baptists of his time either through the lens of individualism or communitarianism have created a binary that has reified both categories.[30] It is insufficient for the camp emphasizing individualism to assert that Leland and Baptists primarily cared about obtaining individual salvation and fighting for the right of individuals to have freedom of conscience without considering the important roles that Baptist churches and associations played in teaching young men the skills needed for political leadership and mobilizing groups of individuals for participation in the political process. Likewise, the communitarian camp ignores or marginalizes some Baptists' fears that ecclesiastical structures like denominations, associations, or even churches could centralize their authority to such an extent that the religious or political opinions of an individual might not be heard or that direct access to a relationship with God might be obstructed. They did not want to trade one burdensome establishment for another. Bill Leonard perhaps said it best when he noted that Baptists "are ever struggling with the tension between individual autonomy and corporate connectionalism."[31] Since that is the case, my work accounts for the unique blend of both individualistic and communitarian elements that motivated New England Baptists without letting those categories drive or frame my analysis.

My thesis is that Baptist ecclesiology and theology played a distinct role in informing and shaping how New England Baptists navigated and performed their duties as citizens. At the same time, the United States' nascent conceptions of citizenship and church-state relations crucially shaped Baptists as well. This approach is a new type of political history of New England Baptists, different from the existing historiography, and happens in four sometimes overlapping stages, each stage corresponding to a chapter.

Chapter 1 explores how Baptist churches in New England afforded mostly uneducated but ambitious young men, of which Leland was one among many, the opportunity to refine their public speaking skills, negotiate between various factions in the church, and connect with like-minded churches in Baptist associations for mutual encouragement, advice, and the achievement of larger goals that one church could not possibly accomplish on its own—such as fighting for religious disestablishment. This fruitful training ground equipped ministers with the necessary tools for activism in the political sphere.

Chapter 2 employs social theorist Michel de Certeau's discussion of the difference between "tactics" and "strategy" as a framework for analyzing how New England Baptist leaders shifted from haphazard and occasion-specific tactics of opposing the Standing Order to building a sustained political movement. This shift gradually occurred between the end of the Great Awakening and the early 1790s. Most notably, increasing disputes between Massachusetts and Great Britain in the 1760s and early 1770s over taxation without representation and the right to self-government provided the context for the consolidation of the Baptist political movement. Like their patriot brethren in the larger cause against Britain, key Baptist media entrepreneurs such as Isaac Backus and Samuel Stillman implemented a strategy of using the increasing availability of newspapers and pamphlets to unite their "constituents" by equipping them with scriptural and pragmatic arguments in favor of religious disestablishment. A second and interrelated part of the strategy consisted of New England Baptists putting their leaders' arguments into practice by forming their first association, the Warren Association (1767), and its political lobbying arm, the Backus-led Grievance Committee (1769), to ensure that Baptists had one political voice. New England Baptists' new political movement was a symbiosis between strong, talented leadership and multiple participating Baptist communities.

Chapter 3 discusses how, building upon the successes of the Warren Association and its Grievance Committee in uniting Baptists, the Baptists of New England, led by John Leland, slowly began to shake off their sectarian insularity by aligning themselves with many non-Baptist citizens into a coalition that comprised Thomas Jefferson's new Democratic-Republican Party. Leland believed that this politically ecumenical approach was necessary because Baptists alone did not have the political clout or numbers to effect change. They needed to partner with non-Baptist allies. He learned this critical lesson while living in Virginia from 1776 to 1791, when he helped Virginia Baptists align with Thomas Jefferson and James Madison to disestablish Anglicanism in 1786 and to accomplish other political goals. The Religious Freedom Act of 1811 represented the high watermark of Leland's and Baptists' legislative influence regarding the issue of disestablishment in Massachusetts. As a member of the Massachusetts House, Leland helped pass an act that, while it did not disestablish the Congregational Church, made public funds available to all religious groups.

Chapter 4 examines how, after almost two hundred years of strained relations between New England Baptists and Congregationalists, both sides put aside their differences and worked together to evangelize the expanding American frontier, fight "infidelity" in America, and carry the gospel to the "heathen" abroad. To accomplish these daunting tasks, Baptists like Jonathan Going and Luther Rice participated in an institution-building bonanza in the early nineteenth century in the form of seminaries and voluntary societies. The creation of these new institutions led to the professionalization of the pastorate and increasing denominational centralization, which transformed American Christianity. It also gave individuals, many of them recent converts to evangelical Christianity, new communities outside of the traditional structure of the local congregation in which to exercise their faith. Leland, however, did not like the blurring of denominational lines and the supposed neglect of the local church's role in accomplishing the work of God. He also feared the centralizing tendencies of Christian groups at the time and had no desire to see Baptists be part of an American Protestant superchurch. Moreover, he did not believe that voluntary societies had biblical warrant. Baptists and Congregationalists finally got along, but by doing so, Baptists lost their status as distinct outsiders, and Leland missed the days when Baptists were dissenters. Following chapter 4 and the conclusion is an appendix that examines various state laws concerning ministers serving in political office. This was a contentious issue for many states in the early nation. Some states viewed ministers just as any other male citizen—fully eligible to run for office. Other states were careful not to allow ministers to be pulled away from their spiritual calling to sully themselves in the grimy world of politics.

WHY READ THIS BOOK?

In its broadest scope, my work goes beyond merely arguing for a different perspective on New England Baptists. It draws attention to other questions of contemporary relevance, such as how to interpret the religion clauses of the First Amendment; whether or not ministers of the gospel should be actively involved in politics, and if so, how much and in what ways; how loyal should Christians be to a political party and those who lead it; what does it mean to be a good Christian citizen of the United States; and who or what authorities should people listen to and why. Thus, my writing contributes to the vast historiography of works that address the multifaceted relationship between religion and politics in the Early Republic.[32]

This work has an additional goal. In the introduction to *Conceived in Doubt*, Amanda Porterfield notes how scholars have spent much time addressing "the shift toward libertarian government and the growth of evangelical religion" in the Early Republic. However, "the codependence of libertarian politics and evangelical religion in the formative era of American politics and religion has not received the attention it deserves."[33] My work will fill this void by honing in on the synergistic relationship that existed between libertarian politics and evangelical religion in the new nation. I will demonstrate how New England Baptists used both Baptist and Jeffersonian Republican principles and practices to participate in a political coalition that attempted to disestablish Congregationalism in Massachusetts. By closely examining the actions of religious Jeffersonians, my work is intended in part to be a mirror of, or companion to, Jonathan J. Den Hartog's excellent book *Patriotism and Piety: Federalist Politics and Religious Struggle in the New American Nation*, which analyzes the origins and development of "religious Federalists," who sought to put their own stamp on defining "the public religious culture of the new nation" vis-à-vis religious Jeffersonians.[34]

1

YOUNG BAPTIST MEN ACQUIRING SKILLS FOR POLITICAL LEADERSHIP

Sometime in 1820, "now in the decline of life," Elder John Leland sat down to reflect on the course of his first forty-five years as a Baptist minister and itinerant preacher.[1] Concerning his entry into the ministry, he recalled: "I finally surrendered, and devoted my time and talents to the work of the ministry, without any condition, evasion, or mental reservation. In myself, I have seen a rustic youth—unacquainted with men, manners and books; without the smallest prospects, or even the thought of gain or applause, turn out a volunteer for Christ, to contest with all the powers of darkness."[2] Leland records that he became resolute in his decision to surrender to God's call to the ministry just a couple of years after converting to Baptist Christianity upon hearing the preaching of the gifted itinerant Baptist minister Elhanan Winchester in September 1772, in Leland's hometown of Grafton, Massachusetts. After his conversion, Leland struggled with assurance of his salvation until Elder Noah Alden of the First Baptist Church of Bellingham baptized him in nearby Northbridge on June 1, 1774.[3] Soon after, Leland gave a satisfactory account of his conversion experience before the entire congregation of First Baptist Church of Bellingham, and they received him as "a member in full communion" on October 2, 1774.[4]

What is fascinating about Leland's account of his conversion, baptism, acceptance into the Baptist community at Bellingham, and the start to his ministry is how unremarkable and common his story was among Baptist ministers in America in the last half of the eighteenth century. It did not matter to First Baptist Church of Bellingham that Leland was "unacquainted with men, manners, and books" since Baptists did not require their ministers to receive degrees like the Presbyterians, Congregationalists, and Anglicans did. Baptists believed that a calling from God and the local church's confirmation of the divine call were the only requirements for pastoral ministry stated in Scripture. In fact, Baptists mocked the desire of ministers from the three major colonial American denominations (especially the latter two because they were established churches) for the gentility and upward social mobility that often came with educational attainment in colonial America.[5]

Moreover, drawing from their English Baptist and New England Congregationalist heritage, Baptists argued that ministers should come straight from the ranks of the laity, which all but collapsed the distinction between clergy and laity. Local congregations selecting ministers was one of the manifestations of the Protestant principle of the "priesthood of all believers" in Baptist life. Every person, man and woman, was a "priest," one capable of performing some sort of role in the church, although God called only a small number of those (usually male) members to the specific role of "pastor" or "elder."

Leland's new church family in Bellingham as well as Baptist churches all over Massachusetts and colonial America sought to maintain a firm boundary between church members, other denominations, and "the world" by emphasizing baptism through immersion as a requirement for church membership (after one related his or her experience of conversion to the church). Baptism by immersion immediately set Baptists apart from most of their colonial neighbors, who were baptized as infants.[6] Baptizing only people (usually adults) who could make a conscious profession of their faith led opponents to accuse them of Anabaptism, or literally "re-baptism." These opponents linked the Baptist practice with continental European Anabaptist groups, especially the revolutionaries who set up a theocracy in Münster in the 1530s by force. Despite paedobaptists' harsh criticisms of the practice, Baptists held fast to believer's baptism because they could find no evidence of infant baptism in the Bible.[7]

In addition to believer's baptism, Baptists also enclosed the garden of the church from the wilderness of the world by policing their members through strict church discipline. All members, pastors included, could undergo the practice of church discipline. Pastors led, but the congregation (theoretically under the leadership of the Holy Spirit) possessed ultimate authority to decide who belonged in the church family and who did not.[8] Baptist congregations in eighteenth-century America operated under the assumption that all members of the church were supposed to be believers. They wanted no compromise on the issue of their churches consisting of the regenerate or "visible saints," an issue that had plagued their New England Congregationalist cousins' churches since 1662 when many Congregational churches adopted the "Half-Way" Covenant.[9] If any member, even a pastor, did not repent of sin and persisted in a state of unrepentance, the Baptist congregation could ban the individual from the love and fellowship of the church.

Just as early Methodist bands in eighteenth-century England functioned as laboratories meant to produce "social holiness" in their members,[10] every local Baptist church "acted as a form of socialization, putting pressure" on members "to conform to certain basic patterns in their spiritual lives."[11] On the surface, such a spiritual environment may seem to be unnecessarily strict on members, but as in those early Methodist bands, Baptist communities gave ordinary men and women the opportunity to "express themselves and find their voices."[12] In mid-eighteenth-century Baptist churches, both men and women could publicly relate their conversion experiences before the congregation, charge other members with sin during church business meetings, and even preach.[13] By the end of the eighteenth century, only men had the liberty to preach in a church,[14] but for those men, Baptist churches provided necessary on-the-job training for those aspiring to be pastors. In other words, churches channeled individuals' ambitions and talents for the good of the church body but also fostered a sense of confidence and opportunity that allowed individuals to carry out those ambitions and talents in the first place.[15]

Most importantly, Baptist churches in the latter half of the eighteenth century, especially in Leland's home colony/state of Massachusetts, provided a distinct training ground and the requisite skills for John Leland, Samuel Stillman, Noah Alden, and Isaac Backus to become political organizers. These Baptists leaders applied their skills to fighting for religious disestablishment on a state level.

COLONIAL MASSACHUSETTS CONGREGATIONALISTS AND BAPTISTS AND THEIR ENGLISH ANTECEDENTS

The unique ecclesiological brew that made Baptist leaders' activism in politics possible in Massachusetts did not come about all of a sudden in the late colonial era. Several developments within English Puritanism and Separatism and New England Congregationalism spanning from the late 1500s to the 1760s coalesced right at the dawn of American patriots' discontent with the British. A brief examination of these elements is thus necessary.

Although the Mennonites played a role in influencing English Separatist pastor turned Baptist founder John Smyth and some members of his church toward accepting the believer's baptism in Amsterdam around 1609, and both the Mennonites and Smyth's group shared similar beliefs concerning the separation of church and state, the Baptists owe their origins more directly to English Puritanism and Puritanism's more radical spin-off, Separatism. In the late sixteenth century, Puritans and Separatists were not satisfied with Reformed Christianity's progress in purging the vestiges of Catholicism from the Elizabethan Church of England. While Puritans (for a time) were willing to "tarry for the magistrate" to reform the Church of England, Separatists contended that the mother church was the Antichrist and sought to cut ecclesiastical ties with the church. Now being outlaws of the state, the Separatists who were able to flee traversed across the North Sea to the more religiously tolerant Netherlands. Eventually, some of those Separatists made it to Plymouth in the New World on the *Mayflower* in 1620. Other Separatists became Baptists, like John Smyth and Thomas Helwys. After Smyth's death in 1612, some of his followers eventually became Mennonites. Starting a Baptist tradition of multiplication through division, Helwys and his followers became the first Baptists to break away from another Baptist church when they cut ties with Smyth's group and went back to England in 1611 or 1612, thereby establishing the first Baptist church in England.

Helwys did not last long as pastor of his Baptist church once they arrived back in England and started worshipping in Spitalfields. He boldly (and rashly) sent a copy of his *A Short Declaration of the Mistery of Iniquity* (1612) to King James I, which criticized the king for not granting liberty of conscience to his subjects. The work is probably the first plea for freedom of conscience written in English. Not surprisingly, James I did not appreciate the work's historical significance and threw Helwys in jail, where Helwys eventually died. John Murton took over leadership of Helwys's church, and the Baptist movement, despite persecution, took root in England.[16]

The small Baptist movement eventually crossed the Atlantic beginning in the 1620s and 1630s, but usually in the form of English Puritans and Separatists who had not yet taken the even more radical step of repudiating infant baptism and embracing believer's baptism. Embracing believer's baptism severed the connection between church membership and political citizenry because English law required all infants in its parishes to be baptized. The New England Puritans wanted to maintain infant baptism in their parishes in the New World, but doing so led to a paradox within their own theology and practice.[17] According to Edmund S. Morgan, the New England Puritans sought "to restrict membership in the church to visible saints, to persons, that is, who had felt the stirrings of grace in their souls, and who could demonstrate this fact to the satisfaction of other saints."[18] How did infants fit into restricting membership to people who could consciously and audibly attest to God working in their hearts to convert them if infants did not have the ability to testify about their faith? The Puritans employed the framework of covenant theology prevalent in Reformed Christianity to explain that infants, while not yet experiencing conversion and thus not entitled to full membership, were still "children of the covenant," a vaguely defined quasi-member of the body of Christ.[19] New England Puritan magistrates were genuinely shocked when dissenters like Baptists, propelled by the same desire for church purity as the Puritans, sought to address the paradox in a manner that departed from the emerging New England way.

But the Massachusetts Bay Colony could brook no compromise or dissent because the stakes were high. As John Winthrop famously said on the *Arbella* on the way to the New World in 1630, the Puritans had covenanted with God to build a "City upon a Hill" that would show all of Christendom, particularly the Church of England, how to establish a godly society.[20] In order to succeed at this difficult task, Winthrop urged that "wee must be knitt together in this work as one man."[21] When Puritan-turned-Separatist Roger Williams first arrived in Boston in 1631, he refused an offer to become pastor because the church did not separate from the Church of England. Throughout his five turbulent years in the Massachusetts Bay Colony and the Plymouth Colony, he promoted his views on the separation of church and state and liberty of conscience, as well as more fair treatment of Native Americans. Since Williams's divisive influence put in danger the Massachusetts Bay Colony's fulfillment of their covenant with God, the General Court banished him to Rhode Island in 1636. Once there, Williams worked to establish a colony that upheld religious liberty. For about four months, Williams became a Baptist and started the First Baptist Church in America in Providence in 1639. Although he did not remain a Baptist, Rhode Island gave dissenters a haven to which they could flee, and Baptists grew unmolested there.

The 1650s were a tumultuous time for dissenters in the Massachusetts Bay Colony as well. In July 1651 the authorities in Lynn arrested Baptists John Clarke, John Crandall, and Obadiah Holmes for holding unauthorized worship services. Each was fined. Clarke's friends paid his fine, Crandall paid his own fine, but Holmes refused to pay his fine out of principle and received thirty lashes for his impudence. Even more so than Baptists, the authorities harassed, jailed, and banished Quaker preachers, and the Massachusetts Bay Colony's punishments culminated in the execution of three Quakers in 1659–1661 for ignoring the decree of banishment from the colony for all Quakers.[22] For Baptists and other dissenters, persecution died down in the Massachusetts Bay Colony after Parliament passed the Act of Toleration (1689) and Massachusetts became a royal colony in 1691.

By 1700 New England had a total of twelve Baptist churches (Massachusetts: five; Rhode Island: six; Connecticut: one), and in 1730, before the first stirrings of the Great Awakening, New England Baptist churches totaled twenty-one (Massachusetts: four; Rhode Island: thirteen; Connecticut: four).[23] In contrast, in New England, the Congregational Church had about 150 churches in 1700, and in 1730, the number reached over 300.[24] What these statistics suggest is that Baptists in Massachusetts and Connecticut, the strongholds of religious establishment, had to add to their number from the much larger ranks of Congregationalists that surrounded them in their parishes.[25] Since many Baptists in New England came from a Congregational Church background, Congregationalist beliefs and practices, especially regarding church discipline and their conception of the ministry described in church covenants, played a formative role in the development and growth of Baptist churches in the region. Thus, I will briefly sketch these themes as they played out in Congregationalist churches and then relate them to the New England Baptist experience in a more detailed section later.

The Congregationalists (Puritans) were a people who believed in the efficacy of covenant-making. According to Charles W. Deweese, "a church covenant is a series of written pledges based on the Bible which church members voluntarily make to God and to one another regarding their basic moral and spiritual commitments and the practice of their faith. A covenant deals mainly with conduct (although it contains some doctrinal elements)" and thus "has close ties with Christian ethics."[26] Everyone agreed to be involved in the regulation of their fellow church members' behavior within the confines of the meetinghouse and out before the world so as to obey God and avoid reproach to the name of God and his covenant people. Regulation especially involved disciplining members who breached the covenant with the professed aim of forgiving and restoring a man or woman to the full privileges of membership according to the disciplinary procedure that they found in Matthew 18.

One example of church discipline occurred in the Old South Church in Boston when members took issue with the unchristian behavior of Nathaniel Wardell on August 14, 1748. After Wardell experienced church discipline for unauthorized preaching and becoming a Separatist back in 1743, the church accused Wardell of "repeated acts of profane swearing and excessive drinking." The church tried a last-ditch effort to persuade Wardell to repent, but two days later, the church decided to excommunicate him because "we apprehend that the rule of God's Word, the Honour of our Lord Jesus, and the Credit of our holy Profession require us to cast said Wardel out of the Church." On August 28, pastors Joseph Sewall and Thomas Prince, who were the church meeting moderators, officially pronounced the sentence of excommunication on the congregation's behalf and sent Wardell a detailed letter explaining why they had excommunicated him. The church now considered Wardell to be an unbeliever.[27]

In addition to providing an impetus to church discipline, Congregational Church covenants also elaborated upon the specific responsibilities that ministers and the congregation had to one another. In the First Church of Hassanamisco, which began on December 28, 1731 and was later renamed Grafton after the new township, church members pledged that "we likewise promise, that we will peaceably submit unto the holy discipline appointed by Christ in His church for offenders, *obeying them that rule over us*."[28] Similarly, the Rowley West Parish church (later renamed First Congregational Church of Georgetown) stated in its 1732 covenant that members were to "submit to the guidance of such as are or shall be over us in the Lord and that watch for our souls."[29]

Both of these churches perceived that the pastor's role was leadership over and responsibility for[30] the congregation, and they were required to follow his lead. However, the pastor's "rule" was not a dictatorship. Solomon Prentice, First Church of Hassanamisco's first minister, became a New Light pastor and admirer of George Whitefield during Whitefield's visit to the area in 1740. From that point on, Prentice was pro-revival, allowed uneducated pastors to preach in his pulpit, and advocated such doctrines as an individual knowing for sure if he or she had been converted. In 1744 other ministers in the area formed a council to urge Prentice to moderate his fervor, but he could not, and the church eventually dismissed him in 1747. After ten years of relative peace with his congregation in 1730s, Prentice failed to navigate successfully presenting his New Light sentiments to a church body that was cautiously pro-revival, at best.[31] Prentice's case demonstrates that not every minister who was a part of a church that subscribed to a congregational polity had the skills to resolve disputes and convince others.[32] This training ground helped to sift out the pastoral successes from the failures.

THE IMPACT OF THE GREAT AWAKENING ON THE NEW ENGLAND ESTABLISHMENT

As the 1730s progressed into the early 1740s, New England Congregationalist churches experienced an ecclesiastical and societal transformation, partly as a result of the event that most scholars label the "Great Awakening."[33] During the Great Awakening in New England, large numbers of itinerant preachers, led by the "Grand Itinerant" George Whitefield, altered people's conception of the relationship between pastors/preachers and the laity. A bevy of young, uneducated men experienced the "new birth" and began preaching and evangelizing in parishes that already had settled ministers. Some ministers, like the famous Charles Chauncy, were unreservedly anti-revival and harshly criticized the preachers' lack of education and emotional histrionics. Other ministers, most notably Jonathan Edwards and Thomas Prince, counted themselves as among those in favor of revival, although they disliked uneducated lay preaching and urged caution concerning emotional expression among preachers and their hearers. A third group, consisting of luminaries such as James Davenport (before his recantation) and Isaac Backus, were staunchly pro-revival and promoted lots of emotional expression and uneducated lay preaching.

From this third faction, the "Separate Congregationalists" or "Separates" originated in, and broke away from, the established Congregational Church. A sizable contingent of the Separate churches then became "Separate Baptists." The transition from being Separates to Separate Baptists in the 1740s and 1750s helped to fuel the explosion of Baptist church growth to 173 churches in New England by 1780 (just four years after a young John Leland left for Virginia), 69 in Massachusetts alone.[34] Despite their schism from the Congregational Church, Separates and their Separate Baptist offspring modeled and then modified Congregationalist solutions to balancing individual and communal concerns in their own churches.[35] Their adjustments ultimately set the stage for Baptist ministers like Leland to learn the crucial networking and lobbying skills that they would need for political action, particularly on the issue of religious liberty.

In November 1739 Anglican itinerant preacher George Whitefield began his first major intercolonial preaching tour of the American colonies in Philadelphia. According to Harry Stout, Whitefield's selection of Philadelphia "was a wise choice." For one, the city was located in Pennsylvania, which, because of its founding by Quaker William Penn, allowed for the toleration of all religions, even Catholicism and Judaism. Although Whitefield was an Anglican missionary and preacher, he prized interdenominational participation in his revivals. Also, Philadelphia "had already grown to be a major port city with a thriving economy."[36] Whitefield used his public relations manager and travel assistant William Seward to write letters to printers and church officials to publicize his arrival in the city. Whitefield had hoped to exploit the growing market economy of Philadelphia to expand the marketing of his message of the "new birth" and to raise money for an orphanage that he had started in Georgia.[37]

Although Philadelphia was perhaps the greatest example of an emerging market economy in the American colonies, it was really part of an Atlantic-wide revolution in trade, travel, and communications that was taking place in the eighteenth century. Great Britain improved its shipping capabilities to the New World, which allowed for safer, faster, and more extensive travel and trade. More effective navigation up colonial American rivers also helped bring trade goods to people in rural regions far away from the coast. Moreover, Timothy D. Hall notes how "an empirewide postal system" helped to knit together increasingly mobile families located in different areas of the American colonies and the British Atlantic. In addition to an increase in written letters sent abroad, the rise of "print-capitalism" allowed for books, sermons, pamphlets, magazines, and newspapers to flood the market. In newspapers in particular, enterprising businessmen in London advertised their products, which created demand for English goods in colonial markets whose own newspapers carried the same advertisements.[38] As Hall astutely notes, "In the rush to obtain these English goods, colonists began to acquire a common set of tastes and experiences that future intensified a sense of kinship with their British fellows."[39] In the hope of converting people to a Calvinist-flavored[40] evangelicalism, Whitefield took advantage of the consumer revolution that was becoming prevalent in the eighteenth-century British Empire by using improvements in shipping, his personal letters, his published journals and sermons, and newspaper advertisements about himself to cultivate a "taste" for evangelicalism among religious consumers in the British Atlantic.

Itinerancy, then, for Timothy H. Hall and for my work, is primarily "a contested metaphor for two very different visions of adapting to eighteenth-century change."[41] For many New Englanders (Hall's study is for the colonies as a whole, not just New England), "itinerants became living metaphors for flux and disorder by violating a wide range of spatial and social boundaries."[42] The anti-revival faction of settled Congregationalist ministers did not like itinerancy for many reasons. They did not like the idea of lay and uneducated itinerant preaching because both the existence of these preachers and their actual words were an indictment of settled ministers' reliance upon education as a means to achieve or maintain high social status. Related to this reason is the fact that, if the settled ministers' own congregants followed Whitefield or his many imitators, then the settled ministers could no longer benefit from the well-established tradition of average people deferring to their social betters. Furthermore, just as the market revolution was transforming relatively isolated communities into stations of consumption for goods from the mother country, itinerancy—whose practitioners evangelized America's countryside and not just major towns—was the religious version of this material goods revolution. Itinerancy, in the minds of detractors, contributed to the breaking up of communities and townships centered on the local churches.[43]

On the other hand, for people in favor of itinerancy and the Great Awakening, itinerancy was a positive metaphor of change. As people eagerly embraced the new consumer culture, so also did many people "buy" the new religious message that the itinerants were "selling." Individual spiritual shoppers throughout New England were anxious to buy a more satisfying practice of their religion. Under the influence of Whitefield, New Jersey Presbyterian firebrand Gilbert Tennant, James Davenport, and other itinerants, people in the Congregational Church began to see their anti-revival ministers as "unconverted."[44] The anti-revival ministers' preaching and lifestyle did not indicate to some hearers that the ministers ever experienced the sudden and emotionally charged work of the Holy Spirit accompanying conversion that itinerants preached about over and over again. Also, itinerant preachers not being bound by parish, colony, or even nation helped create an "imagined community" of evangelicals all over the British Atlantic who believed that they were a part of one big work of God. The rise of "print-capitalism" simultaneously fueled and constructed this emerging transatlantic community of evangelicals through reports about revivals in published sermons, journals, books, and newspapers.[45]

Although the Great Awakening ruptured the churches in New England, Hall observes that "itinerancy provided a means of adapting to a weakly structured, rapidly changing colonial environment by inviting people into close-knit, voluntary local expressions of the transatlantic revival community. The ties of affection that linked members to a long-distance imagined community also bound them to live with one another according to strict standards of internal commitment and moral behavior."[46] Religious entrepreneurs like George Whitefield and his imitators understood how to successfully exploit the new social landscape of the eighteenth-century British Atlantic to produce converts to evangelicalism.[47] These entrepreneurs were more adaptable to the times than the settled ministers of New England who were anti-revival/anti-itinerancy. Most ironically, itinerancy produced new local communities like the Separates and Separate Baptists, who embodied a communitarian ethic while still embracing a transatlantic awareness of communities similar to themselves. Itinerant John Leland helped to knit together Baptist and non-Baptist communities into a network of constituents that comprised the Democratic-Republican Party, a new type of "imagined community" that arose in the United States in the 1790s along with Federalism.

THE RISE OF THE SEPARATES AND SEPARATE BAPTISTS

After preaching throughout the Middle Colonies and parts of the South like Charleston, South Carolina, George Whitefield finally arrived in New England when he disembarked in Newport, Rhode Island, on September 14, 1740, and went right away to Boston. Pastors, lay people, professors, politicians—pretty much everyone in New England knew that he was coming. Whitefield and Seward's publication efforts had paid off. Whitefield ended up touring parts of Massachusetts, Connecticut, and Rhode Island, preaching twice a day wherever he went. His first itineration in New England lasted only about two months.[48] When he came back to New England in the autumn of 1744 for another preaching tour, Whitefield found the churches of New England in turmoil. According to Baptist historian William L. Lumpkin, "Those New Lights who stayed for a time in the old churches agitated for the reinstatement of the concept of the pure church, but since they composed minorities in most churches they failed."[49] Numerous pro-revival churches who were accepting scores of newly awakened members did not see the need to denounce the Half-Way Covenant. An increase in piety and numbers was what these churches sought.

The irony, C. C. Goen observed, was that it was "in those very churches where the revival was strongest that separatism most frequently appeared."[50] The Separates, as this group came to be called, thought that the established churches of Massachusetts and Connecticut who embraced revival did not go far enough in ecclesiological reforms. In response, by 1744, the Separates started to form their own churches, in which they emphasized a wide gamut of beliefs and practices: regenerate church membership, strict church discipline of wayward members, itinerant preaching, lay preaching, having ministers "properly" converted, the priority of sovereign grace in electing people for salvation, assurance of one's salvation, and the idea of a church consisting of members who voluntarily gave to their own church rather than having to give to the established churches from which they separated.[51] The Separates believed that in their new communities they were bringing New England back to the theological and practical ideals

Rev. George Whitefield. Frontispiece,
Memoirs of Rev. George Whitefiled:
By John Gillies, D.D. Middleton, Revised
and Corrected with Large Additions and
Improvements . . . Hunt & Noyes, 1838.

that made the original Puritan and Separatist colonies distinct from the Church of England and all other churches in Christendom.

But the Separates did not depart from the churches of their birth very easily. Their decisions to depart were a mixture of sorrow, joy, a sense of duty to Christ, and fearfulness in starting over. One gets a glimpse into the Separates' drama in the case of the First Church of Sturbridge. The church started in 1736 when Caleb Rice became its pastor and members signed the church covenant. The Great Awakening impacted Sturbridge in 1740, but fifteen Separates did not break away until seven long years later. The non-separating members of the church inquired into why the Separates decided to leave, and the defectors wrote (or had someone write for them) in 1749 their "relation," or narrative, on why they had to leave the church.[52] Their reasons correspond remarkably well with the Separate's beliefs and practices that I listed in the previous paragraph.

One Separate, Hannah Cory, had been in church one day when various scriptures suddenly came into her mind urging her to leave her church: 2 Corinthians 6:17, Amos 3:3, and Matthew 21:13.[53] Pondering these verses, she exclaimed that a "sudden fear came over me" and that she left the meetinghouse to clear her head. She then walked around the church graveyard and thought that she was better off staying in the graveyard than going back into the church. However, she ended up re-entering the church, but the church "seemd to be a dark place Ministers deacon and people lookt Strangely as if they were all going Blindfold to destruction." Cory believed that her pastor, the deacon, and the church members were all unconverted and on their way to Hell. She remained in that particular service filled with spiritually dead people, but she explained that, "tho my body was there, my soul was with the Separates, praising God as soon as I was dismysd at the meeting house I went to Brother Nevils where my soul was sweetly refreshed." Cory was relieved to make it out of the service still alive and sought to go to a Separate preacher, a "Brother Nevil."[54] Although he was probably a layman, in Cory's mind Brother Nevil had the advantage of being a "converted" minister, and Cory received the spiritual edification from him that she desired.

Other Separates were at first hesitant to receive preaching from unlearned lay preachers. Congregationalists were used to their ministers being college educated or at least having an informal months- or years-long mentorship with a wise, experienced pastor. But many Separate preachers did not have a college education. For example, the Separate Sarah Marten (or Morton) said that she "was a fraid also of the Separate teachers because they had no larning. Then was I led to Acts 4.13 and when they se the boldness of Peter and John being unlarned and ignorant men took knowlidg of them they had been with Jesus."[55] What she probably understood from this verse in Acts is that it did not matter that the Apostles Peter and John did not have a former education. The most important "qualification" was that the apostles knew Jesus Christ personally, and they learned directly from Christ's own example and teaching. As long as the Separate preachers knew Christ just like Peter and John did, that was enough for Sarah.

Moreover, in the opinion of Separates, their former churches were dens of spiritual laxity. In his short relation, Sturbridge Separate Jonathan Perry claimed that the church was "not walking according to the order of the Gospel as you ought to dwo and in perticular that

Transaction Committed and Countenanced by maney of you on the 16th of May last which the Lord made use of to open my eyes and to Shwo me what you ware and what your Religion was and he has showon me that you are not a Church of his according to the order of the Gospel." Despite Perry's intention to be "perticular" about the church's misdeeds, his specific accusation is a mystery. Later in his relation, he cites 2 Thessalonians 3:6–18 to substantiate his charge, which may give the readers some hints about his criticism.[56] The passage concerns the Apostle Paul reminding the Thessalonian church that, when he and his companions were there, they worked for their food and did not expect the church to pay them. However, since Paul left, some members of the church had not been working to support themselves, and such laziness was causing trouble in the church. Paul urged the lazy people to work if they expected to eat. Perhaps the "transaction Committed and Countenanced" by Perry and others was the church's willingness to take care of people who could take care of themselves financially but did not do so. We do not know. Regardless, the First Church of Sturbridge was full of "disorder," and, obeying Paul's injunction in 2 Thessalonians 3:6 to leave brethren who walked disorderly, Jonathan Perry left the church.

At least one Sturbridge Separate, Naomy Ward, returned to the First (Congregational) Church of Sturbridge thirteen years later,[57] but many of the Sturbridge Separates took the next step to separate from the established church and become Baptists by submitting to baptism by immersion. The Sturbridge Separates became the foundation for the Sturbridge (or Fiskdale) Baptist Church, started in May 1749.[58]

The most comprehensive extant records of a person in eighteenth-century New England who made the spiritual journey from Congregationalist to Separate to Separate Baptist belong to Isaac Backus (1724–1806).[59] When he was seventeen years old, New Light itinerant all-stars like Benjamin Pomeroy, Eleazar Wheelock, and James Davenport came to Backus's hometown of Norwich, Connecticut, to convert people to evangelical Christianity. Many did convert, but Backus did not, at least not immediately. One day, while doing some yardwork, Backus felt that the "Justice of God Shined so clear Before my eyes in Condemning Such a guilty Rebel that I Could say no more—but fell at his feet." God had made it clear to Backus that there was nothing he could do to ensure his own salvation and that Christ's righteousness "fully Satesfies the Law that I had broken." His conversion was complete when "my Whole Heart was attracted and Drawn away after God and Swallowed up with Admiration in viewing his Divine glories."[60] Backus was now a New Light.

The problem was that the pastor of the established church in Norwich, Benjamin Lord, was not a New Light minister. Lord soured to itinerant evangelical preaching quickly after originally being in favor of it. His church's membership had grown as a result of the Great Awakening, but Lord eventually banned itinerants from his church for unusual behaviors like calling out sinners who were present in the room by name. Backus, one of the eighty-one converts who joined the church in between the years 1741 and 1744,[61] recalled his years at the established church at Norwich as "[having] now and then Some refreshments but generally was Cold and dull. But about the End of the year 1744 the Lord brought me to See that though they had a form of Godliness yet they did Deny the Power there-of and therefore I was commanded to turn away from them."[62] Backus was not alone in his negative assessment of his church, and, spurning the authority of their "unconverted" minister, he and some others formed the Bean Hill Separate Church in 1746.[63]

Not content to be only a member of a Separate Church, Backus felt God was leading him to engage in itinerant preaching, despite his

Isaac Backus. Library of Congress.

lack of college education. He eventually became pastor of a Separate Church in Titicut, Massachusetts, in 1748. As their new minister, he authored the church's articles of faith and the covenant. The covenant is very brief, but the articles of faith spell out in some detail the doctrinal and practical emphases of the Titicut church. For instance, the church believed in the predestination of the elect (part I, article 9) and limited atonement (part I, article 11), marking the church as Calvinistic. Also, the "visable Church" could only consist of "true Believers" (part II, article 1), and only true believers as well as their infant children were the proper subjects of baptism (part II, article 3). Moreover, pastors had the authority to lead the congregation, but they "hath no more power to Decide any Case, or Controvercy, in the Church than any private brother" (part II, article 6).[64] Every person had a voice in making decisions and solving disputes within the church.

Like many other Separate churches, Backus's church and Backus himself were in constant conflict over the matter of infant baptism verses believer's baptism. In 1749 a portion of his church came to Baptist views on baptism, and so did Backus. Backus then quickly changed his mind again, leaving the congregation confused and angry. Backus did eventually undergo immersion in 1751 and tried to pastor a church filled with both paedobaptists and credobaptists for a while. However, the arrangement did not work, and the Separates and Separate Baptists parted ways in 1756. Backus became the pastor of the Baptist faction, and they entered into covenant together as the First Baptist Church of Middleborough, Massachusetts. Backus was the pastor there until he died in 1806.[65] During his long tenure in Middleborough, he became the chief advocate for religious liberty in New England and throughout the American colonies and the early United States and served as the key model for Leland on how to fight and network for religious liberty.

THE NEW ENGLAND BAPTIST TRAINING GROUND FOR POLITICAL PARTICIPATION

For much of the colonial era, politicians did not put a lot of effort into campaigning for office, since according to Robert J. Dinkin, "the common person's deference toward members of the elite was particularly strong." A lot of political offices that the elites held came from appointments from the king or a colonial proprietor, thereby making elections irrelevant. Additionally, candidates who had to run for office could not appear to actively appeal for votes since those who did seemed hungry for political power. They had to appear disinterested in the office they sought. Nevertheless, in colonial times, two forms of politicking were still acceptable: throwing large buffets and drinking parties for constituents and meeting many voters (white male landowners) in person at social events to ask for their votes.[66]

The 1760s and 1770s significantly altered campaigning in America. Regular citizens demanded that the British Crown uphold their rights as Englishmen, which indicated that "those who had passively accepted rule by the rich and wellborn in the past were no longer willing to do so."[67] They wanted to speak out against a political elite class that denied them participation in government, and more and more they sought candidates who claimed to represent ordinary people. After the Revolution, candidates for office adjusted their "vote-getting tactics" by mastering the art of public speechmaking. Having precedent in protests against the British during the Revolutionary War (think of Patrick Henry's "Give Me Liberty or Give Me Death" speech in 1775, which asked Virginia's provisional government for troops), candidates entreated their listeners to vote for or against the new Constitution in the 1780s, and later of course, to vote for the candidates themselves. Political debates between candidates also came into practice during this time.[68]

The Early Republic, then, was a time when effective public speaking assumed a larger degree of importance in political participation than it had in colonial America. The speechmaking abilities of politically active Baptist ministers like Isaac Backus and John Leland had been cultivated in the context of the Baptist communities in which they participated, which meant that they and other Baptist ministers fit the emerging political climate perfectly. Looking back in 1820, Leland contended that "the number of sermons which I have preached, is not far from eight thousand." Five years later, he added that "I have preached in four hundred and thirty-six meeting-houses, thirty-seven court-houses, several capitols, many academies and school-houses; barns, tobacco-houses and dwelling-houses; and many hundreds of times on stages in the open air."[69] Even if Leland's sermons and where he preached them were a fourth of the totals he gave, the numbers are still staggering. Also, notice that Leland's preaching, for political reasons and otherwise, took place in several different locales. He learned the lessons well from other itinerants like Whitefield, who preached whenever and wherever they had the opportunity.

Before Leland left Massachusetts for fifteen years, beginning in 1776, he did some itinerant preaching in Massachusetts, Connecticut, New Jersey, and even as far south as Virginia,[70] but there are no extant sermons or writings by Leland during his first tenure in Massachusetts. Because only scant details from Leland's autobiography exist concerning his own training for public speaking, the records from other Baptist church records in Massachusetts from the latter half of the eighteenth century will show how other young men like Leland came to be ministers and learned how to preach.

The records from the First Baptist Church of Medfield have a particularly rich account of a man being installed as a minister and the role of preaching in that calling. On September 3, 1786, Amos Wood transferred his membership from a church in Haverhill to First Baptist Church of Medfield. Possibly learning from the letter of good standing that they received from Wood's previous church (which the church at Medfield did not record in the record book),[71] the church at Medfield declared that Wood "is distinguished in natural & acquired abilities which promise usefulness for the ministry." Although the records do not say, Wood's acquired abilities were probably a result of being self-taught and not a result of having a college education. He also possibly had some natural charisma and people skills. Seeing his potential, the church at their meeting that same day examined Wood on his beliefs about being a gospel minister and on some general areas of doctrine; he answered their questions in "satisfactory" fashion. Then, the church urged him to preach to them immediately from a text in the Bible to demonstrate his "aptness for teaching," a qualification for pastoral ministry listed in 1 Timothy 3:1. He chose Galatians 6, and the church was impressed with his preaching. To the church, he "[appeared] to be endowed with ministerial talents."[72]

Wood was not out of the woods yet in terms of becoming a minister. To make him a better preacher, the church "proposed to encourage the improvement of his gifts" by requiring him to preach again the following Sunday. After his second sermon, the church agreed that God called Wood to the pastorate, and on September 10, 1786, they voted to license him for the ministry.[73] Wood preached well, but if he could not preach well, then the church would have refused to license him. The ability to preach was one of the most important, if not the most important, skills or "gifts" that a person had to have to be an effective Baptist minister.

Ordination sermons given at the ordination of a candidate also provide a helpful window into how central preaching (and preaching well) was for Baptist ministry. For instance, First Baptist Church of Boston pastor Samuel Stillman (1737–1807), in a 1797 sermon that he preached at the ordination service of Stephen Smith Nelson in Boston, emphasized several characteristics that made one a "a good minister of Jesus Christ" (1 Timothy 4:6). For this preacher influenced by the Great Awakening, the most important characteristic was that a minister must be born again, or "a man of real religion, who has felt the transforming power of the gospel upon his heart and has imbibed its spirit."[74] He added, "If destitute of this qualification, whatever may be his talents and learning, he will be like a sounding brass, or a tinkling symbol."[75] In other words, one being talented at preaching, studying, or other ministerial tasks was worthless if evangelical-style conversion did not first happen to the minister. One could take such a comment as evidence of another Baptist minister simply being critical of higher education, but in Stillman's and Nelson's case, such an assumption is incorrect. Contemporary Baptist ministers as well as some Congregationalist ministers viewed Stillman as a man of extraordinary learning and eloquence, and Stillman even received an honorary master's degree from Harvard and an honorary doctorate from Brown University, the first Baptist college in America, of which Stillman was a founding trustee in 1764.[76] The ordination candidate, Stephen Smith Nelson, graduated from Brown University in 1794 before serving under Stillman as an assistant minister.[77]

Stillman listed other necessary characteristics for a minister of Jesus Christ: being willing to study Scripture, praying regularly, etc.[78] However, Stillman spent more time than on any other subject (four pages) discussing *how* one should preach. One should, according to Stillman, preach sermons that change the life of the preacher first before entering the pulpit. Public speakers speak most effectively when they believe what they are saying. Also, Stillman noted that the preaching should adhere to the tenets of Calvinist and evangelical orthodoxy: the necessity of regeneration, human depravity, divine sovereignty, the atonement (likely he means the penal substitutionary view), Christ's deity, and living lives of holiness. Moreover, Stillman exhorted Nelson to identify with his audience, remembering that he, too, was a sinner like them. Stillman further encouraged Nelson to "study *expression* as well as *sentiment*."[79] A minister of Christ could not afford to be "vul-

Rev. Samuel Stillman, D.D.
Public Domain.

gar," careless, or imprecise with wording. For Stillman, expression also included not preaching over the congregation's level of understanding. Drawing from the Puritans and the Separates, a preacher's dress and manner of speaking should be "*neat* and *plain*."[80] The implication was that too much ostentatiousness in speech or dress echoed the type of ceremonialism characteristic of Catholic and Anglican priests and even overly fancy Congregationalist ministers. Additionally, a preacher should not expect to preach on too much material, as it would confuse his listeners. Finally, a preacher should get his audience to "feel" by preaching to the emotions or the "affections," like Jonathan Edwards and George Whitefield did.[81]

While not every Baptist minister was nor could they be so refined and educated a speaker as Stillman and Nelson, the ideals of a preacher identifying with the audience; working on delivering sermons in a clear, understandable, and emotionally stirring way; and preaching with confidence and conviction were incumbent upon all Baptist ministers. Church members as well as other Baptist ministers would help ensure that their preachers could preach well. When Massachusetts Baptists started to become more involved in colonial politics in the late 1760s with the beginning of the Warren Association, leaders like Isaac Backus and Noah Alden successfully articulated their grievances concerning paying taxes to the established church and undergoing persecution partly through sermons and speeches to their congregations.

In addition to Baptist churches giving uneducated ministers like Leland the opportunity to hone their public speaking skills, these Baptist communities gave ministers a chance to navigate among different factions and competing interests within the church to form a consensus among a community of believers. Individual pastors' peacemaking and group-uniting skills were on clearest display when they led their churches in administering church discipline, for they usually served as moderators of church meetings where church discipline took place.[82]

An example of pastors managing the affairs of the church to maintain unity occurred at a meeting at the First Baptist Church of Norton (also known as Taunton), Massachusetts, on Friday, August 29, 1783. At the house of a widow named Sarah Briggs, the church met together to decide who was fit to partake of communion on the following Sunday. To ensure that the church remained free of sin and was worthy to enter into communion together, Elder William Nelson (the church's pastor) mentioned the troubles that had been brewing between Brother James Wetherel and Sister Azubah Williams. At this point in the church records, the clerk James Gilbert records that they had pledged to marry one another but that they did not get married. As a result, the couple did not feel right about participating in communion until the church could help them settle the matter. Then, the church created a committee to "labour" with, or convince, the couple to reconcile. When the original attempt at reconciliation failed, the church performed the very Baptist act of adding two more people to the three-person committee, but they had not resolved the case by the following Sunday.[83]

Though the problem at first seemed to be a matter of two young church members having cold feet, a later entry in the church book indicates that the issue was a serious ordeal for the church, so serious that the church tried to resolve the problem on and off for over a year. Elder Nelson could not stand by and let Sister Williams and Brother Wetherel marry because Sister Williams had already married Brother Seth Williams instead! Sister Williams asked God, the church, and Brother Wetherel for forgiveness for breaking her promise to Brother Wetherel. The church forgave her, and Wetherel claimed to forgive her, but he still felt that "she had sind in marrying another man and that she still persists in her wickedness."[84] Still bitter at losing Sister Williams,

Brother Wetherel did not want her to go back to church and partake of communion.[85] Realizing that the dispute was not going away, Elder Nelson urged the church to call on two sister churches in the Warren Association to help them to resolve the matter between Williams and Wetherel.

One of these churches was First Baptist Church of Middleborough, Backus's church. He was chosen as the moderator of the interchurch committee. Backus was a greatly sought-after fount of biblical wisdom among New England Baptists. Baptist historian Keith Harper observes in his work on the Elkhorn Association of Kentucky that there was a "pecking order" amongst ministers in that association. Each minister had a voice in an association, but "some voices carried more weight than others."[86] The same was true in New England's Warren Association. Backus's voice was just about the most influential. It was no mistake other Baptist leaders chose him to be in charge of the Grievance Committee and encouraged him to write pamphlet after pamphlet on behalf of all Baptists for religious liberty. Though he was not formally educated, he was well-read, a gifted writer, and an adept speaker. The church asked Elder Job Seamans and his church to be a part of the committee as well.[87] At the advice of the two churches, the First Baptist Church of Norton accepted Williams to full communion and continued to hope that Wetherel "would come and walk with the church."[88] Apparently, Wetherel had left the fellowship of the church, and First Baptist Church of Norton wanted him back. On October 24, 1784, the date of the last entry in the saga, Williams gladly reentered the church, and Wetherel remained dissatisfied with the entire situation.[89]

The records do not say if Wetherel was ever excommunicated, but he did not heed the advice of his own pastor, Elder Nelson, Elder Backus, Elder Seamans, or any members of their churches to reconcile with his church. In this protracted incident of church discipline, three elders used their position as leaders in the church to guide members of the First Baptist Church of Norton in deciding on the course of action that would lead to the minimum amount of damage to the church body and shore up unity within its ranks. The elders could not unilaterally decide which solution was right and make the church follow them; they had to lead by persuasion, concern, patience, and a strict adherence to the rules of Baptist polity that governed the role of pastors. Strong individual leadership thus always existed in tension with the expectations of a given congregation.

Most important for my argument, Massachusetts Baptists and Baptists in wider New England became skilled at uniting together to form associations of like-minded churches for mutual encouragement, advice, and the achievement of major goals like religious freedom. The story of Baptist association-building in colonial America does not begin in New England, however; it begins in the Middle Colonies (Pennsylvania, New Jersey, Delaware, and New York) with the advent of the Philadelphia Baptist Association (PBA) in 1707. In the late seventeenth and early eighteenth centuries, the Middle Colonies enjoyed a high level of religious toleration as a result of William Penn founding its largest colony, Pennsylvania, as a religious haven for his fellow Quakers and all people. The Jerseys (later New Jersey) and Delaware were heavily influenced by their larger neighbor, and New York had a history of religious toleration starting with Dutch rule of what was then called New Netherland. Additionally, the Middle Colonies housed a wide variety of different ethnicities like the Dutch, Scotch-Irish, Swedes, various German groups, and the English, which allowed pluralism to flourish. In this relatively free environment, especially as compared to the colonial religious establishments of Connecticut, Massachusetts, and Virginia, Baptists flourished in the Middle Colonies.[90] In July 1707 five churches around the Philadelphia area united "to regularize Baptist life in the Middle Colonies, solving congregational disputes, testing ministerial candidates, and sponsoring new churches and missionary journeys into unevangelized areas."[91]

According to Horatio G. Jones, as the eighteenth century progressed, the Philadelphia Baptist Association extended over four hundred miles, reaching to Virginia in the South and New York and Connecticut in the North, with its hub in Pennsylvania.[92] Eventually, the PBA's members organized efforts to start other associations beyond the scope of the mother association. Pennsylvania minister Oliver Hart (1723–1795) moved to Charleston, South Carolina, to become a pastor there, and he founded the Charleston Baptist Association in 1751, the South's first Baptist association, which he modeled after the PBA.[93]

The PBA also helped to form the Warren Association in 1767. Leading this effort was James Manning (1738–1791). He attended and was the first graduate of the Hopewell Academy (established in 1756) in his home state of New Jersey. The PBA had started the academy to educate boys and prepare them for the ministry. Manning then continued his studies at the College of New Jersey in 1758. After he graduated from college in 1762, he became the pastor at the Baptist church in Warren, Rhode Island, two years later. Building on their success in establishing the Hopewell Academy, several leaders in the Philadelphia Baptist Association wanted to establish a Baptist college to train ministers. The leaders urged the creation of a college despite some Baptists who opposed an educated clergy because they were afraid that too much education would stifle the work of the Holy Spirit in these pastors' ministries and because of the clear ties between established churches and an educated ministry. Nevertheless, the association selected Rhode Island as the ideal place to start a college because the colony did not have a college and because approximately twenty thousand Baptists lived there. Rhode Island also had the advantage of having PBA disciple James Manning pastoring in one of its churches. In 1764 the Rhode Island College, the first Baptist college in the New World, was founded, and James Manning became its president.[94]

To facilitate fundraising efforts for Rhode Island College and unite the loosely affiliated Baptist churches of New England, James Manning sought to combine the churches of New England into one association: the Warren Association. The name of the association came from the town in Rhode Island where Manning was a pastor. His efforts to organize the Baptist churches of New England into an association encountered resistance. When ten churches (most of them from Massachusetts) met in September 1767 in Warren to form an association, only three churches joined Manning's church: Second Baptist Church of Middleborough, First Baptist Church of Haverhill, and First Baptist Church of Bellingham.[95] Too many Baptist churches feared losing congregational autonomy because Manning's proposed association would have the authority to make decisions to which the church had to submit.[96] For New England Baptists, such an association sounded awfully close to the authority that presbyteries exercised over Presbyterian churches and was reminiscent of the authority that the Standing Church in Connecticut claimed over local churches as a result of the Saybrook Platform in 1708. In Massachusetts, associations did not have "official" authority over churches as they did in Connecticut, but the fear was present, even in Massachusetts's established churches, that associations would overstep their juridical bounds.[97]

Eventually, Manning rephrased his explanation of the power of associations in his *The Sentiments and Plan of the Warren Association* (1769), to make clear that "that such an association is consistent with the independency and power of particular churches, because it pretends to be no other than an *Advisory council* utterly disclaiming superiority, jurisdiction, coercive right and infallibility."[98] In the opinion of an increasing number of Baptist churches, Manning's promises helped to calm their fears of the association engaging in ecclesiastical overreach. As William G. McLoughlin notes, "the Association grew from four members in 1767 to thirty-eight in 1780" and spawned off several other associations in New England: the Stonington Baptist Association in Connecticut (1772); the New Hampshire Baptist Association (1776); the Woodstock (Vermont) Association (1783); and the Shaftsbury Association (1787), which included churches mainly in western Massachusetts.[99]

In addition to the easing of anxiety about the power of associations, the Warren Association gained the respect of a lot of churches by spearheading the fight for religious liberty in New England. In 1769 the Warren Association created the "Grievance Committee," which collected accounts from Baptist churches that detailed persecution from the state and drafted legislation to lessen or eliminate discrimination. From 1772 on, the able Isaac Backus led the efforts of the Grievance Committee. New England Baptist ministers and the churches they led formed one of the first organized religious lobbies in America, but their lobbying efforts could not have taken place without these churches voluntarily uniting into an association to speak a unified message to Massachusetts on why legislation guaranteeing religious liberty should be passed.

2

FROM "TACTICS" TO "STRATEGY"

BECOMING A UNIFIED POLITICAL MOVEMENT

On October 15, 1752, an unexpected commotion interrupted the otherwise normal, if dreary and rainy, evening at the house of a widow living in Norwich, Connecticut. Widow Elizabeth Backus, mother of eleven children, most notably Baptist champion for religious liberty Isaac Backus, found herself in trouble with the law. According to a letter that she wrote to her not-yet-famous son, "tax collectors came to our house, and took me away to prison about nine o'clock" for failing to pay parish taxes.[1] Baptist historian and pastor Frederic Denison later added that, while she was in prison, "she was sick, and, thickly wrapped in clothes to produce perspiration, sat near the fire by her stand, reading the family Bible. The officer thought that, under the circumstances, she would yield and pay the rates. But Mrs. Backus was not the woman to abandon her religious principles."[2] Suffice it to say, the experience filled her with dread and fear, but she relied on God's strength to get her through the ordeal. She continued to her son, "But, O the condescension of heaven! though I was bound when I was cast into this furnace, yet was I loosed, and found Jesus in the midst of the furnace with me. O then I could give up my name, estate, family, life and breath, freely to God. Now the prison looked like a palace to me." After having a "furnace" experience of God's deliverance akin to that of Daniel's three friends, Backus then gleefully made it through the rest of her thirteen-day stay in the Norwich prison.³

In addition to the divine presence, widow Backus had human company in prison when fellow church members Hill and Sabin joined her the following day. The Norwich authorities had been arresting people for a few months before the widow's own arrest, and continued to do so for several months after. Among others arrested were Isaac's brother Samuel and his maternal uncle Isaac Tracy.⁴ Altogether, Denison estimated that the agents for the Standing Order arrested about forty people over the course of a year.⁵ The prisoners believed in a way to go to Heaven different than the Congregationalist path. They were Separates, who because of conscience refused to pay taxes to the established church. Elizabeth Backus and some of the other Separates had not paid their parish taxes since they broke away from Benjamin Lord's Congregationalist church in Norwich in 1745 and formed their own church, the Bean Hill Separate Church, a year later.⁶ Interestingly, Norwich became such a haven for Separate adherence that the Separates and their allies defeated supporters of the established church in a town meeting and voted not to have to pay taxes to Benjamin Lord's church anymore. However, some representatives of the losing party appealed to the Connecticut General Assembly, and the assembly created an act forcing the town's majority to pay Lord and to keep up the parish church. When the original winners refused to pay, the arrests started.⁷

By the end of the 1740s, the Separate Baptists, many of whom were once Separates, were no longer in a mood to sit idly by and see their rights to worship and property endangered. This chapter will analyze the ways in which New England Baptists shifted from using haphazard and occasion-specific tactics in opposing the Standing Order to building a sustained political movement. Such a shift gradually occurred between the end of the Great Awakening and the early 1790s. Most notably, increasing disputes between Massachusetts and Great Britain in the 1760s and early 1770s over taxation without representation and the right to self-government provided a fruitful context for the consolidation of the Baptist political movement. While New England Baptists overwhelmingly sided with the patriots, they actually fought a war "on two fronts: against Britain for civil liberty and against the Standing Order for religious liberty."⁸ Baptists engaged in battle on the latter front by using "no taxation without representation" and the "right to self-government" as tropes against the Standing Order, to the consternation of dedicated

New England patriots (and Congregationalists) like John and Samuel Adams, who were suspicious of Baptist fealty to the rebel cause.

Ironically, this Baptist revolution within a revolution owed its growing strength to one of the major, if not *the* major, reasons that the patriots were able to persuade enough colonists continue fighting through a long war: the increasingly important role of the printing press in consolidating public opinion against Britain. Several Baptist leaders, most notably Samuel Stillman, James Manning, and Isaac Backus, embraced the use of printed materials, namely newspapers and pamphlets, to bind together a growing number of staunchly autonomous Baptist churches throughout New England into both an imagined community of like-minded supporters (some of whom never met each other) and actual organizations like the Warren Association. Through the press, the Warren Association and its Grievance Committee informed their "constituents" about the progress, or lack thereof, that Baptists were making in the fight for religious liberty and sought to persuade the wider public on the importance of ensuring liberty of conscience in the Massachusetts Constitution of 1780. These leaders' fledgling efforts at fostering religious and political unity at the associational level set the stage for their colleague John Leland, who later arrived back in his home of state of Massachusetts in 1792, to go beyond the groundwork that they laid and successfully align with non-Baptists by using partisan politics of the First Party Era to his advantage.

LAWS FAVORING THE CONGREGATIONAL ESTABLISHMENT

The Great Awakening led to the rapid growth of the Separates and Separate Baptists, which challenged the Congregational establishment by siphoning off church members. The exodus from the parent church potentially lessened each parish's tax base. Every family who resided in a given parish was responsible for supporting the parish church and the official or "settled" minister. But what if a parish's residents no longer believed that the parish pastor was their surest spiritual guide? Did they have to pay taxes that supported a false or erring church? Of course, the establishment's critics answered in the negative.

The establishment did not view its opponents' distaste for ecclesiastical taxes as a matter of conscience, which entitled the dissenters to refuse to support the central institution of its covenantal society and endanger the establishment's existence.[9] As a result, Massachusetts passed or renewed a series of exemption laws throughout the eighteenth century that ostensibly allowed for Separate Baptists to submit paperwork claiming that their consciences did not permit them to support the parish church any longer. Separate Baptists could thereby avoid paying ecclesiastical taxes. However, the legislature of the Standing Order intended the requirements for Baptists obtaining exemption status to be extremely difficult for most churches and members to meet, so it was a token law, at best. For example, Massachusetts's tax exemption law of 1753 required that a person purporting to be a Baptist minister find three other Baptist churches that could vouch for him being an actual minister (this portion of the law only stayed in effect until 1758). In turn, the attested minister could legally provide certificates to those who had two other members sign a document substantiating the person's interest in and frequent attendance to Baptist churches. If a person had all the proper paperwork, this person could then (theoretically) become exempt from all parish taxes.[10]

The problem with the 1753 law from the Baptist perspective was that the Baptist churches that came out of Congregationalism and the Separate movement were relatively new and were theologically Calvinistic. Conversely, the Baptist churches that existed in Massachusetts and other parts of New England before the Great Awakening, with members who Isaac Backus and William G. McLoughlin called the "Old Baptists," were Arminians[11] and/or anti-revivalist. Such churches were not always inclined to help Baptists of another theological persuasion.[12] Another complication arose in 1758 when the legislature passed a new version of the tax exemption law. Each conscientious objector had to obtain signatures from three other Baptists, instead of two, and had to be church members, rather than just frequent visitors or attendees of Baptist churches.[13] Throughout the mid-1740s and the 1750s, "church membership" was a contentious concept in Baptist churches. Separate Baptists throughout New England were still trying to distinguish themselves ecclesiologically from both their Congregationalist and Separate neighbors. Also, Baptists would sometimes renounce their "re-baptism" and return to Separate or Congregationalist churches.[14] With the Separate Baptist movement in a state of flux in its early years, it was impossible to have any sort of overarching denominational organization that united the churches on ecclesiological and legal matters.

BAPTISTS' EARLY TACTICS

Massachusetts Congregationalists took advantage of Baptist disunity by continuing to collect their parish taxes, oftentimes even when Baptist churches or individuals met the stringent requirements of the exemption laws. Although there was a wide diversity on how the authorities in each parish treated the Baptist dissenters, characteristic penalties against Baptists included fining them for not paying taxes, imprisoning them, seizing their property, and selling their land and possessions at auction. Until the mid-1760s, Baptists adopted several largely ineffective tactics to fight having to pay parish taxes. The failure of these tactics would eventually lead Baptists to embrace a counterstrategy that sought to consolidate relatively isolated Baptists communities into an association with political goals, a kind of "protoparty" that foreshadowed Baptists' later involvement in actual party politics during the First Party Era.

In discussing Baptist tactics, I am employing as a framework Michel de Certeau's discussion of the difference between "strategy" and "tactics." According to Certeau, a strategy is "the calculus of force relationships" that "assumes a place that can be circumscribed as *proper* (*propre*) and thus serve as the basis for generating relations with an exterior distinct from it (competitors, adversaries, 'clienteles,' 'targets,' or 'objects' of research)."[15] The Standing Order of eighteenth-century Massachusetts and Connecticut implemented a strategy of maintaining its religio-political authority over its major religious competitors like the Separates and Baptists through the passage of self-serving civil and ecclesiastical laws, punishing noncompliance, and trying to deny access to the political process. In contrast, Baptists made use of tactics, or "[calculi] which cannot count on a 'proper' (a spatial or institutional localization), nor thus on a borderline distinguishing the other as a visible totality. The place of a tactic belongs to the other."[16] Because Congregationalists controlled the political, religious, and social space of eighteenth-century New England, Baptists were always the "weak" faction looking for opportunities to act on the "strong" Congregationalists' home turf. As William G. McLoughlin put this dynamic in spatial terms, "The Baptists were in New England but not entirely of New England;" they were the consummate outsiders.[17]

Petitioning

Baptists took advantage of one opportunity to fight the religious establishment by exercising one of the few rights that the Crown gave them as English subjects: petitioning the colonial government, and if necessary, the king and Parliament, to enact more fair laws. Throughout the late 1740s and 1750s, as the need arose, Massachusetts Baptists attended conferences comprised of Baptist pastors and laymen who sought to address specific crises that their churches faced by drawing up petitions together. Most of the time, parish officials and the General Court ignored the petitions because of lack of concern for Baptists, or they became distracted by more pressing matters such as the outbreak of war. When the efforts of a given Baptist conference failed, the conference would eventually dissolve. For example, in 1747 the General Court allowed for Baptists and Quakers to be exempt from paying parish taxes but reversed itself with the harsh 1753 tax exemption law. Massachusetts Baptists did not like this curtailment of rights, so "twenty-two elder and lay delegates from eleven churches" met together in Medfield on March 14, 1753, and formed a committee to draw up a petition to pressure the General Court to reverse the 1753 law. The Baptists had also decided that they would petition the king if the General Court would not listen. The conference then met two more times, once in Bellingham in May 1753 and once in Boston in February 1754. At the latter conference, they collected almost two hundred pounds to fund an agent to travel to England to meet the king. Ultimately, Baptists did not appeal to the king directly because the French and Indian War also started in 1754, and they did not want to appear disloyal by complaining about the actions of one of his royal colonies.[18]

The General Court read the petition on June 5, 1754, and rejected it because they thought that the Baptists misrepresented the actions of the Massachusetts legislature. Over the next few years, the committee submitted similar petitions to no avail. However, the General Court did modify the 1753 exemption law with the 1758 exemption law. According to William G. McLoughlin, "no record exists of any Baptist petitions by the denomination as a whole or by any committee chosen by it against this [1758] act," although individual churches still appealed to their parishes or the General Court for tax relief.[19] The Baptist ad hoc conference meetings and accompanying petition committee collapsed just a few years after starting to meet. Baptists had not yet successfully devised a permanent and unified organizational strategy conducive to challenging the establishment in a consistent, systematic way. The Congregationalists thus held firm to their Certeauian "proper" domain in New England. As a result, Baptists languished under persecution for another decade without much change.

Going to Court

A second major tactic that Baptists employed involved going to local and provincial courts to seek restitution for loss of possessions from imprisonment. True to their steadfast belief in local church autonomy, individual Baptist churches usually faced the courts alone, and most of the time, the churches failed to receive a fair hearing from the courts.[20] Essentially, the courts sought to maintain the status quo by deciding in favor of the parish. As William G. McLoughlin observed, "the function of the courts was to serve as a bulwark of the old order not as a battering ram for the new."[21] Also, judges, lawyers, and most jurors were Congregationalists, and there was a widespread prejudice against Baptists in Massachusetts. Moreover, individual Baptists churches often lacked the funds they needed to pay for a protracted legal battle against the parish. Finally, McLoughlin astutely pointed out that "By waging their battle in the courts the Baptists were acknowledging the legitimacy of toleration, and the more radical among them gradually began to feel that the established structure itself had to be changed."[22] In order to change what they perceived to be an oppressive structure, Baptists eventually figured out that they would need to devise a strategy to attack the establishment with a unified voice. Situational, scattershot tactics did not work.

MAKING USE OF THE PRINTING PRESS
TO FURTHER THE BAPTIST CAUSE

A turning point in the Baptists' struggle against the establishment, unknown to most New England Baptists at the time, occurred when Baptist leader Isaac Backus published a book-length pamphlet in 1768 in response to the sermon series that Congregationalist minister Joseph Fish published the year before, which roundly criticized the Separate and Separate Baptist movements. Although on the surface it appears that a Baptist was yet again responding in an ad hoc fashion to mistreatment from a Congregationalist, the debate that ensued between Backus and Fish hints at the beginning of a Baptist move away from ineffective tactics and toward an actual strategy. Beginning in the mid-1760s, Isaac Backus and other Baptist leaders used the printing press, a technology that played an essential role in the American colonists' larger fight against Britain, as a strategy to foster an imagined community of Baptists throughout New England. They did this in part by relating common stories of persecution. They also used the press to communicate arguments for religious freedom to their congregations. Creating an imagined community was intertwined with the formation of the Warren Association (1767) and its Grievance Committee two years later. Both the imagined community and the new organization gave Baptists a sense of denominational and political unity that they had been lacking until that point.

Joseph Fish certainly did not want to play a part in strengthening the Baptist position in New England. As the longtime pastor of the North Stonington Church, one of three Congregationalist churches in Stonington,[23] he viewed Baptist churches as a threat to the established church. In 1765 Fish preached to his congregation a series of nine sermons on what characteristics composed the visible[24] churches of Christ and whether or not one should consider Separate and Separate Baptist churches to be true churches. It was this same sermon series that he published two years later. If the Separate and Separate Baptists churches were not bona fide gospel-centered churches, then the members of said churches should repent and return to the established churches, Fish reasoned.[25] Ever since the social and ecclesiological upheaval of the Great Awakening in the 1740s, church members and attendees had been defecting from Fish's church and embracing the Separate and Separate Baptist movements. According to Fish, the number of those who left his church was "not less than two thirds of the congregation."[26] His immediate purpose for preaching the sermons was to "instruct the *young* and the *ignorant*, and to establish those that are *wavering*."[27] Fish felt obligated to combat the apostasies because many in his remaining congregation were still sympathetic to the Separates and Baptists. He also was aware that some who attended his church had forgotten about or were too young to remember the Great Awakening and the beginnings of the troublesome Separate movement, which spawned the Separate Baptists. In his sermons, Fish also gave his hearers his recollection of the past twenty-five years of the church's and New England's history.[28]

Had Fish not published his nine sermons, his words would have had the potential to be influential only among his congregation. However, Fish noted that by publishing his sermons, "by the blessing of God upon them, they may be, in some measure, useful to the churches."[29] Although people leaving his church was a very local and personal problem, Fish knew that other Congregationalist churches throughout Connecticut and Massachusetts had been experiencing the same types of problems with the Separates and Separate Baptists. In his own small way, Fish sought to shore up the entire establishment from religious interlopers.

As was common with the writings of the time, Fish asked his readers to report to him any errors that he inadvertently made in his sermons.[30] Most likely, Fish did not expect the long and critical response that he eventually received from Backus. At first, Backus did not even want to respond to Fish. But Backus noted how "I have been requested by Christian friends to write some reply." Backus did not identify who his "Christian friends" were, but they were almost definitely fellow Baptists and maybe even some old Separate friends, groups whom Fish attacked. Even after his friends asked him to refute Fish, Backus still did not agree to do so because he believed a few of his previously published works already addressed Fish's criticisms. His friends did not take no for an answer, however. They reminded Backus that he was an early leader of the Separates and was one of the few people still living who could give an accurate account of the Separates' history. Backus relented, and after reading Fish's book, he concluded that he must respond.[31] Backus published his 129-page *A Fish Caught in His Own Net* in 1768, the title an obvious pun on his opponent's last name. The text was an apologia for the Separate and Separate Baptist causes. According to William G. McLoughlin, it was also the first of Backus's many tracts that "dealt with the specific problem of separation of church and state in regard to religious taxes."[32]

What is significant is not the content of Backus's response, but the fact that his "Christian friends" begged him specifically for help. But why Backus? By 1768 other Baptists in New England already saw him as a prominent leader, perhaps even on top of the "pecking order." Undoubtedly, part of the reason was that Backus, like many of his Baptist ministerial brethren, was an itinerant preacher who encountered many church members during his travels. Also, Backus was involved in ordaining other ministers. Third, Backus was a founding trustee of the first Baptist college in the American colonies, Rhode Island College, which was founded in 1764. Finally, Backus fully embraced the easier and cheaper opportunities for getting his message out that arose because of the increasing importance of the printing press in the American colonies as a whole in the 1760s. In turn, American printers and booksellers helped make Backus the most influential Baptist in the colonies by frequently advertising his writings in their newspapers and/or by selling his works in their shops. It is this last reason, which no other historian of New England Baptists, not even William G. McLoughlin, has adequately explored, that is pivotal in understanding how New England Baptists became a unified movement. They did so by slowly and unevenly distancing themselves from the use of ineffective tactics that characterized their efforts through the 1750s and early 1760s.

The Rise in Importance of the Printing Press in Late Colonial America

Before examining Backus and other Baptists' strategic use of the printing press for the purpose of uniting Baptists ideologically and organizationally, a discussion of the rise in importance of the printing press in the late colonial era is in order. Two forms of printed media, newspapers and pamphlets, were the most prevalent and merit analysis. Concerning newspapers, Benjamin Harris, a newspaper publisher and printer from London, printed the first newspaper in the American colonies in 1690. He printed his first and only issue of *Public Occurrences, Both Foreign and Domestick* in Boston. The paper did not last because it did not have a government license, and it criticized the colonial government for mistreating Native Americans.[33] The number of newspapers grew slowly until the outbreak of the French and Indian War in 1754. According to journalism historian Carol Sue Humphrey, "The French and Indian War provided a major encouragement for the future growth of newspapers in the American colonies because of the desire for information about the conflict." The colonists feared that if the French gained control of the colonies, their lucrative trade with the British would cease, and the French would force them to convert to Catholicism. As a result, the colonists were intensely interested in the course and outcome of the war.[34]

Because their audience wanted to have up-to-date and accurate information about how the war was going, printers also changed their policies on distributing and collecting information. In 1758 deputy postmasters general Benjamin Franklin of Philadelphia and William Hunter of Virginia "established a system of postage-free exchange of newspapers, thus encouraging a broader exchange of news and information throughout the colonies." This policy allowed for news to reach worried citizens much more quickly. Also, printers tried to ensure the accuracy of the reports that they printed in their papers by receiving firsthand accounts from soldiers or other eyewitnesses of key battles. As much as possible, they sought not to rely on hearsay about how a battle fared until they could authenticate the information.[35] Wartime was a boon for the newspaper industry. By the end of war, there were twenty-three newspapers in the American colonies, as compared to eleven just a few decades before.[36] The French and Indian War had taught newspaper printers how to cover successfully an intercolonial and international event, which served the colonists well in their impending war against Britain.[37]

The Stamp Act in 1765, along with the Sugar Act the previous year, were the first major taxes that the British government passed to extract funds from the colonists to refill the Crown's coffers after an immensely expensive war against the French. The Stamp Act was particularly odious, for the law required that all paper—including newspapers, official documents, and books—be taxed. Each taxed piece of paper needed a stamp on it. Colonial newspaper printers would obviously be negatively affected by the new law. Most printers charged subscription fees that were only slightly above the costs of production; most printers did not become wealthy like Benjamin Franklin. An added tax to every news sheet would decrease the already meager profits that printers earned.[38] The Stamp Act also had the potential to ruin the printing industry because its taxes hampered maritime commerce in general. In 1765 New England's eleven printers were located in port cities or in towns along major rivers, areas of major trade. In another book, Carol Sue Humphrey observes how "a certain level of commercial activity was essential if the paper was to get enough advertising to survive."[39] If merchants, lawyers, and other tradesmen who used paper for contracts and other documents could not stay in business because of the stamp taxes, then they could not advertise in the local paper, which meant that newspapers would lose revenue and go out of business themselves.

In addition to concerns over losing income, the colonists voiced displeasure over "taxation without representation" because the British government did not receive the consent of the colonists before taxing them. The colonists wanted a voice in government, but Parliament was not listening, so the colonists sought to make Parliament aware of their complaints about the Stamp Act in various ways. Merchants, who had been boycotting British trade goods since the Sugar Act, increased their boycotting efforts. In churches, clergymen criticized the British government's perceived overreach. Colonial governments, most notably the Virginia House of Burgesses, passed resolutions against the Stamp Act in the summer of 1765. (Virginia was the oldest and most populous of the American colonies. It was thus very important to the rebel cause that Virginia sided against England). The Stamp Act crisis also led to the creation of the Sons of Liberty throughout the colonies. The Sons of Liberty were groups of men who dedicated themselves to making sure that the Stamp Act would never be enforced. In Boston in particular, the Sons of Liberty resorted to mob violence to prevent the Stamp Act from going into effect. They destroyed the home of stamp master-delegate Andrew Oliver and royal Lieutenant Governor Thomas Hutchinson.[40]

Newspaper printers joined in the struggle against the British by reporting on the protests that occurred throughout the colonies. Within a matter of weeks, people in South Carolina could know how successful the Sons of Liberty in Boston were and vice versa. Also, prominent Boston printers like the Thomas and John Fleet (Boston *Evening-Post*) and Benjamin Edes and John Gill (Boston *Gazette*) were actively involved in printing articles that argued against the Stamp Act. Edes was even a member of the Boston Sons of Liberty.[41] The printed word thus both mediated and reinforced public distaste for the Stamp Act. Eventually, the Crown and Parliament decided that they could not enforce the Stamp Act and repealed it in March 1766.[42]

As each new crisis like the Boston Massacre, the Boston Tea Party, and the passing of the Quebec Act ensued, the colonies' relationship with the mother country deteriorated further. All the while, newspapers were there to report events, influence public opinion, and unite enough colonists to fight a long war against a superior military force. Newspapers, then, helped to create a sense of American nationalism.[43] The roles that newspapers played had an inordinate impact upon society in contrast to the actual numbers of newspapers there were. At the start of the Revolutionary War in 1775, almost forty newspapers existed in the American colonies. However, media historian David A. Copeland argues that this small number of newspapers reached about 2.5 million people. Not everyone could read or had the money to afford a newspaper subscription, but nearly everyone interacted with newspapers in some form. He observes that "in colonial America, the same stories were printed, read and debated aloud, then re-read and re-debated in practically every town and home. Political debate fed into the idea of being American, too. Lack of stature in a community did not necessarily lessen a person's knowledge or understanding in America's eighteenth-century public sphere."[44]

Based on Copeland's description of colonists' open access to newspapers, it is not difficult to see why such a medium could benefit the Baptist cause. Generally, New England Baptists were less wealthy, less educated, and had second-class status as compared to their Congregationalist cousins. However, their leaders and some Baptist advertisers formed a strategy that involved using newspapers to make the political situation in New England a more equal playing field and to inform Baptists on issues that mattered to them most: obtaining liberty of conscience from the Standing Order and civil liberty from England.

In addition to newspapers, pamphlets were another printed form that rose in significance in the late colonial era. According to Bernard Bailyn, "much of the most important and characteristic writing of the American Revolution appeared" as a pamphlet. The influential nature of such pamphlets as James Otis's *The Rights of the British Colonies Asserted and Proved* (1764) and Thomas Paine's *Common Sense* (1776) bears Bailyn's point out. One chief benefit that pamphlets had over books and even newspapers was that they were cheap and easy to produce. All a printer had to do was to take a few sheets of paper and fold the sheets into smaller sizes to create the desired number of pages for the pamphlet. Printers also did not have to spend a lot of effort binding the pamphlets like they would books; they only had to stitch the loose pages together. Printers could produce many copies of pamphlets for a fraction of the cost of books and newspapers.[45] So, even groups like Baptists who did not have a lot of money could afford to distribute pamphlets containing their arguments for religious liberty to their churches and to the wider public.

Pamphlets were not only cheap and easy to create but could also contain almost any bit of information that the author(s) wanted on them. Bailyn classified the vast majority of the pamphlets of the era into three major categories. The first category was "direct responses to the great events of the time." For example, as they did in newspapers, people responded in pamphlet form to the Stamp Act to argue why the Stamp Act was not a fair policy. Bailyn described the second category as "chain-reacting personal polemics: strings of individual exchanges—arguments, replies, rebuttals, and counter-rebuttals—in which may be found heated personifications of the larger conflict."[46] The Backus/Fish pamphlet war fits this category perfectly because Joseph Fish and Isaac Backus responded to one another intermittently for six years.[47] At stake in the exchange between Fish and Backus was whether the Separate Baptists could form true churches and if those churches had a place in New England's future. The final major category addressed by pamphlets were important days of commemoration or observance like an election sermon, or increasingly, other noteworthy events like the anniversary of the Boston Massacre. Although election sermons had existed in New England since the mid-seventeenth century, they took on new emphases in the worsening political climate against Britain.[48]

Just like their fellow Patriot leaders, Baptist leaders took advantage of the popularity of the pamphlet medium, but for different purposes that fit their strategy. For example, Samuel Stillman, pastor of the First Baptist Church of Boston, was considered a well-known and erudite preacher, even among Congregationalists, so he frequently published his sermons in pamphlet form. Also, Baptist leaders printed and distributed the yearly minutes of the Warren Association to keep New England Baptists informed on regular church business and the struggle for religious liberty, thereby knitting together a previously loose and fiercely independent number of churches into the beginnings of one denominational body. Finally, the Baptist pamphleteer extraordinaire Isaac Backus crafted several treatises that argued for liberty of conscience and an end to religious taxation, which were very popular among New England Baptists.

Charts Describing Baptists' Use of Newspapers with Analysis

Now that the essential role of the printing press in the American colonists' efforts to gain independence from the British has been explored broadly, Baptist leaders', especially Isaac Backus's, use of the printing press as a strategy to foster Baptist unity and disestablish the Standing

Order deserves closer examination. Two tables will aid in this analysis. What is perhaps most surprising concerning the data in table 1 is that no Separate or Baptist leaders published or advertised their writings at all from 1745 to 1759 (actually, not until 1763, which I will discuss later). However, as stated earlier, the newspaper industry in New England and the rest of the American colonies did not grow much in number and influence until at least midway through the French and Indian War (1754–1763) and especially not until the Stamp Act crisis in 1765. The dearth of Separate and Separate Baptist publications mentioned in newspapers of the time thus makes sense.

Notice also that there is only one advertisement for the works of Separates shown in either table, that from Ebenezer Frothingham.[49] Throughout the 1750s and 1760s, Separates "stood in an unstable 'halfway house' between churchly and fully dissenting positions," according to C. C. Goen. While some Separates returned to the churches of the Standing Order, most Separates took the final step of dissent by embracing believer's baptism and thereby became Baptists.[50] Their longing for a church consisting of only regenerate believers and an ecclesiology that promoted lay preaching overrode their initial scruples against believer's baptism. By the 1780s the Separates as an independent movement had all but collapsed, which is the most likely reason Separate leaders did not advertise their writings nearly as frequently as Baptists. It is also possible that Separate Baptists were more media savvy and commercially aware than their Separate brethren, and therefore were more willing to take advantage of the opportunity that advertising their works afforded them when it came to perpetuating and consolidating their movement.

Furthermore, both tables indicate that the writings of and advertisements for the writings of Baptist leaders James Manning (thirty-nine total) and Samuel Stillman (nineteen total) were popular among newspaper printers. Other than Isaac Backus, James Manning and Samuel Stillman were arguably the most noteworthy Baptist leaders in New England. James Manning was the first president of Rhode Island College, and the ads relating to him reflect his role as president. In several of the ads, Manning endorsed such textbooks as *The American Latin Grammar* for use at Rhode Island College[51] and Noah Webster's *The American Spelling-Book* for anyone "who [wishes] to write or speak the English language properly."[52] More importantly, James Manning was instrumental in Rhode Island College's continued existence after

Table 1
Frequency of Writings and Advertisements for Writings of Key New England Baptist and Separate Leaders Found in Colonial/Early Republic Newspapers, 1745–1792

	1745–1759	1760–1764	1765–1769	1770–1774	1775–1779	1780–1784	1785–1789	1790–1792	Total
Noah Alden (B)[a]	0	0	0	0	0	0	0	0	0
Isaac Backus (S then B)[b]	0	13	8	14	11	23	11	2	82
Ebenezer Frothingham (S)	0	0	1	0	0	0	0	0	1
Israel Holly (S)	0	0	0	0	0	0	0	0	0
James Manning (B)	0	0	1	3	5	19	2	9	39
Solomon Paine (S)	0	0	0	0	0	0	0	0	0
Hezekiah Smith (B)	0	0	0	3	0	0	0	0	3
Samuel Stillman (B)	0	0	2	11	3	0	0	3	19
Total	0	13	12	31	19	42	13	14	144

Notes: a"B" is for Baptist; "S" is for Separate. Concerning my methodology for both tables, I compiled the statistics from the Florida State University Libraries America's Historical Newspapers, 1690–1922 online database in the years 2016 to 2017. I selected the year range of 1745 to 1792 and conducted a search of all newspapers printed during that time. I searched for results by placing the leaders' first and last names in the search box. Sometimes having the leaders' names in quotation marks yielded more (or different) results, but oftentimes not using quotation marks yielded the most results. I searched just the last names as well. bBackus became a Baptist in 1751, three years before he published his first work. Neither he nor anyone else advertised his first work in the newspaper at that time.

the war. According to Manning's biographer, Reuben Aldridge Guild, "from Dec. 7, 1776, until May 27, 1782, the course of studies was suspended" at the college. The British invaded Newport and occupied the college's only building in Providence for over three years.[53] After the British left Providence, Manning made use of a newspaper advertisement to urge the college's corporation members to attend a meeting in order to help the college to resume classes.[54] Although the meeting occurred, Manning had to wait even longer to get the college back on its feet because America's allies, the French, used the college's building for a hospital from June 25, 1780, until May 27, 1782.[55] Once Rhode Island's role in the war was essentially over, Manning, with the assistance of the corporation and donations from the Warren Association and the Philadelphia Baptist Association (PBA), ensured the survival of the college after the war. On September 4, 1782, Rhode Island College joyously had its first public commencement in six years.[56]

Although many Baptists still had misgivings about the utility of ministers receiving a college education, Manning's efforts in starting and continuing Rhode Island College were one of the first steps in helping Baptists to achieve a measure of social respectability through educational attainment.[57] Sometimes, Baptists delighted in their alterity and used it to disparage the Standing Order for preventing religious freedom. However, they also longed for the acceptance in New England society that their educated Congregationalist ministerial counterparts experienced. Founding a college was an example of the weak Baptists "[turning] to their own ends forces alien to them" in order to become respectable.[58]

Samuel Stillman (1737–1807), pastor of the First Baptist Church of Boston from 1765 to 1807, also served New England Baptists in several important ways. He was one of the original trustees of Rhode Island College and was a longtime member of the Grievance Committee. He was also a bit unusual for a Baptist minister in New England. First, Stillman received two honorary college degrees. Second, he enjoyed cordial relations with the Congregationalist clergy in Boston. For instance, one of Boston's Congregationalist ministers, the Rev. Dr. Andrew Eliot, participated in Stillman's installation as pastor of First Baptist Church of Boston.[59] Congregationalist ministers did not usually involve themselves with the ordination of Baptist preachers.

Whereas Manning had a presence in the newspapers of his day because of his work as president of Rhode Island College, Samuel Stillman's popularity and influence among Baptists rested on his reputation as an excellent pulpiteer.[60] All but one of Stillman's nineteen works shown in table 2 involves advertisements for various sermons that he preached throughout his long tenure as pastor of First Baptist Church of Boston. Stillman particularly earned the admiration of Bostonians, Baptist and non-Baptist alike, by successfully converting a convicted criminal named Levi Ames on his walk from prison to the gallows. Stillman included an account of his conversion efforts in two sermons that he preached, one before the day of the execution and one the day after. Bostonians John Kneeland, Philip Freeman Sr., and Philip Freeman Jr. advertised the sale of Stillman's sermons in their shops a total of eight times in several newspapers throughout Boston in November and December 1773.[61] A month later, in Rhode Island, Solomon Southwick advertised the sermons in his Newport *Mercury*, added in his advertisement that Ames was executed for burglary on October 21, 1773, and actually asked Stillman to preach the sermon that took place the day before his death.[62] Advertisements like these promoting Stillman's pastoral concern for a thief and his wish that his main audiences not live a similar criminal life made Stillman a fixture in New England.

Leading Separate and Separate Baptist leaders in just about every category in both tables is Isaac Backus. The eighty-two writings and advertisements of his writings is approximately *57 percent* of the total data. Moreover, table 1 demonstrates that Backus's pamphlets and other writings appeared consistently in the newspapers of his era from the early 1760s to the late 1780s.

Though absent from the newspaper records of the late colonial era from 1745 to 1763, Backus's works first made their appearance in an advertisement in the February 12, 1763, issue of the Providence *Gazette; and Country Journal*. William Goddard, the newspaper's printer, published Backus's pamphlet *Spiritual Ignorance Causeth Men to Counteract their Doctrinal Knowledge. A Discourse from Acts xiii. 27* and advertised that he was selling copies of the sermon. Goddard also mentioned that Philip Freeman of Boston would be selling the same work in his shop on Union Street. The advertisement further informs readers that both shops also carried Backus's first published work ever, *A Discourse Shewing the Nature and Necessity of an Internal Call to Preach the Everlasting Gospel* (1754).[63] Either Backus's 1754 sermon remained popular enough to his Separate and Baptist readers for the shop owners to keep copies on hand, or they were reintroducing Backus's first work as a

Table 2
Types of Writings and Advertisements for Writings of Key New England Baptist and Separate Leaders Found in Colonial/Early Republic Newspapers, 1745–1792

	Ads Written by Leaders	Ads for Selling Leaders' Writings	Excerpts of Leaders' Own Writings in Newspapers	Works of Others Endorsed by Leaders	Miscellaneous	Total
Noah Alden (B)	0	0	0	0	0	0
Isaac Backus (S then B)	11	63	3	0	5	82
Ebenezer Frothingham (S)	0	1	0	0	0	1
Israel Holly (S)	0	0	0	0	0	0
James Manning (B)	24	0	3	12	0	39
Solomon Paine (S)	0	0	0	0	0	0
Hezekiah Smith (B)	0	0	1	0	2	3
Samuel Stillman (B)	0	18	0	0	1	19
Total	35	82	7	12	8	144

companion to the newest publication. Moreover, observe the two locations where Backus's works were being sold, according to this 1763 advertisement: Providence and Boston. Providence (and later Newport), Rhode Island, were important places to sell Backus's works because Rhode Island was the center of Baptist numerical strength and influence in New England. Rhode Island College would eventually move to Providence in 1770. Boston, of course, was the most important city in New England overall, having more printers and booksellers than anywhere else in the region. Selling Backus's works and getting out the Baptist message in Boston and the towns that orbited that city was pivotal for the Baptist strategy of consolidating Baptists' political voice.

As the 1760s progressed, Backus's sermons and other treatises remained in demand in Rhode Island and Boston. William Goddard, printer of the Providence *Gazette; and Country Journal*, again led the way. In his May 5, 1764, issue, he urged anyone interested in subscribing to buy Backus's *A Letter to the Reverend Mr. Benjamin Lord, of Norwich*[64] to contact him and a few other associates—two in Providence and one in Newport—to determine how many copies Goddard needed to print.[65] Apparently, enough people responded to the original advertisement, leading Goddard to print an unknown number of copies and advertise them four more times from July 7 to August 11.[66] Samuel Hall, printer of the Newport *Mercury*, also became involved in the increasingly lucrative sale of Backus's works in 1766 when he published and promoted Backus's new discourse *Family Prayer not to be Neglected*, as well as Backus's sermon on the necessity of an internal call, his letter to Benjamin Lord, and his discourse from Acts 13:27. As with William Goddard's advertisements, Hall's advertisements informed his readers that the same four works by Backus could be purchased in Philip Freeman's shop in Boston.[67]

By 1768, when Backus responded to Joseph Fish in *A Fish Caught in His Own Net*,[68] both Backus and his works were a known commodity among the newspaper printers and shop owners of Providence, Newport, and Boston. These printing press entrepreneurs knew that they were likely to turn a profit if they continued to advertise and sell Backus's writings. Although the newspaper advertisements do not explicitly name who among the readership was demanding Backus's works, clearly Backus's "Christian friends" had created a market for his writings. They had urged Backus to write, but through their demand for his works, they also urged printers to print and sellers to sell.

Although not listed in the two tables like Backus, Stillman, and Manning, Philip Freeman (1712–1789) played an indispensable role as a disseminator of Baptist thought in Boston in the late colonial era and Early Republic. Yet, historians of Baptists have not paid attention to Freeman's contributions. According to Isaiah Thomas, the Boston and Worcester newspaper printer who founded the American Antiquarian Society in 1812, Philip Freeman was a deacon in Stillman's First Baptist Church of Boston. He came from England, where his family had taught him how to make leather gloves and pants. In 1762 he began selling soft leather in a shop on Union Street in Boston.[69] Hugh Amory, a former senior rare book cataloger at the Harvard University's Houghton Library, classified Freeman as an "importing [bookseller]" who peddled other English goods and sold American books and pamphlets as well.[70] Some of the other items that Freeman sold included maps, astronomical prints, microscopes, candle screens, and scales,[71] some items that comprised T. H. Breen's "empire of goods." Since he was not a printer, Freeman did not print his own copies of American writings. Instead, he relied on the newspaper printers in Boston to supply him with works to sell.

Freeman used his vocation as an importing bookseller in the commercially active port city of Boston to execute Baptists' strategy of disseminating their viewpoints through the organ of the press. He had advertised and sold Backus's polemical treatises and sermons since 1763 as well as his own pastor Samuel Stillman's sermons since 1769. Freeman's leadership role in supporting disestablishment in Massachusetts only grew with the advent of the Grievance Committee in 1769. Some of the *Minutes of the Warren Association* throughout the 1770s and early 1780s explicitly name Philip Freeman as being one of the members of the Grievance Committee, which collected accounts of Baptist oppression and was the political lobbying arm of the Warren Association.[72] He thus actively took part in the committee's strategic planning discussions to address religious discrimination. Freeman and his shop, then, served as a hub where Baptists and others passing through Boston could purchase Backus's and Stillman's writings.[73] These writings, primarily Backus's, repeatedly exposed Baptists to stories of persecution as well as scriptural and political arguments against maintaining a religious establishment. The Baptists of Boston and its environs absorbed what their leaders had to say, which helped create a common outlook on the problems they faced and the goals they should achieve. In more than

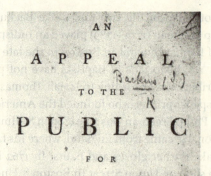

Copy of title page of Isaac Backus' pamphlet, "An appeal to the Public for Religious Liberty, Against the Oppressions of the Present Day" (1773).

one way, Freeman (and his son) helped Stillman and Backus sell to other Baptists the merits of standing together for religious freedom.

THE WORK OF THE WARREN ASSOCIATION'S GRIEVANCE COMMITTEE

Selling Associationalism among New England Baptists

Interconnected with and supported by Baptist leaders' use of the printing press, New England Baptists also formed the Warren Association and its Grievance Committee as a strategy for unifying disparate and independent Baptist churches into an entity with the political clout necessary to challenge the Congregational establishment, even as they remained unified with their Congregationalist cousins against their common foe, the British, in the Revolutionary War. Forming *organizational* unity would be trickier than forming an imagined community of the persecuted, however. Baptists in New England were nervous about having an association because they worried that individual churches would lose their decision-making autonomy to the power of an associational body. Associational bodies of ministers with the authority to make decisions against the will of an individual church already existed among the established churches in Massachusetts and especially Connecticut.[74] Many Baptists were loath to adopt the heavy-handed ecclesiastical practices of their oppressors. Baptist leaders thus had the uphill task of convincing churches through scripture-based and pragmatic arguments to come together as an associational body. They chose a strategy of selling the benefits of associationalism to other Baptists by arguing that Baptist churches needed a sustained and unified voice to combat the Standing Order. The old tactics of individual Baptists or individual churches merely petitioning the government or going to court from time to time did not accomplish their goal of religious disestablishment.

Masterminding the formation of the Warren Association was Elder James Manning. As president of Rhode Island College since 1764, he saw firsthand how fractured and beleaguered the churches in Massachusetts and Connecticut were. The reality of the New England Baptist churches' situation contrasted sharply with his experiences in the Middle Colonies. In the Middle Colonies, Baptists churches had the opportunity to grow in number without hindrance from the civil government because of the religious toleration that reigned in those colonies. The PBA, the Baptist body responsible for sending Manning to Rhode Island to start a college in the first place, had been around since 1707. Manning and leaders of the PBA were veterans of the associational model and wanted to guide their uneasy New England brethren into forming an association of their own.

In 1766 the PBA got its chance. The group heard that their northern confreres had decided to meet the following year to explore the utility of creating an association. At its October 1766 annual meeting, the PBA decided to send renowned pastors John Gano, Morgan Edwards, and Samuel Jones as delegates to the New England Baptist association's meeting at Warren, Rhode Island, the following September to encourage their northern counterparts and presumably to answer any inquiries

"A S.W. View of the College in Providence, together with the President's House & Gardens," c. 1795. Original at John Carter Brown Library at Brown University.

about forming an association. The PBA also appointed Samuel Jones to write a letter to the Baptists at Warren.[75] The letter served as an introduction from the elders and messengers of the PBA. Speaking for his fellow Baptists in the association, Jones expressed joy that the Baptists of New England were at least considering uniting together under the banner of one association. The PBA and the new association in New England would be able to form tighter bonds of intercolonial fellowship as a result. They could more easily by letter and in person share pulpits and stories of church growth, for example. Jones then got right to the point, elaborating the reasons Baptists in New England should have an association. Just as a local church could "answer those ends and purposes which could not be accomplished by any single member," he argued, "so a collection and union of churches into one associational body, may easily be conceived capable of answering those still greater purposes, which any particular church could not be equal to." Jones even had plans to form a "union of associations" that could come together as a colonies-wide denomination. With the "weight and strength" of churches, associations, and unions of associations working together to accomplish God's will on earth, such a "threefold cord [would not be] easily broken," he contended.[76] The "greater purpose" of enacting religious freedom could become the norm in New England like it was in the Middle Colonies if Baptists in New England followed the PBA's example and united together into one association.

The biblical passage that Jones alluded to comes from Ecclesiastes 4:12: "And if one prevail against him, two shall withstand him; and a threefold cord is not quickly broken."[77] The wider context of the passage, Ecclesiastes 4:7–12, talks about the benefits of two people laboring together, supporting each other, and keeping each other warm when necessary. Jones's application of this passage to his readers at Warren would have been unmistakable. Jones noted the futility of an individual, or individual church, standing alone to labor for the Lord. Churches needed to band together to "withstand" the enemy, which the New England Baptists would have understood to be the churches of the Standing Order.

The meeting at Warren did take place in September 1767. Representatives of eleven churches appeared to consider forming an association.[78] Isaac Backus recorded the minutes for the meeting. The minutes noted that John Gano preached a sermon from Acts 15:9.[79] Gano preaching from Acts 15:9 is significant because Acts 15 was the *locus classicus* for Baptists who favored the associational model. Although a copy does not exist of Gano's Acts 15:9 sermon, one can get a sense of the ideas that Gano probably preached by looking closely at the 1749 *Minutes of the Philadelphia Baptist Association.* During this annual meeting, the delegates voted to include Elder Benjamin Griffith's "essay on the power and duty of an Association of churches" in the association's record book. Thus, his essay served as an official statement on what the association thought about the scope of its own authority in relation to individual churches.[80]

Griffith's primary scriptural justification for the existence and benefits of an association arose from his understanding of Acts 15:1–33.[81] Griffith contended that the practices of the early church in Acts 15 were "imitable" in three ways for associations today. First, the council declared that the Judaizers were heretics. Associations should always stand for biblical orthodoxy. Second, the council sent representatives from its home church in Jerusalem to Antioch to testify to the decision of the council regarding Gentile converts. Any association worthy of the name should aid its churches when they have doctrinal or practical disputes by sending other believers to help. Third, the decision of the council was final, and Antioch as well as other churches were to abide by the decision (Griffith cited Acts 16:4 here). At this point in his argument, Griffith moved from scriptural exegesis to historical example. He stated that bishops in the early church would call a council "to make head against any error or disorders, when in any particular church, such things grew too big for a particular church peaceably to determine." Uniting to solve doctrinal quarrels helped the bishops to maintain the ideal of one universal church body.[82]

As C. C. Goen incisively observes, all of Griffith's talk about the universal body of Christ and the authority of bishops "[sounded] to Separate ears suspiciously like an attempt to erect a Baptist catholicism."[83] Baptists were primitivists and biblical literalists by instinct. Any appeal to the corrupt traditions that Christians from the second century on added to the pure ecclesiological system spelled out in the New Testament was not welcome in Baptist churches. Since Griffith's essay was the official statement of the PBA, and since Gano likely preached his Acts 15:9 sermon with Griffith's view of associationalism in mind, New England Baptists less than enthusiastically embraced the idea of an association. Only four out of the eleven churches in attendance formed the Warren Association in 1767.[84]

Leaders of the PBA had failed to convince most New England Baptists to join the new Warren Association through scriptural arguments. But in 1768, when the future of the new association was bleak, Backus suggested to James Manning that he reword the PBA's view of the authority of associations to reassure skittish Baptists that the Warren Association would not violate local church autonomy.[85] Following Backus's advice, Manning addressed Baptists' concerns in a 1769 essay by declaring "that such an association is consistent with the independency and power of particular churches, because it pretends to be no other than an *Advisory council* utterly disclaiming superiority, jurisdiction, coercive right and infallibility."[86] Manning's willingness to alter the highly structured associationalism of the PBA for New England Baptists did help the association to grow from seven churches to eleven churches at the 1769 annual meeting of the Warren Association.[87]

However, the Warren Association did not ultimately become a lasting organization because of Manning's and the PBA's keen use of scripture to persuade wary Baptists. *Realpolitik* concerns won the day. Baptists *needed* the Warren Association in order to fight the political strength of the Standing Order as one body.[88] One important prong to the Baptist strategy of "poaching" upon the religious, social, and political territory owned by the Standing Order was the creation of the Grievance Committee in 1769.[89] In the minutes of the annual meeting for the Warren Association that year, the delegates stated that their "humble remonstrances and petitions have not been duly regarded" by the legislature when they felt that a law discriminated against them. As a result, the Warren Association decided that they would actively "seek remedy for their brethren where a speedy and effectual one may be had." The association appointed six members to comprise a committee that would "receive well-attested grievances" of persecution against Baptists and draft legislation to lessen or eliminate discrimination.[90] Although the association did not start publishing its minutes until 1770[91] to distribute to their churches more easily, in 1769 the delegates presumably made handwritten copies of the call to receive grievances so that they could share this information with their churches after the meeting was over.

MINUTES

OF THE

Warren Aſſociation,

HELD AT *SUTTON*,

In the Province of

Maſſachuſetts-Bay,

SEPTEMBER, MDCCLXXI.

IN the year 1770 the aſſociation was held at Bellingham, when three churches joined it, viz. the firſt and third churches in Middleborough, and the church of Aſhfield. This year, viz. 1771, the following churches joined the aſſociation, of Royalſton, Cumberland and Wrentham, South-Brimfield, Richmond, the firſt of Attleborough.

BOSTON:
Printed by JOHN BOYLES, in Marlborough-Street.
MDCCLXXI.

Cover page to the *Minutes of the Warren Association,* 1771.

Of course, Baptists did not resort merely to handwritten copies to spread the word about the Grievance Committee and its purpose. As they had beginning in 1763, Baptists opened their pocketbooks and made use of newspaper advertising. William G. McLoughlin notes how the Grievance Committee "took advantage of the increasing availability of newspapers," but he mentions Baptists using newspapers only in passing and not as a part of an overall strategy to thwart Congregationalism.[92] From August 2 to September 3, 1770, Grievance Committee members used five different newspapers in three different towns to advertise ten times, some with slightly different wording.[93] For example, in the August 11, 1770, issue of the Providence *Gazette; and Country Journal,* the Grievance Committee reassured its audience that they were aware of their sufferings at the hands of the establishment: "your purses have felt the burthens of ministerial rates, and when these would not satisfy your enemies, your property hath been taken from you, and sold for half its value." Thus, it was imperative for churches to "collect [their] cases of suffering, and have them well attested." To have one's stories "well attested," the Grievance Committee suggested that church members bring in such documentation as evidence of taxes paid to the standing minister or proof of lawyer fees when they went to court. Churches had to get their accounts of persecution ready quickly because, a month later, the Warren Association and its Grievance Committee would meet again, this time in Bellingham, Massachusetts.[94] The Grievance Committee would then act based on the stories and other documents that they collected.

Although the next section will explore the successes and failures of the Warren Association and its Grievance Committee, it is instructive to note the parallels and differences between the Warren Association and the much more famous Boston Committee of Correspondence (BCC). After the crises of the Stamp Act and the Boston Massacre, the American colonies' relationship with the Mother Country continued to deteriorate, particularly in Boston. Most Bostonians felt that the Crown and Parliament were violating their constitutional rights as Englishmen. According to historian Richard Brown, Boston leaders concluded that citizens "needed ... a recognized, systematic method to make sure that every town, and every person in every town was thoroughly acquainted with their rights and the essential features of the constitution" so that people could fight for their rights.[95] After Governor Thomas Hutchinson criticized Bostonians in a letter for having town meetings to talk about exercising their rights, the "freeholders and other inhabitants of the town" met anyway on November 2, 1770. In the meeting, Samuel Adams, the most famous New England patriot until quarterback Tom Brady, made a motion:

> [T]that a Committee of Correspondence be appointed to consist of twenty-one Persons—to state the Rights of the Colonists and of this Province in particular, as Men, as Christians, and as Subjects; to communicate and publish the same to the several Towns in this Province and to the Word as the sense of this Town, with the Infringements and Violations thereof that have been, or from time to time may be made—Also requesting of each Town a free communication of the Sentiments on this Subject.

The motion carried without trouble.[96]

The BCC would be the "systematic method" that Bostonians were looking for. Twenty-one prominent and at least moderately wealthy men served as members of the BCC[97] and were responsible for bringing the three aspects of Samuel Adams's motion to life. A subcommittee of three, led by Adams, crafted a statement of their rights. Another subcommittee of three functioned as the organization's grievances branch. They listed how the British government's "infringements and violations" were detrimental to their liberties. The third subcommittee of three had the task of corresponding with other towns in Massachusetts to encourage local political involvement.[98] The subcommittees worked hard at their assignments and, by the time townspeople met on November 30, 1772, they had combined their efforts into one document, *The Votes and Proceedings of the Town of Boston*. The Committee of Correspondence employed the power of the press to print six hundred copies of the pamphlet. They distributed copies to local clergy and other notable citizens of Boston and mailed them to other towns. As Richard Brown remarked, "When the distribution was completed, the pamphlet had been placed in the hands of hundreds of opinion leaders, especially elected public officials, all over the province."[99] Towns throughout Massachusetts read the pamphlet and debated it in their own town meetings. Some of these towns formed their own Committee of Correspondence. Remarkably, towns in other colonies adopted the practice and functioned as parallel patriot governments to the royal governments until American representatives met in the First Continental Congress in the autumn of 1774.

The function of the Warren Association and its Grievance Committee was similar in many ways to the BCC. Like the BCC, the Warren Association utilized the printing press to distribute their own literature: associational minutes and polemical pamphlets that informed their "constituents" of the growth of the association and its efforts to secure religious liberty. Also, both the Warren Association and the BCC had a subcommittee solely responsible for addressing grievances. The Warren Association's Grievance Committee even predated the Committee of Correspondence by three years. One should expect such similarities between the two politically active organizations. According to Carl Bridenbaugh, the Committee of Correspondence "took the tried-and-proved ecclesiastical organization of the Nonconformist churches and adapted it to secular affairs with great though hardly surprising success." When he mentions "Nonconformist churches," he is primarily talking about Presbyterians and Congregationalists,[100] but Baptists in England and America fit into that category as well in terms of their relationship with the Church of England. (In New England, Baptists were the major nonconformist group to the established Congregationalist church). Bridenbaugh's observation points to how blurry the lines between the "religious" and the "political" were during the Revolutionary era. The more "religious" organization, the Warren Association, mediated Baptist actions of resistance in the political realm, while the more "political" organization, the BCC, fought for the right for all Protestant groups to enjoy religious toleration.[101] The BCC also had the related goal of keeping an Anglican bishop away from America so that he did not persecute other Protestants and strengthen the Crown's temporal authority.[102]

However, there were key differences between the Warren Association and the BCC as well. First, the members of BCC were well-to-do citizens in their communities, being a higher social class than the vast majority of the Baptist pastors, deacons, and other lay members who participated in yearly associational meetings. (Hence, Baptists were not likely to be members of their given town's Committee of Correspondence if their town had one). Most importantly, while one could sum up the general goals of both the Warren Association and the BCC as seeking to achieve "civil and religious liberty," these concepts meant different things, depending upon the organization's perspective. For the BCC, the obstacle to obtaining civil and religious liberty was the British government. For the Warren Association, the obstacle was two-fold: the British government and the government of the Standing Order. As both Baptists and the Congregationalists (who were the prominent citizens on the BCC) moved further into rebellion against the British in the 1770s, the Baptists' and Congregationalists' competing notions of liberty clashed with each other again and again in several different affairs.

The Ashfield Case

Perhaps the most (in)famous early case that tested the utility of the new Grievance Committee and showed great animosity between Baptists and Congregationalists was the Ashfield case. In the summer of 1750, Chileab Smith, a member of the Congregationalist church in South Hadley, Massachusetts, embraced New Light sympathies and protested when his church did not require members to relate verbally their conversion experiences to partake of communion. His church did not accept his Edwardsean emphasis upon members having and declaring a new birth experience as a requirement for communion. (The nearby Northampton church had recently fired Edwards for the same reason). In 1751 Smith and his large family of eight children made it to Huntstown, a plantation several miles west of Deerfield, and became one of the founding members of an area that had virtually no residents for the first sixteen years of Huntstown's existence. In the frontier town, Chileab and his son Ebenezer felt called to become New Light ministers, and they gathered a church that survived despite the tumult of the French and Indian War. By 1762 the Smiths and several townspeople embraced believer's baptism and formed a Baptist church.[103]

The situation for the Baptists who predominated in the early years of Huntstown changed when the Standing Order forced Ebenezer Smith, who should have been the settled minister of the town, to pay ecclesiastical taxes. Settled ministers were exempt from such a tax. According to Isaac Backus, fifteen out of nineteen families living in Huntstown wanted Ebenezer to be the town's official minister. However, with the war over, some Congregationalist settlers moved into town, and they called Jacob Sherwin, a Yale graduate, to be their minister. From then on, Sherwin demanded that Smith and the Baptists pay their ecclesiastical taxes to him and to the Congregationalist church instead of using their money to build their own meetinghouse and pay their own pastor. The Baptists refused and wanted to claim tax exempt status, but they could not do so because the tax exemption laws only applied to towns officially incorporated by the General Court. The General Court did eventually incorporate Huntstown and changed its name to Ashfield in 1765. With tax exemption now a possibility for Baptists, they sought this status, but Sherwin and the parish taxed the Baptists anyway.[104]

Then, Backus noted, Baptists experienced some relief from taxation after 1765 because there was some confusion over voting rights between the citizens of the town and the original proprietors of the town. Normally, the citizens of towns in Massachusetts voted on taxes, but the incorporation act of 1765 gave both proprietors and citizens of the town the right to vote. Proprietors' votes counted more than those of average citizens because their voting power was based on how much land they owned. For instance, a proprietor who owned five hundred acres of land had the voting power of ten town voters who owned fifty acres each. In 1767 the proprietors and the town voters wanted the General Court to clarify the relationship between the two groups of voters. In response, in the following year, the General Court passed an amendment to the 1765 incorporation act that became known as the "Ashfield Law."[105] The new amendment gave all voting rights to the proprietors instead of to the town's inhabitants, and the proprietors immediately raised taxes to support Mr. Sherwin and build the Congregationalist meetinghouse. Yet again, the Baptists did not pay.[106]

Essentially, the General Court decided to let the proprietors engage in taxation without the inhabitants' consent. Parliament passed the unpopular Sugar Act (1764) and Stamp Act (1765), which, to New England Congregationalist radicals like Samuel Adams, amounted to taxation without representation. Time and time again, Baptists pointed out the irony and hypocrisy of their Congregationalist neighbors decrying the oppressive power of the monarchy, while simultaneously oppressing Baptists who wanted the right not to give religious taxes because doing so violated their conscience.[107] Circumstances only worsened for the Ashfield Baptists. The proprietors taxed the town again in the fall of 1769, and the Baptists still refused to pay. This time, the authorities took the Baptists' land and sold it at auction on April 4, 1770, just a few days after the General Court received and ignored another Baptist petition.[108]

The Baptists of Ashfield were in dire straits, so they appealed to the new Grievance Committee for help. In the fall of 1770, the Grievance Committee addressed Lieutenant Governor Thomas Hutchinson and the General Court to plead on behalf of the Baptist church at Ashfield that "our brethren may be saved from threatening ruin, who have suffered much in their persons and estates, to the great disquietude of their minds and distress of their small and chargeable families." More specifically, the committee related how the local authorities sold at auction 398 acres of land that Baptists owned, including 10 acres that the Baptist minister Ebenezer Smith himself owned. Altogether, the land was worth 363 pounds and 13 shillings, but the authorities sold it for the bargain-basement price of 19 pounds and 3 shillings. The petition also mentioned that the Baptists did not deserve such treatment because they were loyal citizens of Massachusetts and the Crown. The Ashfield Baptists had previously fought hard and built a fort without government funds to defend their homes and the frontier during the French and Indian War. Beyond enumerating the difficulties that the Ashfield Law brought upon the Baptists, the Grievance Committee advised the General Court to take three steps: repeal the Ashfield Law and give the Ashfield Baptists restitution for taking their land; let any Baptist from the entire province of Massachusetts receive compensation for any similar acts committed against them; and give all Baptists tax exemption from parish taxes so "that we may all enjoy full liberty of conscience."[109]

In response to the Grievance Committee's petition, the General Court tweaked the Ashfield Law but it did not give full liberty of conscience like the Baptists had hoped, and it did not repay the Ashfield Baptists for the loss of their land.[110] During the same September 11–13, 1770, meeting in which the Warren Association approved the Grievance Committee's petition to the Court, the Warren Association also made plans to appeal directly to King George III in England if the petition failed. In the association's circular letter, James Manning urged the churches in the association to donate money to help with the costs of sending someone to London to represent them to the king.[111]

Once their last petition failed, Baptists did eventually appeal to the king but not before experiencing some abuse from their opponents in the newspapers back home. One anonymous defender of the establishment from Cambridge wrote an opinion piece in response to the Grievance Committee's advertisement for Baptists to send them accounts of their hardship in paying taxes and enduring persecution from the Standing Order. The writer argued several points in his essay. First, the author of the essay stated that it was fully reasonable for the provincial government to require certificates from any Baptists who wanted to avoid paying ecclesiastical taxes. If Baptists did not provide proper certificates from their churches or pastors, then the government could not accurately identify them as Baptists and thus give them exemption. Concerning Baptists' dealings with the courts, the writer was confident that "no such instance I am persuaded can be produced" of a Baptist who suffered injustice at the hands of the courts if he had his required certificate. Regarding the contentious Ashfield case in particular, the writer claimed ignorance of the plight of the Baptists of Ashfield: "What their circumstances are I know not—few are acquainted with them." He then challenged anyone to provide a reliable account of what really happened in Ashfield. Finally, the contributor to the newspaper contended that Baptists experienced more freedom in New England than anywhere else in Christendom and that they should be grateful for the kindness that the government had bestowed to them.[112]

Backus read the man from Cambridge's attacks on Baptists, and as was his custom, he responded in pamphlet form, which he dated March 14, 1771.[113] Interestingly, he did not respond directly to his anonymous critic in the newspaper but to a representative in the Massachusetts General Assembly whom he assumed had also read the smear piece and who was in a position to have the General Assembly reconsider the Baptists' petition. First, Backus rejected the editorial's claim that Baptists did not suffer at the hands of the courts or the established church in general. He cited several instances in the following towns where Baptists experienced persecution: South Hadley, Montague, Shutesbury, Colerain, and Chesterfield. Backus reassured his readers that "All these Accounts I had from the Persons own Mouths."[114] For the infamous Ashfield case, for which the anonymous writer wanted proof, Backus provided the representative with an entire letter written by Ebenezer Smith, one of the Baptist ministers in Ashfield, detailing the difficulties that the Baptists of that town had faced.[115] Although I have no direct evidence, I suspect that Backus's pamphlet reached more than just the General Assembly representative, given Backus's history of making his works available to the wider public through the press to influence opinion.

As the war in the press was dying down, Baptists were making progress in England. An English Baptist friend of Grievance Committee members named Samuel Stennett, who was also close friends with the king, argued that the king should overturn the Ashfield Law, and the king did so on July 31, 1771. The General Court, upon hearing of the king's decision later in 1771, gave the Ashfield Baptists a three-year tax break on all taxes and let the Baptists repurchase their land once they paid a few fees and some interest. The Ashfield Baptists never fully recovered their lands, but the Grievance Committee flexed its organizational muscle by convincing the king to decide in favor of the Ashfield Baptists. The Grievance Committee succeeded, whereas the ad hoc committee from the 1750s failed. Baptist leaders' strategy to consolidate Baptists into a permanent association with one political voice was working. Their victory was not without cost, however. Their Congregationalist neighbors believed that the Baptists were loyalist sellouts. Congregationalists' growing suspicion of Baptists did not bode well for Baptists in the Revolutionary War years.[116]

Before the First Continental Congress

Attempts by the Warren Association and its Grievance Committee to accomplish their inextricable religious and political goals arguably reached their eighteenth-century apex during the autumn of 1774.[117] On September 13–14, 1774, at the annual meeting in Medfield, Massachusetts, the Warren Association decided to send Grievance Committee chief Isaac Backus as its representative to its sister association in Philadelphia for the PBA's annual meeting in October. The Warren Association also asked Backus to address the First Continental Congress (which began meeting on September 5 in Philadelphia) to urge Massachusetts to end religious persecution against the Baptists and to allow for religious liberty.[118] Backus and the New England Baptists had come to believe that the Continental Congress was now their "highest civil resort" for obtaining religious liberty since Massachusetts did nothing to alter its oppressive religious establishment, and relations with England and the king were souring even more by 1774.[119]

Once in Philadelphia, on October 11, 1774, Backus and James Manning met with lawyer Robert Strettle Jones and other leaders of the PBA to discuss the best approach for the Warren Association to use in addressing the First Continental Congress. Notable Philadelphia Quakers also attended the meeting, and the Quakers[120] advised that the Baptists not address the Continental Congress as a whole "but . . . seek for a conference with the Massachusetts delegates, together with some other members who were known to be friends to religious liberty."[121]

Backus and Manning, as well as the PBA, decided that the Quakers' plan was the best course of action. So, on October 14, the Warren and PBA representatives had an audience at Carpenters' Hall with Samuel and John Adams, Robert Treat Paine, and Thomas Cushing, the four representatives from Massachusetts to the Continental Congress. Also present were Samuel Ward, a Baptist and governor of Rhode Island, and Samuel Hopkins, protégé of Jonathan Edwards and pastor of the First Congregational Church of Newport. Quakers James and Isaac Pemberton and Quaker Joseph Fox attended the fateful meeting as well.[122] According to Robert Treat Paine's later description of the meeting to Newport pastor Ezra Stiles, about forty people were present in total.[123] Manning started the meeting with the Massachusetts delegates by reading a memorial of the New England Baptists' grievances against the General Court and the parishes. In the memorial, the Baptists sought "the liberty of worshipping God according to our consciences, not being obliged to support a ministry we cannot attend, whilst we demean ourselves as faithful subjects. These we have an undoubted right to, as men, as Christians, and by charter as inhabitants of Massachusetts Bay."[124] Probably intentionally, the language of the memorial was reminiscent of Samuel Adams's own motion to form a Committee of Correspondence "to state the Rights of the Colonists and of this Province in particular, as Men, as Christians, and as Subjects."[125]

As Backus recounted the meeting, the Massachusetts delegates did not respond to the memorial favorably. The Adamses and Paine thought that Massachusetts had only a minor religious establishment and argued with the Baptists over how much persecution they endured as a result of their failure to pay parish taxes. Backus retorted that the persecution was indeed real and contended that giving taxes to the parish church was a violation of conscience. Both sides were at an impasse and concluded their four-hour meeting. On the next day, Backus and Manning met with members of the PBA, and none of the Baptists thought that the Massachusetts delegates adequately addressed their concerns. The new Grievance Committee of the PBA expressed its solidarity with the New England Baptists and promised to support them in their fight for religious liberty.[126]

Backus eventually returned to New England in November, just in time to respond to Robert Treat Paine's rumor that the New England Baptists and Philadelphia Quakers were in league together to divide the patriot cause. Of course, most Quakers were pacifists and were neutral, if not outright loyalists, during the impending Revolutionary War.

However, New England Baptists (unlike some Baptists in the PBA) were ardently on the side of the patriots. Backus then wrote a petition to the Massachusetts Provincial Congress to defend the Baptists' reputation as patriots and to push for religious liberty. The next year, at a meeting of the Massachusetts Provincial Congress, John Adams (somewhat surprisingly) asked the Provincial Congress to consider Backus's petition in order to maintain unity in America against the Crown, but the Congress just asked Backus to send his petitions to the General Court.[127] Although Backus and the New England Baptists would continue to push for religious liberty in the coming months, the Provincial Congress and the General Court's attention became more fixed on the "shot heard round the world." The Battles of Lexington and Concord occurred on April 19, 1775, and plunged the American colonies into war with England.

THE RE-ENTRENCHMENT OF THE RELIGIOUS ESTABLISHMENT IN 1780

As a result of their rebellion against the British, Massachusetts had no official form of government to rule the young state. About one month after the first battle of the American Revolution, state political leaders sought the help of the Continental Congress in figuring out what form of government to adopt. Taking the Congress's advice seriously, the people of Massachusetts elected members of a House of Representatives to run the government under the conditions of the Charter of 1691. Soon after, the House elected a council that assumed the executive responsibilities that the former royal governor and lieutenant governor possessed. The House and council formed the new General Court, and the General Court directed legislative, executive, and judicial business for the state.[128] This governmental arrangement had the potential of being favorable to religious dissenters of the Congregational establishment like Baptists, for the Charter of 1691 spoke of "a liberty of Conscience allowed in the Worshipp of God to all Christians (Except Papists)."[129] However, the General Court quickly realized that operating the government according to the Charter of 1691 would be "unworkable." Unlike Massachusetts's colonial arrangements, wartime government had no royal governor to enforce the king's decrees. So, in May 1777, the General Court decided to create a new state constitution.[130]

Almost instinctively, Massachusetts Baptists did not trust the new state government because of the Standing Order's less than stellar record of treatment of Baptists. From 1777 to 1780, the Warren Association and its Grievance Committee led the charge to have a "popularly written and ratified constitution" so that the Congregationalist-controlled "legislature that administered the old corporate system [would] not be allowed to frame a new government."[131] Still acting as "agent" for the Grievance Committee, Backus hoped to persuade pastors and legislators of the Standing Order as well as Massachusetts voters at large to adopt some statute in the constitution that would establish religious freedom. The three key pamphlets that Backus wrote during the state constitutional controversy were all sold in Philip Freeman's shop. The works in his shop were, of course, available to the general public, not just to fellow Baptists.[132]

After more than two years of intense debate over the content of the state constitution, 293 delegates gathered to create a more complete draft of the document in a state constitutional convention that met in September 1779.[133] Written mainly by John Adams, who was part of a three person subcommittee for drafting the constitution,[134] the state constitution consisted of three major parts: the preamble, a thirty-article "Declaration of the Rights of the Inhabitants of the Commonwealth of Massachusetts," and six chapters outlining a "Frame of Government." Concerning matters of religious establishment, two articles, Article II and Article III, engendered the most heated debate during and after the convention. Article II declared that all people should worship God and that "no subject shall be hurt, molested, or restrained, in his person, liberty, or estate, for worshipping God in the manner and season most agreeable to the dictates of his own conscience, or for his religious profession or sentiments, provided he doth not disturb the public peace or obstruct others in their religious worship."[135] Article II actually had much in common with the Charter of 1691's guarantee of religious freedom (for Protestants) when it emphasized worshipping God according to one's own conscience.

The new constitution's Article II by itself was not a cause of concern for Baptists. However, Article III, when compared with Article II, negated the right to liberty of conscience altogether. According to Article III, "the people of this commonwealth have a right to invest their legislature with power to authorize and require, and the legislature shall, from time to time, authorize and require, the several towns, parishes, precincts, and other bodies-politic or religious societies to make suitable provision, at their own expense, for the institution of the public worship of God and for the support and maintenance of public Protestant teachers of piety, religion, and morality in all cases where such provision shall not be made voluntarily."[136] Also, the article required citizens to attend some sort of religious meeting in the parish and to support "public teachers" of the gospel. The article then ended with a promise to treat Protestants of various sects equally under the law and have no established sect over the others.[137]

Essentially, with Article III, the Congregational Church reinscribed its authority into the new constitution. Despite claims of treating everyone equally, Article III maintained a system of taxing dissenters (and everyone else) for the support of ministers within a parish and legislating compulsory church attendance for the "common good." As Johann Neem observed, "Because republics require virtuous citizens, the public church served a vital role by providing all citizens access to moral education," which served the common good.[138] While theoretically a parish could consist of mainly non-Congregationalist churches and thus tax money could go to those ministers and churches for support, what ended up occurring most of the time was that the Congregational Church was supported anyway after the constitution was ratified.

Upon hearing of the adoption of Article III of the constitution by the Massachusetts constitutional convention, most Baptists were mortified. If the constitution was ratified, then the Congregational Church would remain the established church. Baptists did not give up trying to change Article III, however. Beginning in March 1780, Baptists, led by Backus, implored voters, who had a chance to vote down any article that they did not like, to vote against Article III before the convention met again in June 1780 to consider alterations.[139] However, at the June 16 meeting of the convention, James Bowdoin, the convention's president, "announced that the entire Constitution had garnered the requisite two-thirds vote."[140] Finally, on October 25, 1780, the Massachusetts state constitution "went into effect" with the controversial Article III included.[141] Baptists had lost.

Despite vigorously petitioning the government and appealing directly to the people to eliminate Article III and establish religious liberty as well as enduring some possible vote-tallying chicanery, Backus and the Warren Association failed in 1780. The Baptists were still the "weak" outsiders who fought for ideological and political space in a Congregationalist-controlled Massachusetts that sought to maintain the status quo. Moreover, out of 293 delegates at the constitutional convention, probably only six were Baptists.¹⁴² Also, as William G. McLoughlin astutely noted, "the Baptists received little visible support from any of the other dissenting sects." Methodists did not make their presence felt in any significant numbers until the late 1780s. New England Quakers and Presbyterians generally supported Article III. Other sects like the Universalists were still very small groups in 1780.¹⁴³ Baptists did not receive help from very many important figures in Massachusetts, either. Major Joseph Hawley, Congregationalist minister Thomas Allen of Pittsfield, and a well-read anonymous author named "Philanthropos" were their only significant allies.¹⁴⁴ At no point in the eighteenth century did New England Baptists have influential elites as allies to the extent that the Virginia Baptists did with Thomas Jefferson and James Madison.

Baptists were ultimately not able to persuade enough non-Baptist to join them in fighting for religious liberty. However, beginning in the 1760s, Baptist leaders, most notably Isaac Backus, embraced the printing press to sell the benefits of religious and political unity to Baptists all over New England. Through the press, they formed an imagined community of the persecuted and informed their "constituents" of key arguments in favor of religious freedom. A second, related aspect to their now-coherent strategy of resistance to the Standing Order was the formation of the Warren Association and its Grievance Committee to lobby for their religious rights. To disestablish the Congregational Church, though, Baptists would need to develop further strategies to connect effectively with people outside of the Baptist fold, to form a strong and diverse antiestablishment coalition. They would get what they were looking for with the rise of Jefferson's Republican Party in the 1790s, and John Leland's political networking skills would help usher New England Baptists into a new era of fighting for religious disestablishment. Baptists still had a long way to go to achieve their goals, but their movement from ineffective tactics to an overall strategy that successfully united Baptists between the Great Awakening and 1792 was a start.

3

BAPTIST "POLITICAL ECUMENISM" IN THE FIRST PARTY ERA

William Bentley (1759–1819), pastor of the Second (East) Congregational Church in Salem, Massachusetts, from 1783 to 1819, was something of an oddity among his ministerial brethren in Essex County. For one, he was a Unitarian Congregationalist who had fully embraced Enlightenment skepticism, whereas most of his colleagues were Trinitarian Congregationalists. Second, while the average Harvard- or Yale-trained minister received a quality education, especially in matters of divinity, Bentley's intellectual interests and talents far surpassed his pastoral neighbors. He could read over twenty languages and speak cogently on matters as diverse as biology, theology, shipping, law, and philosophy. Bentley's enormous library of four thousand books was almost as large as Thomas Jefferson's, one of the few men in the Early Republic who was in the same intellectual stratosphere as Bentley. In almost every respect, Bentley was a gentleman whose biography, upon first inspection, read a lot like a typical New England Federalist clergyman.[1]

The sage of Salem also differed from his local colleagues because he was a Democratic-Republican, and they were Federalists. Although Bentley did not enjoy the harsh partisanship of the era, he appreciated that the Democratic-Republican Party upheld religious tolerance, freedom of the press, and free thought. In his famous multivolume *Diary*, Bentley took notice of another group of people who found a lot to like about Jefferson's party: the Baptists. In a January 24, 1802, entry, Bentley observed:

> The Baptists by attaching themselves to the present administration have gained great success in the United States & greater in New England than any sect since the settlement, even beyond comparison. This seems to be a warning to the Churches of the other denominations. The late address of the Danbury Association of Baptist Churches to President Jefferson with his answer of the present month are before the public. The president is in full consent with them upon the use of civil power in the Church.[2]

The Baptists' "great success in the United States & greater in New England" to which Bentley referred is a little ambiguous. One of his possible meanings for Baptist success could be that Baptist adherence to Jeffersonian politics contributed to numerical growth of the denomination after Jefferson's election to the presidency. Such a possibility is difficult to prove given the prevalence of other factors that explain Baptist growth. For example, the impact of the Second Great Awakening and the diffusion of American citizens to the western frontier spurred exponential Baptist growth throughout the nineteenth century. All denominations using the name "Baptist" grew from 125,000 members at the beginning of the nineteenth century to over 3 million members by the beginning of the twentieth century.[3]

A second meaning of Baptist "success" is the more likely explanation for Bentley's contention: Baptists grew in political clout throughout the country, particularly in New England. According to Bentley, no other denomination benefited more from a devotion to Jeffersonian politics than the Baptists. To support this claim, Bentley argued that Jefferson's election to the presidency in 1800 emboldened Baptists because Jefferson's views of church/state separation were "in full consent with them [Baptists] upon the use of civil power in the Church." The general public had read Jefferson's response to the Danbury Baptist Association of Connecticut from earlier that January,[4] and it was clear to all that Jefferson was against any governmental body interfering with the worship practices of a religious group. The Standing Order's constant meddling into the affairs of Connecticut Baptist churches through imprisonment and burdensome parish taxes and fines was what originally led the Danbury Baptists to complain to Jefferson by letter in the first place.[5]

Bentley's favorable opinion regarding Baptists' participation in the Democratic-Republican Party was ironic because Bentley hated virtually every Baptist with whom he came into contact.[6] Despite his strong personal feelings against Baptists, he admired the fact that "the Baptists are in their constituencies more republican than the Methodists," while "Monarchy is the soul of John Wesley's scheme." To Bentley, Baptist congregational polity closely resembled the way Americans believed government should work: by the consent of the governed without the ultimate authority of a king. In contrast, Wesley's Methodist church had a bishop who made all the decisions for the denomination like a king would for his subjects. As a Unitarian Congregationalist, Bentley shared Baptist distaste for episcopal government.[7]

Begrudging respect for Baptists aside, evidence for a closer partnership between Bentley and Baptists under the banner of the Democratic-Republican Party is lacking, though not a complete impossibility. For instance, Bentley recorded how he accepted an invitation to dine with one hundred other guests at a place in Essex County called "Osgood's in South fields" on the evening of March 4, 1803, to celebrate the two-year anniversary of Thomas Jefferson becoming president. Only citizens who were Jeffersonian Republicans could come to the party, and it is plausible that Bentley conversed with his fellow partisans, the Baptists, that night, though such an interaction is completely undocumented.[8]

Baptists' alliance with a diverse coalition of Jefferson's supporters beginning in the late 1790s was the critical next stage in the development of a coherent strategy to disestablish Congregationalism in Massachusetts. New England Baptists shifted from haphazard and occasion-specific tactics of opposing the Standing Order to building a sustained political movement. Beginning in the 1760s, key Baptist leaders, most notably Isaac Backus, employed the printing press to sell religious and political unity to Baptists all over New England. Through the press, they formed an imagined community of the persecuted and informed their "constituents" of key arguments in favor of religious freedom. A second and related aspect to their strategy of resistance to the Standing Order was the formation of vital organizations, specifically the Warren Association and its Grievance Committee, that lobbied for both an individual's right to liberty of conscience and a religious community's right to practice its faith as it saw fit. Although Backus and other leaders succeeded in consolidating a political movement that was a thorn in the side of the Congregationalist establishment during the American Revolution, their actions did not accomplish the disestablishment of the Standing Order. Instead, Congregationalists reestablished their position as the official church of the new state of Massachusetts in its Constitution of 1780, partly because Baptists did not have enough political leverage to stop them.

Fortunately for Baptists, the United States underwent major political changes after 1780. George Washington became the country's first president, but very quickly disagreements arose among his Cabinet members Alexander Hamilton and Thomas Jefferson concerning such issues as how much power the federal government should possess or whether the young United States should ally itself with England or France, or remain neutral. These issues led to the development of the first two-party political system in American history and the bitterly contested presidential election of 1800.

As leaders like Samuel Stillman and Isaac Backus approached the twilight of their labors, and with the recent death of James Manning in 1791, the younger, vigorous John Leland took the mantle of Baptist leadership in the fight for religious liberty. He saw the change in political climate as an opportunity to increase Baptist influence in the political process. Like William Bentley, Leland perceived the similarities between Baptist polity and Jeffersonian political emphases. He used those commonalities to help other Baptists transition to a more partisan approach to political involvement. This transition resulted in Massachusetts Baptists shaking off their sectarian insularity by partnering with non-Baptist constituents into a coalition that comprised the Democratic-Republican Party to disestablish religion on the state level.

Convincing Baptists to align with non-Baptists was a tall order for Leland. Only thirty years earlier had Massachusetts Baptists agreed to unite *with each other* into one association and that with much difficulty! Leland making use of such a political strategy should not be too surprising, however, when one considers the insights of Michel de Certeau in his discussion on how the "weak" use tactics to contravene the "strong." According to Certeau, "the weak must continually turn to their own ends forces alien to them."[9] Believing strongly in the autonomy of local churches, Massachusetts Baptist churches hesitated to unite for fear of creating an ecclesiastical hierarchy, but they ultimately did so. Even more foreign for Baptists in the eighteenth century was to unite with non-Baptists to accomplish their ends. Baptists were sectarians who believed in baptizing only adults, the necessity of a conversion experience for church membership, and exercising strict church discipline for wayward members. Some of these strong views put them at odds with their Congregationalist neighbors and other Christian denominations. Leland, however, was crucial in helping Baptists to embrace participating in "political ecumenism" with other religious groups in the nascent Democratic-Republican Party.[10] Leland engaged in various townwide, countywide, and statewide endeavors from the late 1790s to 1813 to knit together Baptists and non-Baptists into a party coalition in the wider context of acrimonious partisan conflict characteristic of the Early Republic. Before analyzing Leland's political activism in Massachusetts, however, a brief discussion is necessary of Leland's political involvement in Virginia from 1777 to 1791, which helped him to see the usefulness of adopting political ecumenism to realize Baptist goals.

A SKETCH OF LELAND'S POLITICKING EFFORTS IN VIRGINIA

In September 1776 the newly married John Leland left his native Massachusetts to live in Virginia for reasons unknown to historians. He had previously engaged in extensive itinerant preaching throughout Virginia from October 1775 to June 1776, so perhaps he thought that the harvest of souls would be more fruitful in Virginia than in Massachusetts. He and his wife Sally settled in Mount Poney, Culpepper County, in March 1777. A few months later, the Baptist church in the town ordained him, but not without controversy. Other Baptist elders did not participate in the ordination ceremony, which would have included laying hands on Leland. In his autobiography, Leland recorded how other ministers not being present to lay hands upon him "was a departure from the use of the churches in Virginia." This purposeful oversight prevented his complete fellowship with other churches at that time.[11] After this inauspicious start, Leland's first pastoral ministry only got worse. His congregation did not like the fact that he was an itinerant preacher and was gone a lot of the time. Also, the twenty-two-year-old Leland himself thought that he "was too young" and inexperienced to lead his flock effectively. As a result, the church split, and Leland moved on to live and minister in James Madison's home county of Orange for the rest of his time in Virginia (1778–1791).[12] Eventually, Leland enjoyed ministerial success in Virginia. According to early Virginia Baptist historian and minister Robert B. Semple, "he baptized between six and seven hundred persons while in the State" and started at least two churches in Orange County, all the while itinerating to various other churches. Semple, who also knew Leland personally, added that "Mr. Leland, as a preacher, was probably the most popular of any who ever resided in this State."[13]

Leland translated his popularity in the pulpit into influence as a lobbyist on behalf of Baptists who sought the disestablishment of Anglicanism, but Semple's account does not mention Leland becoming an official agent for the Virginia Baptist General Committee until August 1786.[14] Although he became perhaps the most prominent Baptist political voice in Virginia by the time he left the state in 1791, Leland did not begin that way; he learned how to participate in politics from his brethren (and later, Madison and Jefferson). When Leland arrived in Virginia in early 1777, Baptists had been involved in petitioning the Virginia legislature for religious toleration since 1772, and for full religious liberty since 1776. The new Virginia state government created the Virginia Constitution in 1776, a document that included a Declaration of Rights. In its last article, patriot George Mason wrote that "religion, or the duty we owe to our Creator, can be directed only by reason and conviction, not by force or violence . . . all men should enjoy the fullest toleration in the exercise of religion according to the dictates of conscience." Mason arguing for full toleration of dissenters was a step in the right direction from the Baptist point of view, but they wanted more. Fellow patriot James Madison agreed with the Baptists. He altered Mason's article by replacing "should enjoy the fullest toleration" with "are entitled to the full and free exercise."[15] According to legal scholar Carl H. Esbeck, "The change from 'toleration' to 'free exercise' is apparently the first occasion in America that this now famous First Amendment phrase was used."[16]

Once Baptists read about Madison's efforts in supporting religious freedom, they petitioned the legislature to adopt Madison's language and its implications of ending the Anglican establishment for good. Thomas Jefferson was on the committee responsible for crafting legislation that would abolish the state church, but his efforts failed. The legislature, while granting tax exemption to dissenters, did not dismantle the Anglican establishment and left open the possibility for a general tax supporting a non-sectarian Christianity. Baptists believed that the new law did not go far enough, so some of them met on Christmas Day 1776 in Dover to create a memorial protesting tax support for ministers.

They then mailed it to Jefferson. L. H. Butterfield observes that the Baptist memorial "was fully in accord with his [Jefferson's] own views, and he may have been responsible for its publication in the *Virginia Gazette* as the earliest Baptist declaration of principles to find a place in a Virginia newspaper." Butterfield further speculates that the letter "may also have been the occasion for the first direct contact between Jefferson and the Baptists, who remained his zealous supporters from 1776 to the end of his political career."[17] Even if one cannot prove that Jefferson actually met Baptists in 1776, Jefferson reading Baptist petitions and the memorial from the Baptist gathering in Dover demonstrates that he knew of the Baptist plight and Baptist views on religious disestablishment. Moreover, by 1776 Baptists were also making essential connections with Virginia elites George Mason and James Madison. Virginia Baptists' willingness to embrace political ecumenism would pay dividends for them in the near future and teach Leland the usefulness of adopting such a strategy in producing political change.

As the American Revolution progressed, Virginia politicians engaged in "piecemeal reform" efforts on matters of religion to entice dissenters like Baptists to enlist in the Continental Army against the British. While politicians were unwilling to disestablish Anglicanism entirely, they relaxed some religious restrictions because of military necessity. For example, John A. Ragosta notes that "in 1777, dissenters were given the right to form their own military companies officered by their own coreligionists."[18] Once the war ended, however, Baptists renewed their attempts to dismantle Anglican privilege. Virginia Baptists created the General Committee to consolidate their political lobbying efforts, and delegates from four associations attended the first meeting of that organization on October 9, 1784.[19] Thus, Virginia Baptists created an organization identical in purpose to Warren Association's Grievance Committee, created by New England Baptists.

Leland had first become an official agent for the General Committee in August 1786, but it is probable that Leland engaged in lobbying efforts before 1786, even if he did not have an "official" position. In his dissertation on Leland, John Bradley Creed points out that the General Committee did not publish its minutes until 1790, right before Leland left. For a record of the actions of the General Committee before 1790, one must rely on Robert B. Semple's account.[20] Creed contends that Semple "did a commendable job in chronicling the basic activities of the group, but his accounts were paraphrased in places and occasionally fragmentary."²¹ Unfortunately, the original records do not exist, but if they did, it would not be a total surprise to see Leland's pre-1786 work described in more detail, given Leland's reputation as a prominent leader among Virginia Baptists.

An occasion that may indicate Leland's pre-1786 involvement in politics is the assessment bill controversy. James Madison led the fight in the Virginia legislature to defeat Patrick Henry's 1784 assessment bill, which would have allowed Protestant Christianity in general, but not the new Protestant Episcopal Church (PEC), successor to the colonial Anglican Church, to receive tax money from citizens to support religion and morality in the fledgling state. Baptists universally supported Madison and opposed Henry by petitioning the legislature not to pass Henry's bill. In 1785 the bill failed to pass. In place of the assessment bill, Madison submitted Jefferson's failed 1779 religious freedom bill, and the legislature passed Jefferson's bill as the Virginia Statute of Religious Freedom in January 1786.²² Legal historian Mark S. Scarberry contends that "it seems highly unlikely" that Orange County resident John Leland was not aware of and did not assist his fellow Baptists in supporting the work of the most notable advocate of religious disestablishment, James Madison, who also happened to live nearby in the same county.²³

Finally, opposing tax assessments to support religion is the same cause to which a post-1786 Leland wholeheartedly committed himself. In his "Virginia Chronicle," Leland argues that "a general assessment, (forcing all to pay some preacher,) amounts to an establishment; if government says I must pay somebody, it must next describe that somebody, his doctrine and place of abode. That moment a minister is so fixed as to receive a stipend by legal force, that moment he ceases to be a gospel ambassador, and becomes a minister of state."²⁴ Without direct evidence from before 1786, one must be cautious about firmly concluding anything about the extent of Leland's political work on behalf of Baptists, but it is probable that he fought for religious liberty at this early point in his life as well.

Leland's role as a leader, lobbyist, and mediator between Virginia Baptists and non-Baptist political allies comes into sharper focus in 1786. In an August 5 meeting at Anderson's meetinghouse in Buckingham County, the General Committee selected Leland and Baptist political veteran Reuben Ford as official agents before the Virginia legislature. Semple commented that, while Baptists had been "well pleased" with the passage of Jefferson's Virginia Statute of Religious Freedom earlier in 1786, they still felt that church/state separation had not been fully accomplished. Leland and Ford's job was to convince the legislature to unincorporate the PEC, and they succeeded in this task the following year. The other issue that Leland and Ford were to address for Baptists was to urge the legislature to sell the glebes, lands and property once owned by the Anglican Church, and subsequently owned by the PEC. Leland and Ford were to push the legislature to make the glebes publicly available.[25] Baptists believed that the colonial established church had exploited people by collecting religious taxes to pay for their lands, and they argued that such lands should rightfully return to the people. It was not until 1799, eight years after Leland left Virginia, that the legislature repealed the glebe laws; in 1802 the legislature officially started selling glebe lands.[26]

During Leland's last five years in Virginia, the General Committee also commissioned him to co-write a history of Virginia Baptists, assist with the establishment of a seminary in Virginia, travel north to unite Virginia Baptists with Baptists there into one denomination, and draw up a controversial resolution condemning the evils of slavery.[27] He was even responsible for crafting a letter to George Washington on behalf of the General Committee that effusively praised Washington, congratulated him on becoming president of the United States, and expressed confidence that Washington would defend every citizen's right to religious liberty.[28] Washington responded by reassuring Leland and the General Committee that he was indeed a firm believer in the right to liberty of conscience and conveyed "satisfaction, that the religious society of which you are members, have been, throughout America, uniformly, and almost unanimously the firm friends to civil liberty, and the persevering promoters of our glorious revolution."[29] Virginia Baptists asking Leland to take up so many responsibilities and having a leadership role among them confirmed their immense trust in him and in his considerable abilities.

However, Leland's most important act of leadership in the Baptist cause was his essential role in getting James Madison elected to the Virginia Ratifying Convention. In September 1787, the Constitutional Convention finished its work on a new basis for government, the Federal Constitution, and sent it to the states for ratification. When Virginia Baptists read the Constitution, it disturbed them greatly. Possessing a polity averse to centralized power, they feared the scope of the new government's authority, in contrast to the weaker Articles of Confederation. On March 7, 1788, they called an emergency meeting of the General Committee to condemn the Constitution. The committee "agreed unanimously" that the Constitution also did not "[make] sufficient provision for the secure enjoyment of religious liberty."[30] For these reasons, Baptists were loyal Antifederalists.

James Madison, one of the major supporters for a new form of government at the Constitutional Convention and the principal writer of the Constitution itself, was in favor of his home state ratifying the Constitution but was in real danger of not participating in the Virginia Ratifying Convention in June 1788. At first, he expressed his reluctance to run in the March 24 election as one of the two representatives for the convention from Orange County. He did not like to give political speeches or treat his constituents to parties containing copious amounts of food and alcohol because he considered such vote-getting behavior "inappropriate" for a gentleman.[31] However, without his presence at the Virginia Ratifying Convention, Virginia may not have approved the document. If Virginia, the most populous and wealthiest state in the young country, did not ratify the Constitution, then other states would have followed suit.

Moreover, his own father, James Madison Sr., suggested in a January 30, 1788, letter that he run and warned that the Baptists of Orange County, a key voting bloc in the county, "are now generally opposed to it [the Constitution]." Antifederalist candidate Colonel Thomas Barbour had already been drumming up support among the Baptists, and it was imperative for Madison, who was in New York at the time, to come to Virginia to persuade the Baptists to vote for him.[32] Madison continued to receive warning letters from friends about Baptist opposition to the Constitution. A few weeks after the letter from his father, he received a letter from James Gordon Jr., Madison's fellow Federalist candidate in the county, claiming that "several of those who have much weight with the people are opposed, Parson Bledsoe & Leeland [sic] with Colo. Burnley."[33]

The final and maybe most important missive came from Joseph Spencer on February 28, while Madison was in Fredericksburg, Virginia. Spencer enclosed a copy of a letter that John Leland wrote to Thomas Barbour explaining his objections to the Federal Constitution, which Barbour probably used when campaigning to the Baptists of Orange. (Scarberry supposes that Leland asked Spencer to deliver the letter to

Barbour. That is why Spencer had a copy of Leland's letter).[34] Leland listed ten objections to the Constitution, which included the lack of a Bill of Rights in general (first), the popularly elected House of Representatives not being able to vote on treaties (third), and no provision that guaranteed freedom of the press (eighth). Most relevant, in his tenth objection, he shared the opinion of the General Committee when he said "What is clearest of all—Religious Liberty, is not sufficiently secured."[35] Given Leland's well-reasoned objections and his undeniable influence among Baptists, Spencer implored Madison, "therefore, as Mr. Leeland Lyes in your Way home from Fredericksburg to Orange [I] would advise you'l call on him & Spend a few Howers in his Company."[36]

Scholars of both Madison and Baptists have never reached a consensus on whether Madison actually met privately with Leland before March 24 to debate the merits of the Constitution as it stood and the possibility of Virginia and the rest of the states adding a Bill of Rights to the document. Without going into the arguments for and against a meeting,[37] the meeting most likely occurred because Madison won. He received 202 votes, while Gordon received 187 votes. The two Antifederalists received 90 votes combined in Orange County. What accounts for this lopsided victory for the Federalist candidates in a county where a major voting bloc, the Baptists, were opposed to the Constitution just seventeen days before? The probable answer is the influence of John Leland among his fellow Baptists.[38] Madison had convinced Leland to support him. Over forty years later, to a crowd in Dalton, Massachusetts, Leland declared, "I was in the vigor of life when the national constitution was formed, and gave my vote for a friend to its ratification, and have never repented it."[39] Once Madison persuaded Leland, Leland went to work for Madison, although the details on his exact methods are lacking. It is quite easy to picture Leland itinerating from church to church and house to house in Orange County to sway reluctant Baptists to support Madison and the Constitution. After Baptists received assurance from Leland to trust Madison, they voted for him. Madison then prevailed over arch Antifederalist Patrick Henry in the Virginia ratification debates in June 1788, and Virginia adopted the Constitution with the promise of a Bill of Rights hanging in the future for the worried Baptists.

Madison would need Leland's and the Baptists' help once again when running for a House position in the First US Congress, which began in March 1789. Patrick Henry, who was a leader in the Virginia

General Assembly and a bitter opponent of Madison, thought that Madison did not stand a chance at winning in a heavily Antifederalist district. Many Baptists who lived in the district were still Antifederalists. As with his work before Madison's election to the Virginia Ratifying Convention, it is not clear exactly what role Leland played in support of Madison. However, it seems that Leland and another Baptist minister named George Eve travelled to several counties to argue before their brethren that Madison was not against Congress adding a Bill of Rights to the Constitution (a charge that Henry and other Antifederalists levelled at Madison and disseminated among Baptists). Madison ended up winning a seat in the House with 1,308 votes, as compared to his friend and Antifederalist rival, James Monroe, who received 972 votes. In a heavily Antifederalist district and despite a horrid snowstorm, enough Baptists came to the polls to vote for Madison. Madison, in turn, kept his promise by fighting to include the Bill of Rights in the Constitution while serving in the First Congress.[40]

Enlightenment rationalists like James Madison and Protestant dissenters like Leland and the Baptists forged a seemingly unlikely alliance, but the rationalists and the dissenters needed one another to fight established religion and win. As Carl H. Esbeck notes, "The rationalists provided the political savvy and legislative know-how. The dissenters provided the petitions in the legislature, election-day votes, and other popular support necessary to keep the rationalists in office and advance the agenda in the legislature. Neither camp acted out of the same motive; both shared the same immediate objective."[41]

Virginia's religious and political context in the 1770s and 1780s was quite an education for John Leland. Through his work as an itinerant preacher, he became a popular, well-trusted, and effective minister throughout Virginia. He eventually used his influence as a minister to play a major leadership role in the politics of religious freedom in Virginia in the 1780s, whether he worked behind the scenes or, later, in an official capacity for the interests of Virginia Baptists through the General Committee. Leland also saw the usefulness of characteristically sectarian Baptists reaching out to non-Baptist elites like George Mason, Thomas Jefferson, George Washington, and especially James Madison to accomplish their goal of church/state separation in Virginia. As he left for Massachusetts in 1791, he would take his speechmaking skills as well as his insights into the utility of political ecumenism to attempt to disestablish the Congregationalist Church during the First Party Era.

LELAND'S POLITICAL ACTIVITIES DURING THE RISE OF THE FIRST PARTY ERA: 1792–1813

Leland's Return to New England

After spending fourteen years ministering and lobbying in Virginia, Leland decided to take his talents back to his native New England in the winter of 1791. Just as it is a mystery to historians why Leland left New England for Virginia in the first place, Leland left Virginia for reasons unknown to historians. Leland's granddaughter and the compiler of his writings, L. F. Greene, noted that "as soon as he landed again on its [New England's] shores, he commenced anew the warfare against religious intolerance, and the defence [sic] of the cause that had so signally triumphed in Virginia."[42] Leland had played an integral part in establishing religious freedom in both Virginia and on a federal level through his politicking for James Madison, who championed the

John Leland. Frontispiece to The Writings of the Late Elder John Leland, Including Some Events in His Life, Written by Himself, with Additional Sketches, &c. by Miss L. F. Greene (New York, 1845).

country's adoption of the Bill of Rights. It is probable that he returned to New England to ensure that the region, namely Massachusetts and Connecticut, disestablished religion too.

His first stop was in New London, Connecticut, from about April to June 1791. The Congregational establishment had been concerned about an increasing number of taxpayers leaving the Church to attend other churches or not go to church at all. The establishment was simultaneously losing revenue and moral authority in the state. As a result, the Connecticut General Assembly passed a new law that required dissenters who sought ecclesiastical tax exemption to apply to the local justices of the peace, many of whom were also a part of the Standing Order, for an exemption. Previously, dissenters could apply for tax exemption by asking their ministers to provide them certificates attesting to their faithfulness as church members. As was customary of Leland, he immediately delved into the controversy during his stay in New London by contributing to the Baptists' and other dissenters' arguments against a religious establishment. William G. McLoughlin contends that Leland was probably the otherwise anonymous "Pandor," or "Candor," who wrote a letter in the May 23, 1791, Connecticut *Courant* castigating the Standing Order because "the style and arguments used in the letter closely resemble those used by Elder John Leland in his tract "The Right of Conscience Inalienable."[43]

Leland's "The Right of Conscience Inalienable," published on August 9, 1791, in New London, is an important work but not only in the controversy itself. It also encapsulates many of his ideas on freedom of conscience and voluntary church membership, rights that included not just Protestants but Jews, "Turks," deists, and "Papists" as well, found in the rest of his corpus. Leland was also passionate about making his arguments using Jeffersonian language and disseminating Jefferson's thoughts on religion to the wider public. Amanda Porterfield observes that, like Jefferson, "Leland owned the modern term 'opinion' as much as anyone."[44] In one of the many instances in his essay in which Leland borrowed from Jefferson's *Notes on the State of Virginia*, Leland argued: "Is uniformity of sentiments, in matters of religion, essential to the happiness of civil government? Not at all. Government has no more to do with the *religious opinions* of men than it has with the principles of mathematics. Let every man speak freely without fear, maintain the principles that he beliefs, worship according to his own faith, either one God, three Gods, no God, or twenty Gods; and let government protect him in so doing, i.e., see that he meets with no personal abuse, or loss of property, for his religious opinions."⁴⁵

Leland continued his discussion on the importance of the state allowing all religious opinions to flourish and not inflicting punishment on dissenters because "it is not supposable that any established creed contains the whole truth, and nothing but the truth. . . . So when one creed or church prevails over another, being armed with a coat of mail, law and sword, truth gets no honor in the victory." If all people are free to express their religious opinions, then a superior argument, and not force, persuades people to believe in what they think is the truth. Truth will thus "stand on its own merit."⁴⁶ With this essay, Leland sought to demonstrate to the Connecticut government the futility and error of suppressing the variety of religious opinions that were becoming commonplace in the state by the 1790s.

After his brief but important stopover in New London, he settled in Conway, Massachusetts, for eight months, until he moved to Cheshire, Massachusetts, in February 1792 to live for most of the last half-century of his life.⁴⁷ The first settlers of Cheshire were immigrants from the colony of Rhode Island in the late 1760s. Cheshire historians Ellen Raynor and Emma Petitclerk pointed out that "they were descendants, some of them of the very men who were the first to follow Roger Williams to Rhode Island, and generally they were men who had inherited and imbibed the spirit of her free institutions, and were educated in the religious beliefs prevalent in that colony rather than in the orthodoxy of the Massachusetts Colony."⁴⁸ C. C. Goen added that Cheshire was "the major center of Separate Baptist activity in western Massachusetts."⁴⁹ Given his previous experience as a political operative in Virginia and Connecticut, it was no mistake that Leland chose to live in a town filled with Baptists and other people sympathetic to religious liberty, a strategic headquarters from which he could launch his assault on the Congregationalist religious establishment in Massachusetts.

On March 24, 1792, Leland, his wife Sally, and his daughter Betsy became members of the church normally referred to as the Second Baptist Church of Cheshire.⁵⁰ Once he became pastor, Leland led the church to vote to join the Shaftsbury Baptist Association (SBA).⁵¹ Baptists in western Massachusetts and eastern New York had formed the SBA in 1781⁵² and maintained cordial relations "through fraternal delegations and exchanges of minutes" with the Warren Association, New England's first Baptist association, in addition to other associations throughout New England and elsewhere. Of course, one of the major goals of New England's associations was to unite to fight for the separation of church and state.[53] Various Baptist associations in Virginia had come together to form the General Committee to spearhead the fight for religious liberty and were slowly becoming one denominational body; Baptists in New England were cautiously evolving in that direction as well. Leland realized this and took a leadership role among the Baptists in the SBA from 1792 to 1808. Sammie Pedlow Strange highlights how Leland "regularly attended associational meetings, authored correspondence and circular letters, preached at annual associational meeting [sic], and represented the Shaftsbury Association at other Baptist association meetings" like those of the Warren Association (in 1794, 1795, 1801, 1808), the Vermont Association (in 1796, 1797, 1800, 1807), and the Philadelphia Association (in 1799).[54] Leland used his letters and associational meeting sermons to encourage fellow Baptists to strive for godliness and evangelize unbelievers, but his involvement in the SBA also illustrates his desire to use an already existing network of Baptist churches to marshal political support for the cause of religious liberty.

Federalism and Democratic-Republicanism in Early National Massachusetts

If Leland simply stopped at encouraging New England Baptists to be more politically active in securing their religious rights, he would not be doing anything very different from what Isaac Backus and other Revolutionary-Era Baptist leaders accomplished. These leaders established a necessary foundation for Baptist associational and political unity by forming the Warren Association and its Grievance Committee, but they did not successfully appeal to enough non-Baptists to put pressure on politicians (who were mostly Congregationalists) to end the establishment when they had the chance to do so in the Massachusetts Constitution of 1780. Baptists needed more non-Baptists on their team.

However, Leland had an ace up his sleeve. Unlike New England Baptists, he had significant experience participating in political ecumenism in Virginia. He was able to encourage Baptists to support the efforts of decidedly non-Baptist politicians like Thomas Jefferson and James Madison to enact laws guaranteeing religious freedom. The rise of the First Party Era gave Leland the opportunity to connect Baptists with non-Baptists in the new Democratic-Republican Party coalition, centered around Thomas Jefferson and a party platform distinct from the Federalists but vague enough to bind together a lot of opponents of the religious establishment. Through his politically ecumenical approach, Leland helped Baptists to enjoy more political influence and come closer to disestablishment in Massachusetts than they ever had before.

Leland faced a daunting task because the establishment in Massachusetts involved a complex agreed-upon arrangement between Congregationalist church leaders, wealthy businessmen, large landowners, and governmental leaders. Church, state, and "old moneyed" (by American standards, as no official aristocracy existed in the United States) interests officially supported one another in colonial and early national Massachusetts. Moreover, with the rise of political parties in the new republic in the 1790s, Ronald P. Formisano estimates that "the Congregational clergy were nine-tenths or more Federal."[55] He goes on to insightfully argue that "before there was anything approaching a Federal party organization, there was a Federal establishment, and the clergy were in effect among the key mobilizers of local political support for the status quo."[56]

The upheaval of the American Revolution did not change the mindset of the status quo. Many of the Congregationalist minsters and wealthy elites were ardent opponents of British oppression and rallied support for the patriot cause during the American Revolution. After the war, it was natural for these elites to reassert their politico-ecclesiastical authority since they believed that they were carrying out the will of the people.[57] Not surprisingly, Leland did not see the Congregationalists' beneficial arrangement with the government in a positive light. In his oration that he gave on July 5, 1802, in Cheshire, Leland laid out seventeen "sketches" that would help his audience reflect on their freedom and independence. In the sixth, eighth, and twelfth sketches, he explicitly voiced his displeasure regarding the religio-political status quo of Massachusetts using spatial language. The sixth sketch contains his most detailed comments. This early national Certeau declared, "the *ins*, generally, are grasping after more power, while the *outs* are complaining of oppression. Deprive an *in* of his office, and he cries out, 'the church and state are ruined.' Put an *out* into office, and government grows better and better every day." According to Leland, the "ins" were the Federalist establishment, who wanted to remain in power in

1800 but did not, and the "outs" were the Democratic-Republicans, of which the Baptists were a part. Since Jefferson's election to the presidency, the place of the "outs" in American society had improved, but the former "ins" wanted to reclaim their power over the "outs" in national politics.[58]

In Massachusetts state politics, however, the "ins" still had the upper hand, even after 1800. The mutual arrangement between church and state continued throughout the anxious and politically divisive years of the 1790s and the early 1800s. The Congregational Church wanted the stream of public money to continue flowing to it for the purpose of performing ministry, and the state of Massachusetts sought the moral principles that church leaders provided in order to promote societal stability and prosperity or, as Amanda Porterfield terms it, to "[manage] and [manipulate] doubt."[59]

Two of the most prominent New England Congregationalist ministers and Federalist Party supporters adept at "[interpreting], [relieving], and [feeding]" doubt[60] were Charlestown, Massachusetts, minister and American geographer Jedidiah Morse and Yale president Timothy Dwight. As Jonathan J. Den Hartog cogently argues in *Patriotism and Piety*, both Morse and Dwight "[typified] clerical support for the Federalists" in New England and united their parishioners and other Federalists around the notion of "infidelity." Morse and Dwight believed that the new republic could only thrive when orthodox Christianity "harmoniously cooperated with the government." Instead, infidelity "combined a rejection of Christian orthodoxy with political views that threatened the very existence of the republic." Several events and ideas, both real and imagined, fell under the category of infidelity for Morse, Dwight, and other Congregationalist Federalist clergymen: anti-religious violence in France as a result of the French Revolution; the irreligious Bavarian Illuminati threat; Thomas Jefferson's religious views; the growth of deism, Unitarianism, and Universalism in the United States; and Democratic-Republican societies that gathered in taverns and other public spaces in opposition to the Adams administration and in support of Jefferson and/or France.[61]

To fight infidelity and express concern over the French Navy attacking American ships, President John Adams, following the practice of countless New England magistrates before him as well as the precedent that George Washington established while in office, proclaimed on March 23, 1798, a national day of humiliation, fasting, and prayer, which would commence on May 9. The document asked God for help in preserving the young and fragile republic in the midst of the French threat.[62] The Adams administration also responded to infidelity in a more heavy-handed manner, by leading the Federalist-controlled Congress to pass the Alien and Sedition Acts (1798). The three Alien Acts—the Naturalization Act, Alien Enemies Act, and the Alien Friends Act—were anti-immigrant measures designed to increase the time it took for immigrants to become American citizens (from five to fourteen years), deport any male adults who were from an enemy country with whom the United States was at war, and deport immigrants who plotted against the federal government, respectively. Since many immigrants were also sympathetic to the Democratic-Republican Party, the laws had the potential to decimate opposition to the Federalist Party. Because America did not end up going to war with France, the government did not systematically enforce the Alien Acts.[63]

However, passing the Sedition Act dramatically altered the political landscape of the United States. The law threatened to jail for six months to five years and fine up to $5,000 any person or entity who criticized the president and his administration through writings or print.[64] The Sedition Act had the opposite effect of its intention; the Democratic-Republican Party and the newspapers that supported and helped consolidate the party *grew* in influence and vociferousness against Adams and the Federalists. Jeffrey L. Pasley maintains that, before the Sedition Act, the Federalists were firmly in control of the press since most newspapers supported the status quo or were apolitical. According to Pasley, "The Federalists saw themselves as the legitimate governing class rather than as a party, and most printers agreed."[65] Before spring 1798, Pasley records that there were 51 Republican-leaning papers out of 185 total papers, with only 10 of the papers being strongly anti-Adams and pro-Republican.[66] Once Congress passed the Sedition Act, Adams's secretary of state and fellow New Englander Timothy Pickering led the suppression efforts against well-known Republican newspapers like Boston's *Independent Chronicle*, the Philadelphia *Aurora*, and the New York *Journal*. Despite fears of jail-time or being fined, printers flouted the law and created more newspapers to criticize Adams's unconstitutional squelching of the freedom of the press and actively campaigned for Thomas Jefferson in the 1800 election. The printers also saw the clampdown on the press as an issue of equality because they sought to make a living just like any other artisan. Pasley notes further that "in all, eighty-five strongly Republican or Republican-leaning newspapers were published in that election year, two-thirds again more that there had been before the Sedition Act was introduced."[67] By 1800 the Federalists no longer controlled the flow of information; voters elected Thomas Jefferson, and he partly had the opposition press to thank for his victory.[68]

The opposition press was more successful at "linking various sectors of the polity" than the Federalist press.[69] Early national newspapers, on an even greater level than newspapers from the Revolutionary era, reached not only subscribers to newspapers but also patrons of taverns and other public places, who shared newspapers with other each other. Moreover, people who were illiterate could hear someone else read the content of the partisan newspapers and form their own opinions based on what they heard. The profusion of newspapers, then, according to Pasley, "contributed in fundamental ways to the very existence of the parties and to the creation of a sense of membership, identity, and common cause among political activists and voters."[70] Newspapers played such a large role in forming party identity because there were not yet the large political party machines in place that would come to characterize American politics after the Civil War.

Moreover, Democratic-Republican newspapers were responsible for transmitting to potential voters Thomas Jefferson's political "platform—a profession of his political principles which he often repeated to correspondents during the course of the campaign and which he reaffirmed in his first inaugural address."[71] For example, the nation's flagship Democratic-Republican paper, the Philadelphia *Aurora*, included a version of Jefferson's principles to sway the public to vote for him. (Of course, pamphlets, handbills, and speeches also informed potential voters about Jefferson's platform).[72] Jefferson's political platform is probably the earliest platform that a national political candidate used to solicit voters.[73] In a January 1799 letter that Noble E. Cunningham includes from Thomas Jefferson to Elbridge Gerry, the Democratic-Republican candidate for governor of Massachusetts in 1800, Jefferson discussed the principles that distinguished his campaign from that of Adams, whom he does not name in the letter. According to Jefferson, he stood for eliminating the national debt, decreasing the size of diplomatic bureaucracy, having no standing army during peacetime and relying upon local militias instead, having a small navy only to protect the American coast, encouraging free trade, avoiding political alliances abroad, and supporting both freedom of religion and of the press. In contrast, Jefferson believed Adams was a big government, fiscally wasteful, warlike autocrat.[74]

The beauty of Jefferson's platform was that it contained memorable, pithy principles like fiscal responsibility, a small government, religious freedom, etc., but did not delve into policy details that could turn off potential voters.[75] Also, since his platform was fairly vague, "fiscal responsibility" and "religious freedom" could mean something different to each bloc of constituents. For example, voters like Leland wanted a complete disestablishment of the Congregational Church, but another Jeffersonian might only want less of his tax money to go to Congregationalist ministers without severing the official relationship between church and state altogether. As a result, the Democratic-Republican Party was able to appeal to a diverse coalition of adherents.

In Massachusetts specifically, two major categories—social class and religion—give some general indications of which groups comprised the Democratic-Republican coalition, vis-à-vis the Federalists, from the late 1790s to approximately 1824.[76] In regard to social class, Federalists tended to be in the highest circles of both civil and ecclesiastical government and thus possessed the most power in the state. Many of the Federalists possessed wealth from the earliest days of the colony and intermarried with other Federalists of the same social station. So, throughout Massachusetts, one could see Federalist marital (and political) alliances between families like the Dwights, Sedgwicks, Worthingtons, and Hookers.[77] In contrast, some Republicans could be quite wealthy, but they were usually *nouveau riche*. Many wealthy Republicans made their fortunes after the American Revolution as shipping and other types of merchants. While they may have had comparable wealth to the Federalists, the Federalists often excluded them from the highest levels of society due to their perceived lack of gentility.[78] Many artisans and "middle-class" merchants were also Republicans, as well as some of the poorer citizens of the state, a group that often, but not always, included members of dissenter sects like the Baptists.[79]

Regarding the religious affiliations of participants of the Democratic-Republican Party, several general tendencies were present in early national Massachusetts. First, dissenting Protestant groups like the Baptists and later the Methodists were almost uniformly Republicans since they sought religious liberty from an oppressive established church. A Methodist pastor named Billy Hibbard from Pittsfield once noted how "I wanted to be a Congregationalist and to be respectable" like his father had wished for him, "but I wanted the love and seriousness of the Methodists."[80] So, he became a Methodist and then a dedicated Democratic-Republican. Another interesting group in the coalition of Democratic-Republicans was the so-called "nothingarians," an indeterminate number of people who were not members of any church and did nothing to support Christianity in Massachusetts unless the Standing Order forced them to support the Congregational Church through taxes. Although not much is known about them, Ronald Formisano estimates that many of these "nothingarians" were likely Democratic-Republicans.[81]

Finally, and perhaps most surprisingly, a large number of Congregationalists were a part of the diverse coalition of Republicans. Although over 90 percent of Congregationalist ministers were avowed Federalists, the Congregationalist laity was much more divided in political affiliation. According to James M. Banner, "the Republican Party could hardly have won a single election without having attracted thousands of Congregational votes."[82] Such is the case because, as William G. McLoughlin observed in his study of statistics from the 1820 state constitutional convention, "probably two-thirds or more" of the state's entire population was Congregational.[83] In contrast, to use the 1810 election for governor as an example, dissenting sects accounted for "25,000, or 28 per cent of the statewide gubernatorial vote."[84] Dissenters like the Baptists did not have the numerical advantage to produce statewide change. They needed some Congregationalist Christians on their side.

John Leland's Circles of Political Influence

As a political ecumenist, John Leland took advantage of the nation's, and specifically Massachusetts's, polarized political situation and an informal but quickly developing political culture to connect Baptists with non-Baptist allies under the banner of the Democratic-Republican Party in the fight for religious disestablishment. His work as a Jeffersonian operative included several overlapping circles of influence: townwide, countywide, statewide, and even nationwide to an extent. His networking efforts within each circle and each circle's interrelationship to one another will illuminate the components of his politically ecumenical strategy.

The first circle of his wide-ranging political influence rests in the town of Cheshire, where he spent most of the last fifty years of his life.

Leland and the inhabitants of Cheshire were a good fit, both religiously and politically. People settled Cheshire, like many towns in Berkshire County, much later than towns on the coast of Massachusetts or in the Connecticut River Valley. Berkshire County was a very mountainous region, which led to several small communities developing their own character, as was the case with Cheshire. The Appalachian Mountains in western Massachusetts also created a natural barrier between it and the rest of Massachusetts. Cheshire was thus the quintessential frontier town.[85]

Under Leland's leadership, his church members and other town residents were the most uniform religious Jeffersonian partisans in the entire state. For instance, from 1800 to 1808, citizens of Cheshire routinely voted for the Republican candidate for governor by a landslide. If one adds up the total number of votes for Republican candidates and Federalist candidates during this nine-year stretch, there were 1,628 votes cast for Republican candidates *and only thirteen* for Federalist candidates.[86] In the only recorded presidential election result during this same nine-year period (the election of 1804), "the town cast 184 votes for the Democratic-Republican electors and none for the Federalists."[87]

What made Leland so successful in shoring up such a uniform voting bloc in Cheshire for Democratic-Republican candidates? Although the church and town were already predisposed to believe in religious freedom and the right to make a living without much interference from the government (hence the settlers' movement to the frontier, far from their new state's capital of Boston), Leland made sure that their *inclinations* turned into political *actions*. Leland encouraged their partisan participation through a couple of "festive" rituals—orations and parades—that were commonplace in the early national era.[88] Jeffrey L. Pasley, in an important essay in *Beyond the Founders*, notes that "Because the early political parties were organizationally almost nonexistent, the work of building support for them was conducted by scattered groups of local activists, with little centralized direction or funding. Necessarily reliant on local resources and personnel, these typically self-appointed activists simply made partisan use of whatever existing traditions, institutions, and practices that they could."[89] Leland perfectly fits Pasley's description of a self-appointed local activist who counted on his or her own abilities and the resources at hand to participate in politics at the time.

One notable example of a practice that Leland used was the oration ritual during the larger ritualized celebration of the Fourth of July. In his book *Celebrating the Fourth*, Len Travers examines the crucial role that Independence Day celebrations played "in the formation and communication of national identity and national consciousness in the early republic."[90] The scope of his work analyzes celebratory practices in Boston, Philadelphia, and Charleston. According to Travers, Independence Day celebrations were "largely an outgrowth of early national urban culture." Rural areas had more difficulty getting enough people to coordinate large processions to a location where an oration would take place. Additionally, the large cities above possess more extensive records of Independence Day celebrations.[91] Despite the urban focus of Travers's study, much of what he discusses about the importance of orations applies to rural Cheshire as well.

Moreover, Travers notes how, in the three cities that he analyzed, "the public oration was the intellectual and hermeneutical focus of Independence Day. In Boston particularly, all the morning's preparations aimed at this event, and the official procession literally led up to it. In its form, the oration ceremony was a secular version of a Sabbath-day service (and was almost always held in church buildings) that preached the 'gospel' of the republic."[92] The oration that Leland gave to the citizens of Cheshire on July 5, 1802,[93] did not record a procession to the site of the oration. There probably was not much of one, given the rural and rugged environment of Cheshire. However, it is quite plausible that Leland's oration took place in his or a neighboring church since he was a minister and many Cheshirites were Baptists.

Travers is mistaken, though, in drawing an unnecessary wedge between the religious and the secular when he calls an oration ceremony a "secular version of a Sabbath-day service." For Leland and the Cheshirites, one of their major concerns was to separate church from state in the sense of no longer having to pay taxes to an established church in Massachusetts and being able to worship as they pleased, free from governmental molestation. This type of separation, however, did *not* mean that their religious and political ideals and goals were separate. In fact, part of the reason why Leland and the citizens of Cheshire were meeting in the "secular" service of the oration ceremony was to reaffirm their commitment to religious disestablishment. During the oration, Leland extolled the Democratic-Republican Party for "contending for the civil and religious rights of all men," while castigating Federalists in Massachusetts for "[admiring] a state-established religion,"[94] for practicing "spiritual tyranny" by "turnpiking the way to heaven by human law,"[95] and for acting like Pharaoh by engaging in the "religious slavery" of the populace.[96]

Expressing concern for the state of religious liberty in Massachusetts was not the only theme that Leland highlighted in his oration. He also gave the citizens of Cheshire in his sketches a summary of the Democratic-Republican political platform that the newspapers made available to voters back in 1800, which demonstrates Leland's close familiarity with the platform. Like Jefferson, Leland espoused fiscal conservatism (rather than the perceived "extravagance" of the Adams administration) through lower taxes, having a smaller overseas diplomatic bureaucracy, and shrinking the national debt.[97] He also believed that the country was on the right track because Jefferson's government allowed for freedom of speech and of the press, instead of punishing critics of Federalism for sedition.[98] Leland understood how well the Jeffersonian governmental aesthetic resonated with his audience. A government that was small, simple, free, and antiauthoritarian matched the ecclesiological tastes of his Baptist audience.

Furthermore, in a creative application of Jefferson's platform, Leland discussed the importance of "self-government," which Leland defined as "the genuine meaning of republicanism." Usually, "self-government" related to a belief in a small or limited federal government. However, Leland stressed the importance of his listeners practicing self-government by not "[swearing] profanely, [drinking] to excess, [cheating] his neighbor, [speaking] falsely and [scandalizing] his fellow creatures." Additionally, the audience was to help the widow, the poor, and orphan.[99] In the oration, Leland put his sermonizing talents to work by reaffirming his, and his audience's, commitment to Jeffersonian politics, just as any pastor might spend time reaffirming a congregation's theological beliefs, as well as encouraging what I call a nascent Jeffersonian personal morality.

Leland thus is an ideal example of one of the "politicized clergymen" who played an important role as "essential intermediaries between would-be national leaders and average Americans."[100] Though not formally educated, Leland had spent around twenty-five years learning Jeffersonian and Madisonian principles regarding religious liberty and quickly consumed the details of the wider Democratic-Republican platform as the presidential election of 1800 drew near. He then effectively communicated his understanding in his characteristic folksy, bold, and humorous style[101] so that regular people in his audiences knew what the issues were and could vote accordingly. Since the 1770s, Jefferson and Madison had recruited ministers like Leland to reach the people who they could not; they knew the utility of having dissenting ministers on their side, and Leland was more than happy to oblige in the dawning era of partisan politics.[102]

In addition to engaging in the early national ritual of the oration, Leland and the townspeople of Cheshire delivered the previously described "Mammoth Cheese" on January 1, 1802, which the ladies of Cheshire made to honor President Jefferson, an event that garnered significant press coverage during the trip and after the delivery. I began my analysis by telling the Mammoth Cheese story, so I will not repeat it here. However, a few more observations about the importance of the cheese are in order.

Jeffrey L. Pasley perceptively argues that the women of Cheshire making the Mammoth Cheese and the town having that cheese delivered to Jefferson in profound appreciation of his republican principles "was not merely a colorful stunt. It was a natural by-product of a political culture that could not stray far from the fabric of everyday life, and that often asked people to exercise their political rights for the first time, to make a choice between alternatives rather than merely give assent."[103] The reason Leland and the Cheshirites chose to make a giant cheese to thank Jefferson was simply because many people in the town were dairy farmers. Making cheese was a prominent Early Republic example of a "producerist language in which ordinary Americans often expressed themselves on public occasions, the tendency for people who made things to speak through the medium of the things that they made." Just as artisans would parade through a large city holding their goods and showing how their goods were essential to the functioning and sustaining of the nation, the Cheshirites expressed their partisanship and usefulness to society through their cheese.[104] Also, note how even though no women from the town came with Leland and Brown to deliver the cheese, they were present through the cheese that they made. In the early 1800s, cheese making was women's work. By making the cheese, the women of Cheshire had found a way to demonstrate their love for Jefferson and America and participate in politics despite not being allowed to vote.

Finally, making such a large wheel of cheese was no small endeavor. It took virtually the entire town, Baptists and non-Baptists alike, to

A modern monument to Leland and the cheese press in Cheshire, MA. Public domain under Wikimedia Commons.

accomplish the task.[105] Planners had to figure out how much milk to use for the cheese making and how to keep curds from being contaminated. Also, they had to use a cider press instead of an ordinary cheese press to make the huge cheese. When July 20, 1801, came around, citizens after church "turned out with pails and tubs of curd for a day of thanksgiving, hymn-singing, and cheese pressing" at a large farm. They then used nine hundred cows to make enough milk for the Mammoth Cheese.[106] Making the cheese was a creative way for everyone to be involved in early national politics and was simultaneously an act of worship.

Since his circle of influence in Cheshire involved predominantly Baptists, Leland's work as a political ecumenist—his efforts to encourage Baptists to unite with non-Baptists to fight for religious liberty in Massachusetts—is not as apparent. However, when one considers his influence in Berkshire County as a whole, his political ecumenism becomes more evident. Democratic-Republicans throughout the county, including in the county seat of Pittsfield, considered Leland to be a party leader. His influence in the county was of a slightly different nature than his role in Cheshire, however. In Cheshire, he was perhaps the most well-known citizen there for decades, as it was a rather small town. In Berkshire County, he was part of a coterie of ministers and other political leaders who, together, led the Democratic-Republican Party; he served as a mediator between Cheshire Baptists and non-Baptists in the rest of the county.

The county's Republican Party and its leaders created a network that was a model for the rest of Massachusetts Republicans. According to Paul Goodman, in Berkshire County, "one of the earliest successful Republican organizations developed in the 1790's." Also, since "Berkshire County was settled later than all other parts of the Commonwealth except Maine," the status quo that favored the Congregational establishment and thus Federalism was not as strongly entrenched as in other areas of the state.[107] The county still had a notable Federalist population, but throughout the first quarter of the nineteenth century, the county tended to vote more Republican than Federalist.[108]

So, who made up the leadership of the Republican Party in Berkshire County from the 1790s through the early 1800s? In short, very strong and diverse personalities networked together in the Berkshires. Two noteworthy figures stand out. Thompson J. Skinner Jr. (1754–1809) was the son of a minister from Connecticut. He became a mechanic and was also a general in the militia. He was something of a local folk hero who successfully beat the wealthy and well-connected Federalist Theodore Sedgwick for the US House of Representatives seat for the First District in Massachusetts in 1797 and 1798.[109]

The Congregationalist minister Thomas Allen (1743–1810) of Pittsfield was also a luminary for the Republican cause and was another remarkable example of a politicized clergyman. He was the son of Joseph Allen, one of the few people who supported Jonathan Edwards at his Northampton congregation before the group fired Edwards. As the son of staunch Calvinists and a graduate of Harvard, Thomas Allen fit the profile of a Federalist Congregationalist minister.[110] Appearances were deceiving, however. In Pittsfield Allen was known as the "fighting parson" because he fought in the American Revolution and aggressively preached both Jeffersonian Democracy and Edwardsean Calvinism from his pulpit, despite having many Federalists in his congregation.[111] His credentials as a party leader in western Massachusetts (and statewide) were further established when the first Democratic-Republican governor of Massachusetts, James Sullivan, invited him to preach the election sermon to begin his second year because Allen was such a dedicated Democratic-Republican. According to Jonathan Sassi, "in the early nineteenth century, the choice of election preacher had become a partisan issue."[112] Through the able leadership of these men, Leland's Baptists, Skinner's followers, and Congregationalists sympathetic to Allen connected with one another to accomplish party goals.

In addition to giving speeches, Leland and Allen influenced voters to adopt Republican principles through the important information organ of the newspaper. For Berkshire Republicans, their major newspaper for forming public opinion and gluing together their constituents was the Pittsfield *Sun*. Reverend Thomas Allen was apprehensive that the only newspaper in Berkshire County was the Stockbridge *Western Star*, established in 1789. This newspaper essentially promoted the views of its Federalist patron and US Speaker of the House from 1799 to 1801, Theodore Sedgwick. So, during the year of the important 1800 election, Allen "persuaded his nephew Phinehas to come to Pittsfield as printer-editor of a much needed Republican journal." The younger Allen did so, and the Pittsfield *Sun* was born the year of Jefferson's landmark presidential victory.[113] Sharing the opinion of many other Republican newspaper editors during the Early Republic, Phinehas Allen from the start "conceived partisan newspapers and partisan organization as integral parts of the electoral process, 'the mode pointed out by the Constitution' by which people could influence their government."[114] The *Western Star* and the *Sun* sparred in print with one another and pleaded for votes virtually alone until other newspapers began to arrive on the scene in Berkshire County by 1825.[115]

Like many other Republican leaders, Leland found the Pittsfield *Sun* a useful means to promote his views.[116] Between 1802 and January 1841, just after Leland's death, the *Sun* printed sixteen different sermons, letters, or articles written by Leland. The newspaper also carried at least eight advertisements of Leland's preaching engagements in various churches that he visited or Independence Day lectures that he would deliver in a given town.[117] In a small opinion piece on August 22, 1839, a contributor even argued that a Boston *Post* writer's suggestion that Leland be nominated for the position of Massachusetts's lieutenant governor be given serious consideration.[118] Leland was eighty-five years old at the time, but his reputation as a "Jeffersonian patriarch" had been well set by then.[119] Moreover, in the twenty-two months after Leland's death, the *Sun* advertised twenty-eight times that it was selling copies of the sermon that Leland's friend, Reverend John Alden Jr., preached at Leland's funeral.[120] Leland's presence in the Pittsfield *Sun* was pervasive, even after his death. That is why Phinehas Allen concluded in his extended obituary of Leland on January 21, 1841, a week after Leland's death, that "no one rendered him more efficient aid than did Mr. Leland" who "[assisted] in the promotion and furtherance of the great and fundamental principles we have constantly and fearlessly aimed to maintain."[121]

Finally, while it was customary for Leland to encounter various groups of people in Massachusetts during his extensive itineracies and to preach to all who would hear the gospels of both Jesus and Jefferson, perhaps his most direct statewide impact occurred during a brief two-year stint as a member of the Massachusetts House of Representatives from 1811 to 1813, the only time he held public office in Massachusetts. Ever since the 1780 passage of the Massachusetts Constitution's controversial Article III, dissenters like Baptists had been required to pay taxes to the state's Standing Order. Nevertheless, there was still enough leeway in the vague wording of some of the clauses of the article to theoretically allow for some sects and denominations who were the majority in a parish to receive public money for themselves. More than any other case before it, the *Barnes v. Falmouth* case that state Supreme Court chief justice and avowed Federalist Theophilus Parsons decided in October 1810 closed the door on these loopholes. In the decision, Parsons argued that Universalist minister Thomas Barnes could not receive tax money from his Universalist congregants whom he served from 1798 to 1805 because the church was not an incorporated entity under state law. Only churches that were incorporated could have "public teachers" who were able to receive tax money.[122] Parsons's decision was a way for the Congregational Church to maintain both its established status and orthodoxy against "heretical" sects like the Universalists. The decision essentially outlawed other churches that were unincorporated. (By being the state church, the Congregational Church was already incorporated). Republicans were outraged and responded that "the state should not determine which churches were legitimate."[123]

Like other Republicans, Baptists all over the state were alarmed at the *Barnes* decision. The Baptists of Cheshire and their non-Baptist neighbors ensured that their most able spokesman, John Leland, represented their interests and the interests of all Republicans by electing him as a member of the Massachusetts House of Representatives in May

1811.[124] In front of the assembled representatives of the state, Leland gave possibly his most famous speech, a well-reasoned and passionate defense of religious liberty. He declared that, in the eyes of the state, "these non-incorporated societies are nobody—can do nothing and are never to be known except in shearing time, when their money is wanted to support teachers that they never hear."[125] Unincorporated societies were defenseless sheep before the power of the state, who harvested the sheep's "wool" as they wished. Speaking for his constituents back home, his fellow Baptists statewide, and many other Republicans, he claimed that *"we* cannot pay legal taxes for religious services."[126] To be forced to do so was akin to "disrobing Christianity of her virgin beauty—turning the churches of Christ into creatures of state—and metamorphosing gospel ambassadors to state pensioners."[127] The legislature needed to alter the state constitution in order to stop the coerced financial support of the Congregational Church, Leland argued.

Following Leland and other speechmakers who argued against the *Barnes* decision, the Republican-led Massachusetts House passed "An Act Respecting Public Worship and Religious Freedom" in late May 1811. This act did not disestablish the Congregational Church, but it allowed for all "teachers of a corporate or an uncorporate religious body to receive" public money.[128] Also, the act declared that only the sect or religious body itself and not the state had the right to determine which minister received money according to the rules of its given polity. Gone was the distinction between "public teachers" and every other minister. Finally, citizens received exemption from paying taxes to the Congregational Church.[129] The Religious Freedom Act of 1811 represented the high-water mark of legislative influence for Leland and other Baptists regarding the issue of disestablishment in Massachusetts. With the aid of their confreres in the Republican House, they severely weakened the establishment in Massachusetts. Leland's politically ecumenical approach had worked for the once sectarian Baptists.

4

RECONCILIATION THROUGH INSTITUTIONALIZATION

The Trinitarian Congregationalists of the first parish church of Dedham could hardly believe what they heard when Massachusetts Supreme Court justice Isaac Parker decided in favor of their rivals, the Unitarian Congregationalists, in the April 1821 *Dedham* case.[1] According to historian John D. Cushing, the "dispute had begun several years earlier when the people of Dedham in town meeting had elected a Unitarian minister over the opposition of two-thirds of the regular Congregational society, which refused to accept the vote of the town, claimed to be the legal church, and sued the Unitarians for title to the church property."[2] In Cushing's description, the "regular Congregational society" referred to full members of the church who were bound together by covenant responsibilities. The voters of the parish, however, were not officially members of the church but still had to support the church financially (a parish system requires that everyone living within its geographical bounds to pay taxes). The contest over church property and which group represented the "true" church of the parish (thus entitling the group to parish tax money) became more heated when one of the Trinitarian deacons walked out the door with the church's "records, communion service, trust deeds, and securities."[3] According to custom, the Trinitarians argued that the parish had to accept the decision of the church members and could not override its decision. In Justice Parker's assessment, however, the majority opinion of the parish, not the church, mattered most.[4]

The *Dedham* case set a dangerous precedent as far as the Trinitarian Congregationalists were concerned. William G. McLoughlin estimates that between 1820 to 1834, almost one hundred parishes "fell under Unitarian control, driving Trinitarians into exile from their own meetinghouses and forcing them either to appoint Unitarian ministers or to proclaim themselves dissenters and certificate men."[5] Outraged at losing the pecuniary and social benefits that the establishment offered them, Trinitarians chose a "Separatist logic" to justify departing from their former brethren, the Unitarians, so that they did not have to follow "heretical" pastors.[6] For the first time since their ancestors lived in England in the 1620s, the Trinitarian Congregationalists had become religious dissenters.

Because of the Trinitarian/Unitarian split in the established church that started in 1805 and became irreconcilable after the *Dedham* case, the longtime dissenter Massachusetts Baptists gained a seemingly unlikely new ally, the Trinitarian Congregationalists, against the official religious establishment. Both groups detested Unitarian theology and political power, but the alliance was more profound than that. In the first quarter of the nineteenth century, both groups created theological seminaries as an antidote to Unitarianism and other forms of religious infidelity present in the Early Republic, as well as to equip men for pastoral and missionary work. Also, since Federalists could not regain the White House in the 1800s and 1810s, many Congregationalist ministers "decoupled themselves from Federalist politics" and focused instead on forming voluntary societies, most notably home and foreign missions societies.[7] According to Jonathan Den Hartog, religious Federalists like Congregationalist ministers had to figure how to be relevant as they were "faced with pluralism and disestablishment." Creating religious societies and a national denominational structure were ways for these leaders to "[channel] the populist religious impulses erupting in the new nation." Den Hartog alludes to a discussion of religious populism in Nathan Hatch's influential *The Democratization of American Christianity* but qualifies Hatch's emphasis upon early national American Christianity's antiauthoritarianism and egalitarianism by calling the religious Federalists' approach "simultaneously democratizing and centralizing."[8] Baptist leaders, like their Trinitarian Congregationalist counterparts, regulated their members' popular religious fervor by centralizing their authority through the formation of voluntary societies and the creation of a national denomination as well.

With both Trinitarian Congregationalists and Baptists building the same types of institutional structures in order to combat heresy, train a more professionalized leadership, and spread the gospel at home and abroad, a sense of interdenominational cooperation started to develop in the first decade of the 1800s and was prominent by the 1820s. Jonathan Sassi aptly called such cooperation a "sort of a religious analogue to the Era of Good Feelings in politics," an era that had only one strong national political party, the Democratic-Republicans, with James Monroe at the helm.[9] Denominational differences and rivalries still existed, hence the need for the Congregationalists and Baptists to run their own missions boards—the American Board for Commissioners of Foreign Missions (ABCFM) and the Triennial Convention, respectively. However, Congregationalists and Baptists generally appreciated each other's efforts in achieving their common goals. Moreover, their mutual respect was a microcosm of the transatlantic cooperation that existed among evangelical Christians in England and America during this time.

As Trinitarian Congregationalists were becoming dissenters and interdenominational cooperation was growing between them and Baptists, Baptists in Massachusetts were also transitioning from being religious outsiders and becoming part of a mainstream "evangelical united front."[10] Various evangelical groups like Baptists in antebellum America "started national organizations that sought to impose their moral norms on law."[11] My analysis will not argue whether or not Baptists and Congregationalists actually succeeded in transforming American society and its laws, just merely that they both created comparable institutions with similar goals. Rather than fighting to change laws to prohibit governmental interference in churches or favoring one religious group over another, almost all Massachusetts Baptists were evolving toward a stance that attempted to alter laws to enforce religious and moral observance among the populace. Thus, a strict separationist view of church/state relations became unpalatable. By the late 1820s and early 1830s, they also abandoned Jefferson's (and Andrew Jackson's) party and identified as "anti-Jacksonian [Whigs]"[12] like most New Englanders did generally.

The influence of John Leland, so prevalent among Baptists in Virginia and Massachusetts in previous decades, diminished as a result of these developments. Leland, who died in 1841, outlived other prominent New England Baptist leaders like Isaac Backus (d. 1806) and

Samuel Stillman (d. 1807). He saw a new generation of Baptist leaders like Second Baptist Church of Boston pastor Thomas Baldwin (1753–1825) and First Baptist Church of Boston pastor and eventual president of Brown University Francis Wayland (1796–1865) exert their influence over Baptists to form them into a national denomination by 1814.

Leland also lived long enough to observe the entire process of Trinitarian Congregationalists becoming dissenters and Massachusetts Baptists becoming part of an unofficial religious establishment. Leland disagreed with many of these changes that occurred in Baptist life and in American evangelicalism generally from the early 1800s to his death. He was a strident opponent of voluntary societies, particularly missionary societies, believing that they had no biblical basis. He resented Baptists' and other evangelicals' efforts to promote Sabbatarianism by enacting a law to prohibit mail delivery on Sundays; Leland argued that passing such a law amounted to establishing Christianity by law. He also dreaded the increasing centralization of denominational authority.[13]

Ironically, the man who led the way in encouraging and modeling for previously insular and sectarian Baptists a politically ecumenical approach that called for them to network with non-Baptist Democratic-Republicans to achieve the goal of religious disestablishment in the political arena was not supportive of Baptists partnering together with members of other denominations in "unbiblical" voluntary societies. Historians L. H. Butterfield, William G. McLoughlin, John Bradley Creed, and Nathan Hatch attribute Leland's contrariness to his eccentric and individualistic tendencies.[14] In contrast, Leland's opposition to new trends in American Christianity derived not from his individualism per se but rather from his unfailing loyalty to Jeffersonian ideals of separation of church and state and citizenship. The increasing concentration of authority taking place in churches was reminiscent to him of the centralized power of his old foes the Anglicans and the Federalists/Congregationalists. He was nostalgic for the time when eighteenth-century Baptists were still small, weak dissenting Davids fighting against powerful, state-supported Goliaths. Through his political ecumenism, he wanted all underdogs to be able to worship freely and maintain the distinctness of their own faith communities, not to join the favorites' "team."

PROBLEMS AND OPPORTUNITIES FACING BAPTISTS AND CONGREGATIONALISTS IN THE NEW NATION

The 1790s were a fractious time in the young republic, as two political parties—the Federalists and the Democratic-Republicans—developed because of opposing perspectives concerning foreign political alliances with France and Britain, the scope of governmental authority under the new federal Constitution, and freedom of the press and religion. In Massachusetts, Congregationalist clergy, as represented by Jedidiah Morse and Timothy Dwight, supported the Federalists' policies of being pro-Britain and having a strong national government, as well as the Alien and Sedition Acts' goal of restricting divergent political and religious opinions, or forms of "infidelity," in order to maintain political unity.[15] On the other hand, many Baptists supported France (until bloodshed in the wake of the French Revolution modified their enthusiasm), favored a limited federal government, and believed in the free expression of political and religious ideas.

Despite these stark differences, however, the seeds of unity and cooperation were already taking root in the 1790s. Although they did not appreciate their Congregationalist cousins including them with "infidels" like deists, atheists, Socinians, and Universalists, many of whom tended to be Jeffersonians as well, Baptists agreed that these groups espoused theological heresy and were just as adamant as Congregationalists in denouncing them in order to preserve their churches and the republic.[16] In the 1793 circular letter of the Shaftsbury Baptist Association, which was part of the approved minutes of the association's annual meeting, John Leland argued that the Bible, and not popes, kings, councils of bishops, or "civil courts," was the only reliable and "infallible guide" for Baptists. What prompted Leland to write the letter was that "we [the Baptists] find ourselves boldly attacked by deists and infidels; who seek to sap the foundation of our religion, by asserting that Moses and the prophets, were enthusiastical cheats; and that Jesus and his apostles were put pitiful impostors:—That all their writings are like modern priestcraft."[17] Leland did not want more New England Baptists to defect to the Universalists, Shakers, or other religious groups, so he provided Baptist churches with twelve arguments to combat skeptics' slanders.[18]

Shaftsbury's sister association, the famous Warren Association, expressed concern over the growth and threat of infidel groups throughout the 1790s into the early 1800s as well. Members of the Warren

Association wrote circular letters and corresponding letters (letters that went from association to association) defending the divinity of Christ against "Socinian and deistical writers"[19] and assuring churches that God was sovereign over the "sons of infidelity waging war with superstition and idolatry," a not-so-subtle reference to the religio-political conflict occurring in France between the secular French government and traditional Catholic power in the country. This second letter added that, despite God allowing the forces of infidelity to eliminate the observance of the Sabbath right after the French Revolution, God would eventually judge them for their blasphemy.[20] Later, as the first few decades of the nineteenth century progressed, Baptists and Congregationalists slowly realized that they had much in common theologically and mostly saved their ammunition for groups who did not adhere to the tenets of American evangelical Protestantism.

Complementing their combined literary fight against rampant infidelity through letters and treatises, Congregationalists and Baptists worked together to make sure that the new republic had an accurate English language edition of the Bible printed in America. Before the American Revolution, the American colonies received all of their English-language Bibles from England. It was much less expensive to print an entire Bible in England throughout the colonial era, so American printers did not compete with cheaper prices. Also, American printers feared lawsuits from printers in England for infringing upon their monopoly over the Bible printing trade.[21] Once America gained independence from Britain, various printers tried to print English-language Bibles, but their efforts contained too many errors. Not having an accurate Bible greatly alarmed the Congregational ministers of Massachusetts when they had their annual meeting in May 1790. They appointed a five-member committee, one of whom was Jedidiah Morse, to draft a petition asking the US Congress to ensure "that no Edition of the Bible, or its translation be published in America without its carefully being inspected and certified to be free from error." The committee was also responsible for contacting other denominations to join them in their petition.[22]

Samuel Stillman, who was friends with Congregationalist ministers in Boston, received the committee's request for help and shared the petition with other members of the Warren Association at their annual meeting in September 1790. The petition prompted four votes from the body of ministers and lay delegates assembled. First, they voted to thank the Congregationalist ministers for caring so much about

Americans having an accurate copy of the Bible. Second, they created a committee of five—three of whom were Stillman, Isaac Backus, and Thomas Baldwin—to draft their own petition. For the fourth and final vote, they asked other Baptist associations to join them in entreating Congress. Of all of the votes, however, the third one stands out the most: "we heartily concur in the measure proposed, and are equally desirous of cultivating a friendly and Christian intercourse with them, and the whole body of Christians; 'believing that such an intercourse between Christians of different denominations and sentiments, especially the ministers of the gospel, will have a happy tendency to harmonize them—remove unreasonable prejudices—to promote a spirit of love and candor, and thus essentially serve the interests of our holy religion: and that it also might have a beneficial influence on the civil affairs of our country.'"[23]

The fact that Congress tabled the Congregationalists' petition in June 1790 and various New England Baptist associations' petitions after January 1791 to avoid establishing religion by regulating the printing of the Bible is beside the point.[24] Congregationalists had reached out to several Protestant denominations, and the Warren Association responded positively to their longtime opponents who comprised the Standing Order. Baptists were hopeful that the focus upon creating an accurate edition of the Bible would bring unity and fellowship between them and the Congregationalists (and all Christians) and help them to break down points of difference. They also understood that interdenominational cooperation "might have a beneficial influence on the civil affairs of our country," if they could work together to transform society.

In the view of early national Baptists and Congregationalists, the largest challenge and opportunity that they faced in the new nation was the reality of an ever-expanding American frontier in need of the gospel. Keith Harper has noted how Thomas Jefferson unintentionally "played a dramatic role in shaping Baptist thought and development in the first half of the nineteenth century" by helping to add over one hundred million square miles to the United States. The country's acquisition of so much land "coincided with an unprecedented zeal for organized missionary work" among Baptists.[25] Although Harper does not apply his insights about how the nation's geographical growth affected Baptists to other religious groups, Congregationalists, too, formed institutions like seminaries and missions societies to engage in more organized missions work on the frontier.

Already in 1789, when he published the first edition of his textbook *The American Geography,* Congregationalist minister and geographer Jedidiah Morse anticipated the importance of the west for the fate of both true (i.e., evangelical Protestant) Christianity and the United States. According to Morse, "empire has been travelling from east to west. Probably her last and broadest seat will be America . . . Here civil and religious liberty are to flourish, unchecked by the cruel hand of civil or ecclesiastical tyranny." He added that "the AMERICAN EMPIRE will comprehend millions of souls, west of the Mississippi. Judging upon probable grounds, the Mississippi was never designed as the western boundary of the American empire." In an early expression of Manifest Destiny, Morse argued that God had a plan for America to expand beyond the Mississippi River. The extensive nation would be a model for the entire world since both civil and religious liberty would "flourish" in America like no place else.[26] New England Baptists and Congregationalists would soon follow in their revered Puritan ancestors' footsteps by going on their own "errand into the wilderness," the West.[27] This time, rather than Baptists being a troublesome element to accomplishing the Puritan errand, Baptists and Congregationalists would set aside their differences and partner together to complete the work before them.

COMMON SOLUTIONS TO SHARED PROBLEMS AND OPPORTUNITIES

To meet the challenges of perceived rampant infidelity in the early United States and evangelize an expanding frontier (which, as the nineteenth century continued, would not include only American territories but foreign lands as well), New England Baptist leaders had to get creative by adopting a new strategy. Inspired by the missions societies that British Baptists and other British evangelicals created in the 1790s, and often borrowing from the ideas and practices of their Congregationalist neighbors, Baptists committed themselves to creating new institutions like a seminary and various voluntary societies to manage the explosion of individual and popular religious zeal resulting from the revivals of the Second Great Awakening.

Time and time again in the American context since 1740, New England Baptists had proven themselves to be keen religious entrepreneurs. During the Great Awakening, Separate preachers, many of whom became Baptists, engaged in extensive itinerant ministry. Because they did not have to wait to receive a college education before ministering, they quickly fanned out to the countryside and preached on the importance of the new birth. They were more effective in converting people than anti-revival religious groups were in keeping their own church members or adding to their numbers. As the American Revolution engulfed the colonies, Baptists, much like patriot leaders organizing opposition against Britain, took advantage of the increasing availability of the printing press to unite fiercely independent Baptists churches into one political voice to fight against the Standing Order. After Americans won independence and eventually formed a stable constitutional government, John Leland demonstrated to other Baptists how participation in the Democratic-Republican Party gave Baptists an avenue for networking with non-Baptists for the first time, to attempt to overthrow Massachusetts' religious establishment. Institutional proliferation (and its accompanying centralization of denominational activities) was simply the next stage in a long trend of religious innovation for Baptists. Congregationalists were involved in the same types of structural change at this time, which helped foster appreciation between the enemy religious groups and initiated a new era of interdenominational affinity and cooperation.

Coinciding with this new stage of religious experimentation for Baptists and Congregationalists, and what made such experimentation possible, was the existence of a "bullish" economic and technological market in the late eighteenth and the early nineteenth centuries in the United States. Steam engines, new canals, better roads, and, later, trains made it easier to travel and communicate across a growing country. An explosion of new books, tracts, and pamphlets also fostered communication and allowed denominations to publish more religious works than previously possible. In New England specifically, textile mills brought many new jobs, especially to rural areas. They manufactured goods using cotton they received from southern plantations. The uptick in jobs meant that New Englanders had more disposable income to fund the two religious groups' different institutions.[28]

Creating Theological Seminaries

Theological seminaries were one kind of institution that church leaders and concerned laity developed with the aid of increased cash flow. Congregationalists' efforts antedated those of Baptists, but they might not have formed a seminary without the controversy that precipitated the school's founding. In 1805 Harvard appointed Henry Ware as the new Hollis Professor of Divinity, the most influential theologian position in all of New England. The college's choice of Ware was problematic because he was a Unitarian, and the chair's original rules for the endowment stipulated that the professor accepting the position would be a Calvinist. Despite Calvinistic Congregationalists' objections, Ware's appointment went forward. As a result, a rift between Unitarian-leaning Congregationalists and Calvinistic Trinitarian Congregationalists began to split the denomination. The latter faction worried about Ware's presence at Harvard because he had the potential to corrupt young men preparing to be ministers, who would then take the Unitarian heresy to their churches and lead average congregants astray.[29]

Since the Trinitarian party could not stop Ware's appointment, they decided to form their own educational institution, Andover Theological Seminary, in 1808. Andover was not only the first theological seminary in the United States; it was the first graduate school of any kind, predating other professional schools like medical schools and law schools.[30] To prevent "heresy" from creeping into Andover and to equip students to battle it outside the walls of the school, Andover had strict requirements for its professors. A professor had to be a pious Congregationalist or Presbyterian who was "a man of sound and orthodox principles in Divinity, according to that form of sound words or system of evangelical doctrines, drawn from the Scriptures, and denominated [in] the Westminster Assembly's shorter Catechism." While providing students with the pure milk of Reformed Christianity, a professor also had the responsibility of teaching explicitly against the spiritually "hazardous" errors of Unitarianism, atheism, deism, Universalism, Judaism, Islam, and so forth.[31]

Expectations for students were likewise high. Each student whom the seminary admitted had to "[complete] a course of liberal education," meaning that he had to have a college education, "and [sustain] a fair moral character." Students could also be from any Protestant denomination.[32] For example, Baptists and future Newton Theological Institution professors Irah Chase and Horatio Hackett were Andover graduates.[33] Moreover, students received a rigorous, three-year, systematic curriculum that included "Lectures on Natural Theology, Sacred Literature, Ecclesiastical History, Christian Theology, and Pulpit Eloquence."[34]

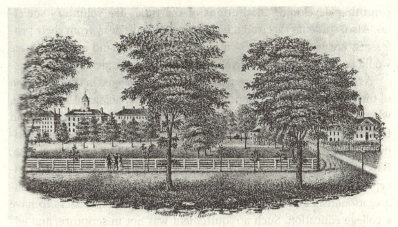

Andover Theological Seminary from the early 1800s. Public Domain under Wikimedia Commons. Original at the Yale University Art Gallery, Yale University, New Haven, CT. Author: J. Kidder (1813–1823).

Ministerial education was entering a new era of professionalization as a result of Andover Theological Seminary. Andover became a model for theological education in the United States, which seminaries still follow to this day. For instance, Harvard (1815), Bangor (1816), and Yale (1822) soon copied Andover by creating their own seminaries.[35] Before the advent of Andover Theological Seminary, most pastors did not receive formalized training. Although some young men went to college, most of them learned their craft through one-on-one mentorship from a more experienced pastor (some participated in both options). The mentor often suggested theology and other books to read, quizzed the novice pastor on his understanding of doctrine, and sometimes critiqued the pupil's sermons. Jonathan Edwards had trained Joseph Bellamy that way, and Bellamy trained other ministers in like manner.[36] With the mentorship method, much depended upon the quality and time investment of the mentor. However, Trinitarian Congregationalist church leaders came to realize that this method was outdated and unable to meet the challenges of the time. In contrast, Andover Theological Seminary exposed students to several professors at once and gave students a much more wide-ranging training that the students would use to lead churches, some of which were mission churches, and run other developing institutions of the time, like voluntary societies. Also, students received a heavy dose of orthodoxy from their professors, ensuring that their churches in New England and elsewhere would be steeled from the deleterious effects of "infidelity."

As compared to Congregationalists, Baptists lagged in the formation of their first theological seminary, the Newton Theological Institution, which opened began in 1825. Unlike Congregationalists, Baptists had to manage a popular, though by no means universal, streak of anti-intellectualism within its tradition. Since at least the Great Awakening, Baptists and their Separate immediate precursors had scorned the concept of a "learned ministry." They believed that it was wrong for Congregationalists and other denominations to require ministers to have a college education. Such a requirement was not in scripture, and education, without accompanying piety, could lead to a spiritual lifelessness in preaching and evangelism. Instead, it was essential that pastors be regenerate and have a clear "inner" call from the Holy Spirit and an "outward" call from a local church body that confirmed the work of the Spirit. As the last half of the eighteenth century ensued, Baptists slowly moved toward acknowledging the importance of a college education. For instance, New England Baptists helped to establish Rhode Island College (1764). To fund Rhode Island College, the Warren Association advised that churches in its association contribute to "a system of annual subscriptions" in 1783. Furthermore, in 1791 the Warren Association created the Education Fund whereby indigent potential students could receive financial help to attend college.[37]

However, until the actual formation of the Newton Theological Institution, the most important step in Baptists embracing a learned ministry was the Warren Association's founding of an Education Society in 1817. Anybody could join the Education Society, provided they gave a minimum of one dollar a year. There was a secretary, a treasurer, and seven members on the executive committee. On this executive committee sat James Winchell (1791–1820), pastor of the influential First Baptist Church of Boston from 1814 to 1820, and chief Baptist apologist for a theological seminary, Worcester Baptist pastor Jonathan Going (1786–1844). To solicit donations, the society attached two mostly blank sheets of paper at the end of the Warren Association's circular letter with columns for a donor's name, residence, annual subscription, and donation to distribute to all churches in the association.[38] At the annual meeting of the Education Society of the Warren Association the following year, the society succeeded in collecting $264.49, which was $179.64 more than Baptists gave to foreign and home missions causes combined ($84.85) that year.[39]

Jonathan Going built upon the success of the Education Society in encouraging Baptists to contribute money to support ministerial education by writing an essay to persuade Baptists to form a theological seminary of their own. Going lamented that "all other denominations are increasing their exertions for the improvement of the ministry among them. It is true, we are not idle; but shall we be contented with doing a little? We profess to believe that our distinguishing sentiments, though not essential to the salvation of the soul, are highly important, and that they will become universal; and we are much concerned in their extension and establishment."[40] He wanted Baptists to catch up with other denominations, namely their Congregationalist neighbors, in creating a seminary. Andover was an excellent model, but it was not a *Baptist* seminary wherein they could have a sense of control over their graduate-level education and feel free to emphasize their "distinguishing sentiments" like believer's baptism.[41] He also acknowledged the important steps that Baptists had already taken in funding ministerial education, but the problems and opportunities that Baptists faced required more effort. Earlier in the essay, he pointed out that Baptists were "suffering through want of ministerial ability; many of our churches are destitute of pastors; and, to say nothing of the number of well-educated ministers necessary to supply the Foreign Mission, the trees of the western forests, with every breeze, wave a Macedonian cry, 'Come over and help us.'"[42] A new era needed a new method to prepare ministers, and establishing a seminary to give ministers thorough and specialized training was that method.

In addition to discussing what he thought was a clear need for a seminary, Going noted the advantages of forming the institution. First, having one place where ministers could train for church ministry and missions work was an efficient use of resources. It would cost more for students and church members alike if Baptists tried to fund numerous institutions and "divide our strength." Second, Baptists had no standardized way of training ministers. Some were able to attend college; others attended academies, post-secondary institutions that were unequal to colleges in scope and duration of education. According to Going, some academy teachers were unbelievers, mocked true religion, and distracted young men by also admitting young girls. Still other ministers, as with the Congregationalists, had one-on-one mentoring relationships with more experienced pastors, and that was the only training they received. Going's dream was to have all young men who showed evidence of piety and intellectual ability receive the same training in one centralized location. In close quarters, such young men would keep each other accountable in their studies and in their devotion to God.[43]

Eventually, in 1825, Going's arguments and the needs of the time convinced New England Baptists to create a seminary. Not surprisingly, Going was an original trustee of the Newton Theological Institution.[44] For $8,000, they purchased eighty-five acres of land in Newton, a town just west of Boston, which had an old mansion on it that they used for a residence hall and classrooms. However, they had to purchase another building for $5,000 (which they did not have) so that the school could have a library, a chapel, and other essential seminary spaces. Newton Theological Institution did not have the financial backing that Andover did and struggled with debt on and off for its first couple of decades. Also, Margaret Bendroth highlights how, in contrast to Andover, "Newton had no constitution, and its leaders made no attempt to set forth a faculty creed, course curricula, or any means of doctrinal oversight of the school."[45] Although Baptists hated Unitarianism and other theological "errors" as much as the men of Andover and would similarly train their students to defend the tenets of American evangelical Protestantism, they did not have to battle with a Unitarian faction within their own denomination like the Trinitarian Congregationalists did.

There were other significant differences between Newton and Andover. Newton did not require students to have a college degree before attending seminary like Andover did. This could have been an allowance for the scarcity of college-educated Baptists in New England. Baptists, while adopting Andover's three-year framework for graduate study, did not stress having their students learn systematic theology as students at Andover did and instead focused on biblical theology.[46] Notwithstanding these important differences, Andover Theological Seminary and Newton Theological Institution, along with similar institutions, were on the cutting edge in terms of providing specialized ministerial training. They would try to stem the tide of infidelity in the new country and provide the plethora of voluntary societies with crucial leadership throughout the nineteenth century.

Forming Voluntary Organizations

In addition to creating seminaries, both New England Baptists and Congregationalists started numerous voluntary societies to inculcate evangelical moral norms on everyday Americans and to urge them to direct their religious impulses into the new societies. Perhaps no one made clearer to early nineteenth-century Protestants the potential of voluntary societies to produce moral transformation and to encourage popular participation in these same organizations than Lyman Beecher (1775–1863). Beecher was born in Connecticut and came under the tutelage of Timothy Dwight at Yale in 1793. He was present for Dwight's work to reverse the prevalence of "irreligion" at Yale and became one of Dwight's biggest supporters. He pastored various prominent Congregationalist and Presbyterian churches in New England and Ohio and became president of Lane Seminary in Cincinnati. Wherever Beecher went, irreligion and immorality concerned him, and thus he committed himself to preaching about the benefits of creating and participating in voluntary societies.[47] He also took his cue about the need to reform America from none other than George Washington. In an 1803 sermon, Beecher quoted at length one of the key statements about religion that Washington made in his Farewell Address (1796): "Of all the dispositions and habits which lead to political prosperity, religion and morals (says he) are indispensable supports." Washington continued, "reason and experience both forbid us to expect, that a national morality can prevail, in exclusion of religious principles." According to Beecher, American may not have a national church, but neither could the young nation survive without the supports of religion and morality. Immoral people running a nation could expect to receive punishment from God.[48]

But how specifically could the American people remain religious and moral enough for the country to prosper? Many people worked on and blasphemed the Sabbath, drank too much, dueled, and had heretical beliefs.[49] The government could not regulate morality by itself. An individual working alone could not accomplish much either. Even popular democratic voting on an issue might not do the job because people might vote in an immoral manner. In his 1812 sermon *A Reformation of Morals Practicable and Indispensable*, Beecher instead suggested that alternative institutions, specifically voluntary societies, could mediate between government and individuals to address societal ills. Beecher contended that voluntary societies "aid the civil magistrate in the execution of the laws [against immorality]. These associations are eminently adaptable to answer their intended purpose. They awaken the public attention, and by the sermons, reports, and the conversation they occasion, diffuse much moral instruction . . . They constitute a sort of disciplined moral militia, prepared to act upon every emergency, and repel every encroachment upon the liberties and State."[50] For Beecher, the lean bureaucratic structure of voluntary societies—as compared to the federal, or even state, government—allowed their members to mobilize support to solve problems efficiently and effectively. Voluntary societies helped to maintain social stability in a new and unsettled nation by encouraging people to depart from their immoralities and crimes and obey the law.[51] Although he did not cite Romans 13:1–7, Beecher was of course operating under the assumption that citizens who obeyed the civil law were ultimately obeying God because God created civil law.

Despite his fears of continuing immorality and infidelity, Beecher saw signs of improvement in America by the time of his 1812 sermon. Probably hinting at the creation of Andover Theological School, he rejoiced that having a learned ministry had become a great priority among Christians. He believed that "the morals of a nation will ever hold a close alliance with the talents and learning, the piety and orthodoxy of its clergy." Revivalism was also bringing droves of new people into churches. "The doctrines of infidel philosophy" were diminishing as well. Finally, he celebrated an increase in missionary activity and what he saw as a reformation of morals. Beecher observed that a focus on missions and starting missionary societies "calls off the hearts of thousands from political and sectarian bickerings, to unite them in one glorious enterprise of love."[52] Possibly more than any other cause in antebellum America, missions to the "heathen" inspired and encouraged interdenominational cooperation. This was especially true in New England, where Baptists and Congregationalists formed parallel state and national missionary societies to one another but were ultimately united in the desire to spread their faith at home and abroad. This partnership also served to lessen animosity between the two religious groups.

The lessening of hostility between the two groups could not be clearer than in the changing relationship that Beecher and New England Baptists had with one another. During the 1810s, before Connecticut's Congregationalist establishment ended in 1818, Beecher loudly and frequently criticized Connecticut Baptists for trying to end the Standing Order and disparaged them for having "illiterate" ministers lead their churches and evangelize the populace. The Baptists, in turn, condemned Beecher for not allowing religious freedom and for ignoring Baptist interest in college education.[53] Although it is unclear exactly when Beecher's views of Baptists changed, they certainly had by 1829. According to First Baptist Church of Boston historian and pastor Nathan Wood, Beecher visited the Baptist church and said in an 1829 sermon, "Your light was kept burning and shining when ours had gone out." Beecher was referencing the fact that many Congregationalist churches in Boston had become Unitarian in the first decades of the nineteenth century, and he was grateful that evangelical Christianity survived in the city because of the efforts of the Baptists' flagship church.[54] Baptists likewise thought well of another sermon that Beecher preached that same year. The Baptist religious magazine *Christian Watchman* lauded Beecher for an address at the Quarterly Meeting of Sabbath School Teachers, which met at Beecher's church. In the sermon, Beecher stressed the importance of the society in educating young children about the Bible, which led to large numbers of children converting to Christianity. Pastor of the Second Baptist Church of Boston James Knowles (1798–1838, pastor from 1825–1832) echoed many of Beecher's sentiments at the same meeting.[55]

The cause that may have united Baptists and Congregationalists the most was missions work. However, the formation of various missionary societies in New England owed itself ultimately to transatlantic influences. The modern missionary movement in Anglo-Protestant churches began in England in 1792, when members of the Northamptonshire Association of Baptists created the Particular Baptist Society for Propagating the Gospel among the Heathen, or the Baptist Missionary Society (BMS). Before the start of the BMS, many Baptist churches in the Northamptonshire Association and throughout England had believed in the "hyper-Calvinist" view that unconverted sinners "were under no moral obligation to repent and believe the gospel, since they were rendered incapable of doing so by total depravity, and could not justly be held accountable for failing to do what they were unable to do."[56]

Kettering Baptist Church minister Andrew Fuller, in his essay *The Gospel Worthy of All Acceptation* (1785), modified this uncompromising version of Calvinism by arguing, like Jonathan Edwards a few decades before, that God's sovereignty did not preclude people from having the moral obligation to respond to the gospel if they heard it. Fuller's essay helped convince Baptists to begin missions work. So, too, did fellow Northamptonshire Association minister William Carey's work *An Enquiry into the Obligations of Christians to Use Means for the Conversions of the Heathens* (1792), which argued that the Great Commission of Matthew 28:18–20 was binding upon all Christians, not just Jesus's apostles. The BMS appointed William Carey and medical doctor John Thomas as missionaries to India in 1793. BMS members collected donations from all over England to support the missionaries, and even had prominent non-Baptists like William Wilberforce and John Newton give to the cause.[57] Inspired by the accomplishments of the BMS, ardor for missions soon spread to other Protestant Christian groups in England, and evangelical Anglicans and various members of Nonconformist churches like the Presbyterians and Congregations united together to found the London Missionary Society in 1795.[58]

Baptist associations throughout the United States heard about British Baptists appointing Carey and Thomas to India. As a result, according to Baptist historian Walter Shurden, "Baptists in America developed enthusiasm for foreign missions." The Philadelphia Baptist Association took up a collection to give to the BMS in 1794. Shurden further observed how the topic of missions was not prominent in American associations' circular letters written before 1793. For Shurden, "this fact is significant because circular letters reflected the contemporary concerns of Baptists to a remarkable degree." From 1793 to 1800, associations mentioned missions more frequently,[59] but, at least in the Warren Association in New England, fears of the spread of "infidelity" in the new nation and the ever-present desire for religious freedom still dominated the content of the circular letters at that time. A shift occurred after 1800, however. Circular letters and corresponding letters began to report about missions work at more length,[60] which not surprisingly coincided with the formation of state missionary societies among Baptists and their Congregationalist neighbors.

Unlike their fellow evangelicals in England, Baptists and Congregationalists did not start with establishing foreign missions societies. They first built smaller-scale institutions, state missions societies, which focused on home missions. Funding foreign missions was more expensive than beginning home missions, prohibitively so—though supporting home missions was a daunting and expensive task in and of itself because of the rapid expansion of the American frontier. British evangelicals had the advantage of using Britain's best-in-the-world naval fleet and its many merchant vessels to go to far-flung areas of the British Empire. In comparison to Britain, America did not have a large navy or a lot of merchant ships, and the country was just beginning to build canals and better roads to cross its own frontier. As with the creation of a seminary, the better-funded Congregationalists beat the Baptists in founding the first state missions societies in New England: the Connecticut Missionary Society in 1798 and the Massachusetts Missionary Society in 1799. Congregationalists on the East Coast wanted to fashion into "typical" New England towns the frontier areas of Maine, Vermont, New York, and Ohio, where New Englanders emigrated. These new settlements needed churches and ministers at the center of society, both spatially and morally, so that they could flourish like New England itself had, Congregationalist society leaders thought.[61]

Baptists were not far behind. Notable Warren Association leaders like Samuel Stillman, Thomas Baldwin, First Baptist Church of Newton pastor Joseph Grafton (1757–1836),[62] and pastor Hezekiah Smith of the First Baptist Church of Haverhill were responsible for creating the Massachusetts Baptist Missionary Society (MBMS) on May 26, 1802, at the First Baptist Church of Boston.[63] In the preamble to the society's constitution, members explained that it was not enough for people to pray for the salvation of lost souls; they also had to be intentional in spreading the message of the gospel. They formed the MBMS in response to perceived spiritual needs. They also were "dominated by the laudable exertions which many of our Christian friends of different denominations on both sides of the Atlantic are making to extend the empire of truth and promote the salvation of dying men." The institution-building efforts of English evangelicals and Congregationalists in New England were making an impact on the methods that Massachusetts Baptists used to reach the outside world.[64]

In this new era of intentional missions activity, the MBMS prescribed how they were going to regulate missions work and run the organization. The society's target group would be "the new settlements of the United States, or further if circumstances should render it proper." The trustees of the MBMS determined how to allocate funds generally and how much to pay missionaries. Moreover, the trustees decided which missionaries to appoint and where to send them. Decision-making for the society, then, did not ultimately rest with local Baptist churches but with a Presbyterian-esque board of trustees elected by

> HISTORICAL SKETCH 9
>
> intention more explicit, we submit to your consideration the following."
>
> The Constitution thus presented for consideration, which was subsequently adopted, reads:
>
> "*Article I.* This Society shall be distinguished and known by the name of the MASSACHUSETTS BAPTIST MISSIONARY SOCIETY.
>
> "*Article II.* This Society shall be composed of such members only as shall subscribe and pay at least *one dollar* annually to its funds.[1]
>
> "*Article III.* The members, at their first meeting, and at their annual meeting ever after, shall by ballot appoint Twelve Trustees, eight whereof shall be ministers, or professing brethren of the Baptist denomination; the other four may be chosen from the members at large; who shall conduct the business of the Society in the manner hereafter described.
>
> "*Article IV.* The object of this Society shall be to furnish occasional preaching, and to promote the knowledge of evangelistic truth in the new settlements within these United States; or further if circumstances should render it proper.
>
> "*Article V.* The Trustees shall have power to apply the funds of the Society, according to their discretion, in all cases in which they shall not be limited by special direction of the Society.
>
> "*Article VI.* They shall have power to appoint and dismiss missionaries, to pay them, and generally to transact all the business necessary for the accomplishment of the important object of the Society.
>
> [1] To Article II. the following foot-note was appended:
> "This small sum, which by this article is made necessary in order to become a member, is not designed to restrict such as have it in their power to subscribe more liberally."

First page of "Constitution of the Massachusetts Baptist Missionary Society," 1802, W. H. Eaton, *Historical Sketch of the Massachusetts Baptist Missionary Society and Convention, 1802–1902: With an Appendix and Other Related Matters* (Boston: Massachusetts Baptist Convention, 1903), 9.

members of the society, who contributed a minimum of one dollar per year.[65] Baptists had drifted away from their treasured belief in the autonomy of local churches by embracing the societal method.

Another crucial aspect of the MBMS was that its missionaries were to remain neutral on political matters. In its 1803 letter of instructions to missionaries, the MBMS warned missionaries to "avoid all interference and allusions to those political topics which divide the opinions and too much irritate the passions of our fellow citizens."[66] In a time of sharp regional and national political divisions, the MBMS did not want to complicate its goal of missionizing the lost by its missionaries taking partisan stands. Just like the "religious Federalists" that Den Hartog describes in *Patriotism and Piety*, religious Jeffersonians like the Baptists were also slowly decoupling themselves from a bitter political climate and focusing more on the higher callings of missions work and society building generally,[67] even if most New England Baptists still remained staunchly Jeffersonian for another couple of decades after 1803.

By the 1810s both Baptists and Congregationalists expanded from state missions societies focusing on home missions to building much larger institutions that concentrated on foreign missions and also consolidated both religious groups into national denominations. Other than important British precursors, the foundation for both groups' foray into international missions was a prayer meeting that took place among a handful of college-aged Congregationalists. During the summer of 1806, five students at Williams College,[68] a school in western Massachusetts, found themselves in an unexpected thunderstorm. To seek cover, they found a haystack and continued their discussion and prayers about what to do regarding the "heathen" in Asia. One of the young men, Samuel Mills, suggested that they should all commit to going overseas themselves and evangelizing the lost. It was a radical notion because college students at that time in American history did not go on foreign missions trips, much less become lifetime missionaries. Also, unlike in England, there was no institutional structure in place to fund and direct foreign missions work. Two years later, five college students, though not all the original five who took shelter under the haystack, created a secret society called the Society of the Brethren. They kept their meetings a secret because they believed that others would find their aspirations to do overseas missions too ambitious.[69]

Eventually, in 1810, Mills, James Richards, and Harvey Loomis became students at Andover Theological Seminary with the goal of being missionaries. Other students such as Adoniram Judson, Samuel Newell, and Samuel Nott became part of this group as well. Mills, Judson, Newell, and Nott, sensing that the time was right, asked some of their seminary professors and key Congregationalist leaders what could be done about their desire to become foreign missionaries. In response to their impassioned request, these leaders formed the American Board of Commissioners for Foreign Missions on September 5, 1810, in Farmington, Connecticut, "for the purpose of devising ways and means, and adopting and prosecuting measures, for promoting the spread of the gospel in heathen lands."⁷⁰ Nine prominent Congregationalist leaders signed on to be the society's board members. The board included Timothy Dwight, Samuel Worcester, and Samuel Spring, a professor at Andover. Jedidiah Morse joined the board a year later.⁷¹

After completing their studies at Andover, Judson, Newell, Nott, Gordon Hall, and Luther Rice were ordained by the ABCFM at Samuel Worcester's Salem Tabernacle Church on February 6, 1812, as missionaries to India. Leonard Woods, Abbot Professor of Theology at Andover, preached the ordination sermon.⁷² Accompanying the ordained missionaries were Judson's wife, Ann Hasseltine, and Newell's wife, Harriet Atwood. This "immortal seven," but especially the Judsons, quickly achieved legendary status in their own time and in the annals of American Baptist and American Protestant missions because they were the first prominent white overseas missionaries.⁷³

The ABCFM also helped Baptists to form their own national mis-

"First Missionary Ordination." On February 6, 1812, the first five ABCFM missionaries were ordained in Salem, Massachusetts, including three members of the Brethren. Frontispiece from James L. Hill, *The Immortal Seven: Judson & His Associates* (American Baptist Publication Society, 1913).

sions organization, the General Missionary Convention of the Baptist Denomination in the United States of America for Foreign Missions, or the Triennial Convention, in 1814, but inadvertently so. The ABCFM missionaries left the United States on February 19, 1812. On the way to India, the Judsons had a lot of time to study the Bible to refute English Baptist William Carey's credobaptist views. (They knew that they would meet Carey in India). However, both Adoniram and Ann became convinced that believer's baptism was true. On another ship bound for India, Luther Rice independently came to the same conclusion. William Ward, a missionary associate of Carey's, baptized the Judsons by immersion upon arriving in India. The Judsons and Rice had a crisis of conscience. The ABCFM was a Congregationalist, and thus paedobaptist, missionary organization, and the three new Baptists did not feel they could receive ABCFM money anymore. They resigned from the ABCFM, and the Judsons sent Rice the bachelor back to the United States to encourage Baptists to form a national missions society like the ABCFM.[74]

Rice was an ideal salesman to and for Baptists. He itinerated throughout the United States and inspired Baptist churches to give donations for international missions through passionate sermons and riveting stories about the lives of missionaries. Upon hearing Rice, Baptists throughout the country like Thomas Baldwin's congregation in Boston started foreign missions societies. According to Baptist historian H. Leon McBeth, "before the end of 1813, at least seventeen local and regional Baptist societies had agreed to share in the foreign missions work." These smaller levels of organization officially coalesced into American Baptists' first national denominational body, the Triennial Convention. The members of the convention met in Philadelphia every three years until 1826, when it moved to Boston. Moving the convention to Boston made it more difficult for Baptists in the South to attend and participate in the Triennial Convention, which is one reason northern and southern Baptists eventually split in 1845. Controversy over the Triennial Convention was in the future, though. The Triennial Convention of the 1810s allowed Baptists all over the country to unite in support of foreign missions. Rice (1783–1836) spent the rest of his life as Baptists' chief fundraiser for missions work and the building of Baptist colleges and seminaries, most notably Columbian College, Newton Theological Institution's short-lived predecessor.[75]

VOLUNTARISM: HERE TO STAY (DESPITE ITS DETRACTORS)

Voluntary societies were one kind of institution used by New England Baptist and Congregationalist leaders to address the common problems and opportunities they faced during the early 1800s: fighting perceived infidelity, evangelizing settlers on the frontier and the "heathen" abroad, and seeking to impact the morals of the American people, by law if necessary. Seminaries were the other kind of institution. This chapter has discussed how interconnected these efforts—creating seminaries and organizing voluntary societies—were to one another, partly by showing that the same leaders participated in all these ventures for their respective denominations. For instance, Congregationalist Jedidiah Morse addressed the challenges and advantages of evangelizing the frontier in his *The American Geography*, was a strident opponent of infidelity, and was a member of the board of trustees at Andover.

However, not everyone saw the emergence of voluntary societies in antebellum America in a favorable light. John Leland was a harsh critic of this trend for three reasons.[76] First, he believed that the establishment of voluntary societies had no biblical basis; they were illegitimate communities for any Christian to participate in. In 1818 he attacked missionary societies in a creative and sarcastic way by pretending to be a "correspondent" living in Palestine who received news from America that "numerous societies, and other societies of a like kind, [were] formed and very zealously supported in New England, and adjoining parts, in North America." To counter this distressing news, the correspondent informed his American audience that Jesus Christ was the founder of a missionary society back in the first century called the church, and the New Testament had extensive records of its minutes and methods for missions. At this point in the "report" back to America, Leland argued that neither New England nor the nation needed to have missions societies because the original blueprint that the New Testament laid out worked just fine. The church did in fact spread after President Jesus sent his twelve top assistants to share the gospel.[77] Leland echoed his biblicist sentiments to an unnamed friend ten years later when he contended that "a missionary spirit and practice is apostolical; but missionary societies and missionary funds are of later date. That missions established on divine impression, are no ways related to those formed by human calculation."[78] For Leland, missions must come directly from God and the Bible and not be a human institutional invention.[79]

Second, Leland objected to voluntary societies' methods of fundraising. Again, in his "report" from Palestine, he noted how Jesus and the apostles did not wait to perform missions work until they were able to collect a large enough sum of money to give them a measure of "permanent security" like the American societies. The apostles simply relied on God to meet their needs. Leland also castigated the presidents and other bureaucrats in the missionary societies in New England for being too focused on money management rather than on evangelizing for Christ.[80] What drew Leland's ire the most, though, was that money "solicitors" (he does not mention Luther Rice by name, but people like him) "[frightened], [flattered], and [deceived]" people into giving to a supposedly good cause.[81] Leland believed that these collectors "even [descended] to obtain from the unsuspecting little children, the few cents which are given them by their friends."[82]

The third and perhaps most important reason why Leland opposed voluntary societies was their potential for centralizing ecclesiastical and civil authority and creating another establishment of religion. In an 1830 letter, he expressed his concerns to his old friend and fellow Baptist minister John Taylor (1752–1833), who he knew in Virginia in the 1770s and who now lived in Kentucky. He sighed to Taylor that "the lot assigned *me*, seems to be, to watch and check *clerical hierarchy*." Leland missed the good old days when all Baptist preachers did was to share how people were sinners and needed God's grace. Instead, Leland had to endure hearing in the churches he visited entreaty after entreaty from solicitors about how one should give to missions, tract, Bible, and other societies. He did not want to sound like a cranky, "bigoted old man" who disapproved of anything new, "but, when I see the same measures pursued that were in the third century, I am afraid the effects will follow." In his allusion to the third century, Leland probably means the fourth century, or the 300s, when Constantine became the first Christian Roman Emperor, and Christianity eventually became the official religion of the Roman Empire. Just like when Christianity became the law of the land in the fourth century, the Christians of his day were pursuing "the same measures" by seeking to change American laws to force Protestant Christian morality upon the populace through the creation of Sabbath societies and societies for preventing vice.[83]

Leland could not have vented his frustrations and worries regarding voluntary societies to a more appropriate person. Taylor, too, distrusted the societal method of organization. In his entertaining and insightful analysis of Taylor's views about voluntary societies, Keith Harper identifies the "New England Rat" to which Taylor alludes in his 1819 work *Thoughts on Missions*.[84] According to Harper, Taylor believed that voluntary societies were a plot that New Englanders devised to spread political and religious hierarchy and centralization throughout the country. Taylor was a fervent southern religious Jeffersonian, and he viewed New Englanders with suspicion because of their ties to Federalist politics, state religious establishments, and growing denominational machinery.[85] Of course, Leland, a staunch Jeffersonian himself, agreed with Taylor's assessment of these three perils because of their "centralizing tendencies." For Leland and Taylor, the connections between these three elements and voluntary societies were impossible to ignore. Federalism still dominated the politics of New England during much of the first two decades of the 1800s. Congregationalists started their missions agencies in Massachusetts and Connecticut, the two states that held on to their religious establishments the longest, and the Baptists' Triennial Convention moved to Boston in 1826. Judson and Rice, the catalysts for the Baptist foreign missions movement, were even former Congregationalists and not steeped in decades of Baptist life and thought like Leland and Taylor.[86]

In the course of Leland's and Taylor's lifetimes, Baptists moved from a sect that experienced decades of oppression at the hands of Congregationalists in New England and Anglicans in Virginia and struggled for religious liberty to a full-fledged denomination that ironically supported the unofficial Protestant religious establishment that voluntary societies helped to produce by the 1820s. Baptists and Congregationalists had finally put aside their differences and worked to accomplish the same goals. However, this interdenominational acceptance and cooperation did not appeal to Leland and Taylor. Leland warned of the threat of "many Christian sects [agreeing] to surrender their distinguishing rituals so far as for all of them to unite" and set up laws to make sure that only Christians could run for office. He also feared the rise of a "nominal Christianity" in which the nonsectarian Protestant superchurch focused on merely increasing the numbers of society members and requiring that these people give outward obedience to Sabbatarian laws in order to be considered Christian.[87] Likewise, Taylor lamented that voluntary societies were replacing the autonomous authority of local Baptist churches and the usefulness of the associational model to do missions work and other activities. Baptists were losing their identity, and most were glad to do it, according to Taylor.[88]

What Leland and Taylor may not have understood, or wanted to understand, however, is that the way a religious group defines itself is never static. Identities constantly evolve, and Baptist leaders, along with their Congregationalist counterparts, embraced an organizational revolution in the early 1800s through building seminaries and voluntary societies. These organizations channeled individuals' religious fervor toward meeting the challenges of evangelizing an American frontier and the "heathen" overseas, combating "infidelity," and fashioning the behaviors of everyday Americans according to evangelical Protestant moral norms. In turn, seminaries and especially voluntary societies were a new type of religious community apart from churches to which individuals could contribute their time, energies, and perhaps most importantly, their money. New England Baptists and Congregationalists thus played strategic roles in helping to transform antebellum American Christianity.

CONCLUSION

THE POWER OF PREACHERS

Baptist leaders such as Samuel Stillman, Isaac Backus, Jonathan Going, Luther Rice, and most crucially, John Leland, shepherded Baptists through a rapidly changing political order in Massachusetts from 1740 to 1833 to help bring about religious disestablishment in the state. The pathway to disestablishment reveals many changes that occurred amongst New England Baptists to make them an important political force in the new nation. In chapter 1, I discussed how their ecclesiological beliefs and practices helped to prepare young men for pastoral leadership. The skills that they acquired in their local Baptist churches—namely, being effective public speakers, resolving internal church conflicts, and networking with other churches—were fully transferable to the political sphere. They helped to fashion Baptist leaders like Leland into the lobbyists they became.

Chapter 2 examined how, after continuing to experience persecution at the hands of the Standing Order, Baptist leaders had to devise a coherent strategy to exercise their religious rights. They formed the Grievance Committee, the political lobbying arm of the Warren Association, to coordinate their lobbying efforts. Isaac Backus, the chief of the Grievance Committee, collected evidence of persecution and presented it to the state legislature and the wider public. The Grievance Committee was so popular that it convinced more and more Baptist churches to join the Warren Association and eventually to create spin-off associations. Backus also took advantage of the increasingly important media—newspapers and pamphlets—to make cogent arguments in favor of religious liberty on behalf of Baptists and to create an "imagined community" of the persecuted. Without non-Baptists to help them in their fight for religious liberty, however, the efforts of Backus and others fell short when it came to influencing the final draft of the Massachusetts Constitution of 1780, which ultimately reaffirmed the state's official relationship with Congregationalism.

In chapter 3, I examined John Leland's return to Massachusetts after experiencing significant political success leading Virginia Baptists' disestablishment efforts throughout the last half of the 1780s. In Virginia, Leland learned the importance of allying with non-Baptists, most notably Thomas Jefferson and James Madison, to effect political change. Building on Backus's, Stillman's, and James Manning's efforts to unite the disparate Baptist churches of New England into associations and lobbies, Leland helped Baptists in Massachusetts to see the benefits of a politically ecumenical approach in which Baptists purposefully partnered with non-Baptists in the new Democratic-Republican Party. Leland identified the potential of political parties as a new vehicle for change perhaps sooner than any other Baptist. He argued that Baptists did not have to give up their religious commitments to work with non-Baptists to achieve political goals. Baptist and non-Baptist Republicans, while not achieving complete disestablishment, successfully passed the Religious Freedom Act of 1811, which made public tax money available to all religious groups, not just to the Congregational Church.

Leland's politically ecumenical approach worked well—too well—as chapter 4 indicates. Baptists eventually embraced partnering with non-Baptists like their former Congregationalist foes for religious as well as political ends. Congregationalism had gradually split in two in the first decades of the nineteenth century. Unitarian Congregationalists took over Harvard College, and both sides argued over which side had the right to receive public tax money and own church property. Trinitarian Congregationalists found themselves to be dissenters in their own denomination. They discovered that they had more in common with their Baptist neighbors, who were also Trinitarians, and who were creating missions societies and seminaries just like Congregationalists were. Both groups had the goal of winning the "West" for Christ, engaging in overseas missions, curbing "infidelity," and creating an unofficial yet powerful Protestant moral establishment in the early 1800s in the United States. Though Leland did not like the blurring of denominational lines and the possibility of forming even an unofficial religious establishment, his earlier political networking efforts played a role in helping Baptists look beyond themselves to clasp Trinitarian Congregationalists' outstretched hand. Political cooperation had in part led to religious cooperation, which Leland ironically did not intend. Following chapter 4 and this conclusion is an appendix that briefly examined various state laws concerning ministers serving in political office. This was a contentious issue for many states in the early nation. Some states viewed ministers just as any other male citizen—fully eligible to run for office. Other states were careful not to allow ministers to be pulled away from their spiritual calling and sully themselves in the dirty world of politics. The argument centered on how much a minster could be "in the world" without becoming "of the world" if he became a politician.

Perhaps the longest-term consequence of the work of Leland and other Baptist leaders in the political arena is that it set a precedent that we still see in the twenty-first century in the United States. Pastors play a major role in endorsing political candidates, running for political office, and giving their opinion on various laws, ranging from laws restricting abortion to vaccine and mask mandates during the COVID-19 pandemic. Despite America's ministers facing a potential "credibility crisis," a February 16, 2022, article from the Barna Group reported that 71 percent of Christians agree "that a pastor is a trustworthy source of wisdom."[1] The power of pastors to influence their congregants' political views and involvement through their own persuasive gifts and political activities is still very much present. Historians of religion in America, political historians, and people on the street ignore the power of preachers at their peril.

APPENDIX

STATEWIDE CLERGY EXCLUSIONS FROM POLITICAL OFFICE IN THE REVOLUTIONARY ERA AND THE EARLY REPUBLIC

A minister like Leland who ran for and held political office did not have widespread approval or acceptance in the Revolutionary era and the Early Republic. According to William Silverman, six states banned clergy from political office during the Revolutionary War (1776–1783): North Carolina, Delaware, Maryland, Georgia, New York, and South Carolina. Five states also adopted the exclusion in their constitutions from the time of the ratification of the US Constitution to 1820: Kentucky, Tennessee, Louisiana, Mississippi, and Missouri[1] University of Tennessee law professor Frederic S. Le Clercq contends that "The minister disqualification clauses in the constitutions of Tennessee and other states can be traced to the English practice excluding clergy from the house of commons."[2] Since the monarchy was ultimately responsible for both ecclesiastical and civil appointments, the English wanted to prevent priests from "dual office holding."[3] Sirs Edward Coke and William Blackstone—England's two most influential jurists of the seventeenth and eighteenth centuries, respectively—also argued against clergy holding political office in the lower house. Framers of American state constitutions almost certainly considered Coke and Blackstone's view on the issue.[4]

It is also significant that philosopher John Locke, a favorite thinker among America's Founders, wanted to keep clergy from serving in political office. It was a part of his larger call for a sharp division between the religious and political spheres. According to Locke, "all the power of civil government relates only to men's civil interests; is confined to the care of the things of this world, and hath nothing to do with the world to come."[5] In a similarly restrictive way, a pastor's authority "ought to be confined within the bounds of the church, nor can it in any manner be extended to civil affairs; because the church itself is a thing absolutely separate and distinct from the commonwealth. The boundaries on both sides are fixed and immovable."[6] Moreover, a minister serving in political office led to ministerial malpractice because his entire being should be focused on ministry and not on worldly ambitions, or what Locke called a "forwardness" to forsake one's pastorate for political power. Locke argued that "the office of a minster of the gospel requires so the whole man, that the very looking after their poor was, by the joint voice of the twelve apostles, called 'leaving the word of God, and serving of tables.'"[7] The "right" type of minister stayed in his lane by only tending to spiritual matters. Several state constitutions agreed with Locke's assessment and banned clergy from serving in political office for the express purpose of keeping them beholden exclusively to their spiritual calling.[8]

Perhaps the most vocal opponent of laws that forbade clergy from serving in political office was John Witherspoon, the embodiment of everything these laws prohibited. As the only clergyman to sign the Declaration of Independence and the Articles of Confederation as a delegate from New Jersey, he was the most well-known clergyman-politician in America in the Founding era. He was an ordained Presbyterian minister and theologian in Scotland before coming to America to become president of the College of New Jersey (Princeton) in 1768. He was a leader in the Presbyterian Church in America as well.[9] According to Witherspoon's modern biographer Jeffry H. Morrison, he saw no conflict of interest with being both a clergyman and a politician, as "He conspicuously wore his large Geneva collar to sessions of Congress."[10]

When Georgia stipulated that "No clergyman of any denomination shall be a member of the General Assembly" in its revised 1789 state constitution, Witherspoon wrote an angry letter against the measure.[11] He retorted that ministers were citizens of the United States and of Georgia if they lived in Georgia before becoming ministers. If such

"John Witherspoon (1723–1794),
President (1768–94)." Public domain
under Wikimedia Commons.

men owned property, then they should be allowed to hold public office. He inquired, "Is it a sin against the public to become a minister? Does it merit that the person who is guilty of it should be deprived of one of his most important rights as a citizen? Is this not inflicting a penalty which always supposes an offence?"[12] It was unjust for Georgia to prohibit ministers from exercising their right to run for office without a legitimate reason to prevent their office-holding. He also rejected the argument that a minister could and should only focus on spiritual matters. If the minister's church or denomination had decided that he could not serve as both a minister and a politician, then Witherspoon would have been fine with the prohibition because he believed in the autonomy of ecclesiastical bodies to set rules for their ministers. However, *civil* authority had no right to exclude ministers from political office because it was not in their authority to determine what was a spiritual matter or even who was a minister.[13] Georgia did not drop its exclusionary law in response to Witherspoon's letter, but his arguments corresponded to those of his most famous Princeton student, "Father of the Constitution" James Madison.[14]

John Leland himself agreed with Witherspoon and Madison's criticism of state laws that excluded the clergy from running for political office. Leland conceded that it was "absurd" to have ministers "entitled to seats of legislation, on account of their ecclesiastical dignity, like the bishops in England" did in the House of Lords. However, he believed that citizens had a right to choose whoever they wanted to represent them, and if they wanted to elect their local minister, then so be it. It was also an unwarranted "check" on the minister's right to run for office.[15] A year later, in another work, Leland elaborated on his stance. He argued that states should scrupulously exercise neutrality toward a minister who ran for office: "ministers should share the same protection of the law that other men do, and no more. To proscribe them from seats of legislation, etc., is cruel. To indulge them with an exemption from taxes and bearing arms is a tempting emolument. The law should be silent about them; protect them as citizens, not as sacred officers, for the civil law knows no sacred officers."[16] Though Leland briefly served in political office, he was more content with participating in mediating political roles such as lobbying, campaigning, and preaching. However, he defended other ministers' rights to be official politicians.

NOTES

INTRODUCTION

1. Daniel L. Dreisbach, "Mr. Jefferson, a Mammoth Cheese, and the 'Wall of Separation between Church and State': A Bicentennial Commemoration," *Journal of Church and State* 43, no. 4 (September 2001): 725–27, quote on 725. The word "mammoth" came into usage as an adjective meaning something that was extremely large during the Mammoth Cheese spectacle. This was just a couple of years after Charles Wilson Peale had reassembled and exhibited the bones of a large Mastodon, or "Mammoth," in Orange County, New York. See L. H. Butterfield, *Elder John Leland, Jeffersonian Itinerant*, American Antiquarian Society, Worcester, MA (October 1953): 220n146.
2. Dreisbach, "Mr. Jefferson, a Mammoth Cheese," 727.
3. "Committee of Cheshire, Massachusetts, [30 December 1801]," to Thomas Jefferson, Founders Online, National Archives, accessed January 13, 2017, https://founders.archives.gov/documents/Jefferson/01-36-02-0151-0002, emphasis original.
4. Butterfield, *Elder John Leland, Jeffersonian Itinerant*, 220.
5. Thomas Jefferson, "To the Danbury Baptist Association, 1 January 1802," Founders Online, National Archives, accessed March 14, 2017, https://founders.archives.gov/documents/Jefferson/01-36-02-0152-0006. For the Danbury Baptists' original letter to Jefferson, see "To Thomas Jefferson from the Danbury Baptist Association, [after 7 October 1801]," Founders Online, National Archives, accessed November 4, 2016, https://founders.archives.gov/documents/Jefferson/01-35-02-0331.
6. Dreisbach, "Mr. Jefferson, a Mammoth Cheese," 737–38, 741–44. The information about the text for Leland's sermon comes from Federalist

US congressman from Massachusetts, Manasseh Cutler. See Manasseh Cutler to Dr. Joseph Torrey, January 4, 1802, in William Parker Cutler and Julia Perkins Cutler, *Life, Journals and Correspondence of Rev Manasseh Cutler, LL D* (Cincinnati, OH: Robert Clarke and Co., 1888), 2:66–67, quoted in Dreisbach, 742. Cutler was also a Congregationalist minister.

7. Monica Najar, *Evangelizing the South: A Social History of Church and State in Early America* (New York: Oxford Univ. Press, 2008), 5.

8. The first ever full-length biography of John Leland was recently published. For more details about his remarkable life, see Eric C. Smith's *John Leland: A Jeffersonian Baptist in Early America* (New York: Oxford Univ. Press, 2022).

9. Sammie Pedlow Strange, "Baptists and Religious Liberty: 1700–1900," (PhD diss., Southern Baptist Theological Seminary, 2006), 257. McLoughlin mentions Leland on the following pages: McLoughlin, *New England Dissent*, 1: 406, 438; 2:926–38, 942, 983, 999, 1013, 1099–1101, 1112–13, 1024, 1109, 1141–42, 1233. See Strange, 257n31. One of the members of Strange's dissertation committee at Southern was Gregory Wills, a critic of Baptist individualism. See Wills's *Democratic Religion: Freedom, Authority, and Church Discipline in the Baptist South, 1785–1900* (New York: Oxford Univ. Press, 1997), a book partly about how great it was that Georgia Baptists once frequently practiced church discipline to ensure that their communities had doctrinal and behavioral purity. Strange's dissertation chairman, Thomas J. Nettles, was a coeditor of a book written to refute the perceived pervasiveness of Baptist individualism in Cecil P. Staton Jr.'s edited volume *Why I Am a Baptist: Reflections on Being Baptist in the 21st Century* (Macon, GA: Smyth & Helwys, 1999). The coeditors wrote: "The query, 'Why are you a Baptist?' seemed to be answered in unison with a simple answer: 'I grew up Baptist, and it gave me the freedom to do and believe what I choose, so I remain one." See Thomas J. Nettles and Russell Moore, preface to *Why I Am a Baptist* (Nashville, TN: Broadman & Holman, 2001), xvi. The disagreements by theological conservatives Nettles and Moore with moderate Staton and his work's contributors was another chapter in the identity politics battle that started with the moderate vs. conservative Baptist controversy that split the Southern Baptist Convention in the 1980s.

For a few standard works of the "Fundamentalist Takeover" or "Conservative Resurgence"—the moderate and conservative camps' terms for the controversy, respectively—see Bill Leonard, *God's Last and Only*

Hope: The Fragmentation of the Southern Baptist Convention (Grand Rapids, MI: W. B. Eerdmans, 1990); Walter B. Shurden and Randy Shepley, eds., *Going for the Jugular: A Documentary History of the SBC Holy War* (Macon, GA: Mercer Univ. Press, 1999); Jerry Sutton, *The Baptist Reformation: The Conservative Resurgence in the Southern Baptist Convention* (Nashville, TN: Broadman & Holman, 2000); Barry Hankins, *Uneasy in Babylon: Southern Baptist Conservatives and American Culture* (Tuscaloosa, AL: Univ. of Alabama Press, 2002); Paige Patterson, *Anatomy of a Reformation: The Southern Baptist Convention, 1978–2004* (Fort Worth, TX: Southwestern Baptist Theological Seminary, 2004). For a concise and well-balanced overview of the controversy, see Thomas Kidd and Barry Hankins, *Baptists in America: A History* (New York: Oxford Univ. Press, 2015), 228–46.

10. William G. McLoughlin, *New England Dissent, 1630–1833: The Baptists and the Separation of Church and State* (Cambridge, MA: Harvard Univ. Press, 1971), 2:934.
11. John L. Thomas, "In Memoriam: William G. McLoughlin," *American Quarterly* 45, no. 3 (September 1993): 427–28.
12. John Bradley Creed, "John Leland: American Prophet of Religious Individualism" (PhD diss., Southwestern Baptist Theological Seminary, 1986), 200.
13. H. Leon McBeth, *The Baptist Heritage: Four Centuries of Baptist Witness* (Nashville, TN: Broadman Press, 1987), 19–20, quotes on 20.
14. Hatch states that McLoughlin's *New England Dissent*, along with L. H. Butterfield's *Elder John Leland, Jeffersonian Itinerant* and a couple of other sources, are "the best assessments of Leland's activities." See Nathan O. Hatch, *The Democratization of American Christianity* (New Haven: Yale Univ. Press, 1989), 271n99. Hatch's emphasis on Leland's individualism shows Hatch's indebtedness to McLoughlin. Hatch does not cite Creed's dissertation, however, even though it examines Leland's life in much more detail than McLoughlin.
15. Hatch, 101.
16. Hatch, 3, 6.
17. For Hatch's extended discussion of Leland, see 93–101.
18. Butterfield, *Elder John Leland*, 214–18.
19. See Smith, *John Leland*, 5, and the entirety of chap. 6. Creed also identifies Leland as "an unofficial whip for grassroots politics," but the term "whip" is not a key component of his analysis. See Creed, "John Leland: American Prophet of Religious Individualism," 200.

20. Duncan Watts, "Whips," in *Dictionary of American Government and Politics* (Edinburgh, UK: Edinburgh Univ. Press, 2010), https://lopes.idm.oclc.org/login?url=https://search.credoreference.com/content/entry/eupamgov/whips/0?institutionId=5865.
21. Butterfield, *Elder John Leland*, 159.
22. Butterfield, 160.
23. Smith, *John Leland*, 5.
24. Smith, 126.
25. Leland's stubborn refusal to participate in and administer the Lord's Supper divided his church in Cheshire and led the Shaftsbury Association to disfellowship from him. His church and the association decided to part ways in 1817 as well. Smith lays out the Lord's Supper controversy in detail in chapter 4 of *John Leland*. Smith accurately shows how this controversy is a prime example of Leland's individualism regarding religious matters. That still does not negate the political activities that he continued to participate in and the network that he still possessed.
26. Barry Alan Shain, preface to *The Myth of American Individualism: The Protestant Origins of American Political Thought* (Princeton, NJ: Princeton Univ. Press, 1994), xvi.
27. Mikael Broadway, "The Roots of Baptists in Community, and Therefore, Voluntary Membership not Individualism, or, the High-Flying Modernist, Stripped of his Ontological Assumptions, Appears to Hold the Ecclesiology of a Yaho," in *Recycling the Past or Researching History?: Studies in Baptist Historiography and Myths*, vol. 11, ed. Philip E. Thompson and Anthony R. Cross (Bletchley, Milton Keynes, UK: Paternoster, 2005), 68. The title of Broadway's essay, as he acknowledges on page 67, is based on Leland's "The Rights of Conscience Inalienable, and, Therefore, Religious Opinions Not Cognizable by Law: or, The High-Flying Churchman, Stripped of His Legal Robe, Appears a Yaho," in *The Writings of John Leland*, ed. L. F. Greene (New York: Arno Press, 1969). Hereafter, this work will be cited simply as *Writings*.
28. Broadway, "The Roots of Baptists in Community," 78–81, quote on 78. See also Mikael Broadway, "The Ways of Zion Mourned: A Historicist Critique of the Discourses of Church-State Relations" (PhD diss., Duke University, 1993), 171–240, but particularly 199–220 for his analysis of Leland.
29. For Strange's discussion of Leland's theology and ecclesiology, see his "Baptists and Religious Liberty: 1700–1900," 262–75. For his discussion of early English Baptists' and Backus's theology and ecclesiology, see 98–245. Both Strange and Broadway quote Leland's definition of

a church: "A church of Christ, according to the Gospel, is a congregation of faithful persons, called out of the world by divine grace, who mutually agree to live together, and execute gospel discipline among them; which government is not national, parochial, or presbyterial, but congregational." See Strange, 274, and Broadway, "The Roots of Baptists in Community," 79. The work that they cite is John Leland, "The Virginia Chronicle," in *Writings*, 108.

Dale R. South, like Broadway and Strange, views individualism as being inimical to the spiritual health of contemporary Baptist churches. See his "Saved for God's Possession: Recovering the Gospel Among Southern Baptists by Guarding against its Syncretization with Autonomous Individualism" (PhD diss., Southeastern Baptist Theological Seminary, 2017). Unlike Broadway and Strange, however, South follows Creed and the majority opinion of Leland historiography that Leland was a radical individualist. According to South, Leland, along with notable Baptist leaders Francis Wayland and E. Y. Mullins, were responsible for setting a dangerous precedent by promoting individualism in Baptist churches in America. See South, 164–84.

30. Historians' portrayal of Leland and the Baptists as individualists or communitarians, or even Early Republic precursors of SBC moderates or conservatives (see endnote 8 of this chapter), is addressing the very specific "religious and cultural needs" of historians and their readers, namely that it is important that Leland and the Baptists are one of us, so that it is ok if, in our own current context, we are X label. In other words, the historians *needed* historical precedent for their own views and practices. Such appropriation of Leland and the Baptists by historians is akin to historians and church leaders in the nineteenth century who crafted various traditions from the life, writings, and thought of the famous eighteenth-century revivalist and theologian Jonathan Edwards for their own ends. See Joseph A. Conforti's *Jonathan Edwards, Religious Tradition, & American Culture* (Chapel Hill, NC: Univ. of North Carolina Press, 1995), quote on p. 5.

31. Bill Leonard, *Baptists in America* (New York: Columbia Univ. Press, 2005), 153.

32. A very small sample of such works include the following: Hatch's *Democratization of American Christianity;* Jon Butler, *Awash in a Sea of Faith: Christianizing the American People* (Cambridge, MA: Harvard Univ. Press, 1990); Christine Leigh Heyrman, *Southern Cross: The Beginnings of the Bible Belt* (Chapel Hill: Univ. of North Carolina Press,

1997); Mark A. Noll, *America's God: From Jonathan Edwards to Abraham Lincoln* (New York: Oxford Univ. Press, 2002); E. Brooks Holifield, *Theology in America: Christian Thought from the Age of the Puritans to the Civil War* (New Haven: Yale Univ. Press, 2005); and Eric R. Schlereth, *An Age of Infidels: The Politics of Religious Controversy in the Early United Sates* (Philadelphia: Univ. of Pennsylvania Press, 2013).

33. Amanda Porterfield, *Conceived in Doubt: Religion and Politics in the New American Nation* (Chicago: Univ. of Chicago Press, 2012), 11.
34. Jonathan J. Den Hartog, *Patriotism & Piety: Federalist Politics and Religious Struggle in the New American Nation* (Charlottesville: Univ. of Virginia Press, 2015), 3.

CHAPTER 1

1. John Leland, "Events in the Life of John Leland: Written by Himself," in *Writings*, 35. Leland wrote most of his autobiography in (or possibly by) 1820. When he realized he was not in the "decline of life" after all, he broke his autobiographical hiatus and started adding diary-like entries to his autobiography in 1824 and continued doing so until 1835, six years before his death at age eighty-six (see pp. 35–40). L. F. Greene, the compiler and editor of John Leland's works and Leland's granddaughter, continued Leland's narrative until his death and added more detailed information about some events in Leland's life that he only briefly commented on or failed to mention at all. See her "Further Sketches of the Life of John Leland," in *Writings*, 41–72.
2. Leland, "Events in the Life," 18.
3. Leland, "Events in the Life," 10–16.
4. October 2, 1774, First Baptist Church, Bellingham, MA, Records 1737–1962, Book "A," from the Trask Library, Andover Newton Theological School, Newton Centre, MA (hereafter *ANTS*). Leland's account contradicts the date found in the First Baptist Church of Bellingham's record for his joining the church. Leland puts his joining the church in the autumn of 1775, rather than 1774. It was in the autumn of 1775 that the church in Bellingham licensed Leland to preach (more on licensing later). Before coming under the authority of the church, Leland had engaged in itinerant preaching on his own around central Massachusetts for about a year. See Leland, "Events in the Life," 19.
5. For Baptist (and Quaker) criticisms of the New England Congregational establishment's educated ministry and its ties with "wealth and social

rank," see David D. Hall, *The Faithful Shepherd; A History of the New England Ministry in the Seventeenth Century* (Chapel Hill, NC: Published for the Institute of Early American History and Culture, Williamsburg, VA, by the Univ. of North Carolina Press, 1972), 182–83. For Baptist's and other dissenters' criticisms of ministerial education, wealth, and desire for high social status in the American colonies in the eighteenth century generally, see E. Brooks Holifield, *God's Ambassadors: A History of the Christian Clergy in America* (Grand Rapids, MI: William B. Eerdmans, 2007), 80, 82–83, 86.

6. Kidd and Hankins, *Baptists in America*, 7. For the New England context specifically, see C. C. Goen, *Revivalism and Separatism in New England, 1740–1800: Strict Congregationalists and Separate Baptists in the Great Awakening* (Middletown, CT: Wesleyan Univ. Press, 1987), 208–13, 258–64.
7. Kidd and Hankins, *Baptists in America*, 1, 3–4.
8. Wills, *Democratic Religion*, particularly the introduction and the first three chapters.
9. Edmund S. Morgan, *Visible Saints: The History of a Puritan Idea* (New York: New York Univ. Press, 1963); Robert G. Pope, *The Half-Way Covenant: Church Membership in Puritan New England* (Princeton, NJ: Princeton Univ. Press, 1970); James F. Cooper Jr., *Tenacious of Their Liberties: The Congregationalists in Colonial Massachusetts* (New York: Oxford Univ. Press, 1999), chap. 5.
10. Kevin M. Watson, *Pursuing Social Holiness: The Band Meeting in Wesley's Thought and Popular Methodist Practice* (Oxford, UK: Oxford Univ. Press, 2014), 2.
11. Watson, *Pursuing Social Holiness*, 163.
12. Watson, *Pursuing Social Holiness*, 122, 163, quote on 163.
13. Wills, *Democratic Religion*, 19–21.
14. Susan Juster, *Disorderly Women: Sexual Politics & Evangelicalism in Revolutionary New England* (Ithaca, NY: Cornell Univ. Press, 1994), 30–31, 42–43, 86, 130–32. Martha Stearns Marshall, Daniel Marshall (her husband), and Shubal Stearns (her brother) spearheaded Separate Baptist expansion from New England into the South in the 1750s. She was the most famous female "exhorter" among Baptists in the eighteenth century. See Catherine A. Brekus, *Strangers & Pilgrims: Female Preaching in America, 1740–1845* (Chapel Hill, NC: Univ. of North Carolina Press, 1998), 61–65.
15. Baptist churches empowering young men from limited means to serve the church as well as make an impact on society has a prominent example in the twentieth century that shows the endurance of this tradition:

Bill Clinton, the forty-second president of the United States. Bill Clinton was originally born William Jefferson Blythe III on August 19, 1946. His father died in a car crash before he was born, and his mother Virginia Kelley married Roger Clinton in 1950. Bill grew up in a home where Roger was an alcoholic who verbally and physically abused his mother. To get away from his rough childhood, his mother urged him to attend Park Place Baptist Church in Hot Springs, Arkansas, less than a mile from his house. His family was not interested in attending, but he started attending at six years old and had a conversion experience at the age of nine. Bill attended church regularly throughout the rest of his childhood, through high school. Presidential historian Gastón Espinosa observes that his Baptist church gave him the opportunity to learn "how to give his testimony in public services, lead small group Bible studies, song services, and public rallies, and preach to the point of moving a crowd to action; all skills that would serve him well on the campaign trail and during his presidency. Clinton applied these skills in the political arena with stunning success." See Gastón Espinosa, "Religion and the Presidency of William Jefferson Clinton," in *Religion and the American Presidency: George Washington to George W. Bush with Commentary and Primary Sources*, ed. Gastón Espinosa (New York: Columbia Univ. Press, 2009), 432–34, quote on 434.

16. Leonard, *Baptists in America*, 7–9; Kidd and Hankins, *Baptists in America*, 4–7; McBeth, *Baptist Heritage*, 24–26, 30–39.
17. Morgan, *Visible Saints*, 128–29.
18. Morgan, *Visible Saints*, 113.
19. Morgan, *Visible Saints*, 125–26.
20. Perry Miller, "Errand into the Wilderness," in *Errand into the Wilderness* (Cambridge: Belknap Press of Harvard Univ. Press, 1956), 11–12.
21. John Winthrop, "A Modell of Christian Charity (1630)," in *The American Intellectual Tradition*, vol. 1, *1630–1685*, 6th ed., ed. David A. Hollinger and Charles Capper (New York: Oxford Univ. Press, 2011), 14–15.
22. Kidd and Hankins, *Baptists in America*, 7–14.
23. Robert G. Gardner, *Baptists of Early America: A Statistical History, 1639–1790* (Atlanta: Georgia Baptist Historical Society, 1983), 20–21.
24. Edwin S. Gaustad, Philip L. Barlow, and Richard W. Dishno, *New Historical Atlas of Religion in America* (New York: Oxford Univ. Press, 2001), 7–9, 24–25. There were a handful of Congregational churches south of New England in 1700 and 1730, so I have approximated the number of Congregational churches in New England itself.

25. Of course, some Baptists immigrated into New England between 1700–1730, and Anglicans had established a foothold in the region by 1750 with the Society of the Propagation of the Gospel planting twenty churches. See Gaustad, Barlow, and Dishno, *New Historical Atlas*, 25. Still, the predominant religious group by far was the Congregational Church.

26. Charles W. Deweese, *Baptist Church Covenants* (Nashville, TN: Broadman Press, 1990), first quote on vii and second quote on ix. Colonial New England Baptists clearly borrowed the format and even the wording from Congregationalist covenants. See Deweese, 39–41, 43–46.

27. August 14, 16, 28, 1748, Old South Church, Boston, MA, Records, 1669–2012, Reel 1, Records from Congregational Library and Archives, Boston, MA (hereafter CLA). For a printed version of this section of church records from the Old South Church, see Hamilton Andrews Hill, *History of the Old South Church (Third Church) Boston, 1669–1884*, 3rd ed. (Boston and New York: Houghton, Mifflin and Co., 1890), 587–89.

28. Emphasis added. Church covenant, December 28, 1731, First Church Record Book, Hassanamisco, 1731–1774, CLA. This is the church that Leland's family attended. According to the record book's list of marriages, John Leland's parents, James Leland and Lucy Warren, were married by Solomon Prentice on June 21, 1744. The record book did not record John Leland's baptism in the list of baptisms, but Leland claimed that he was baptized after the age of three. See his "Events in the Life of John Leland: Written by Himself," in *Writings*, 9–10.

29. Church Covenant, 1732, First Congregational Church (Georgetown, MA) records, 1731–1866, CLA.

30. I.e., "watching." Watching, or being a "watchman" referred to the Old Testament principle that God's spokesmen were to speak his truth and warn their hearers of the potential of God's judgment for disobedience. See Ezekiel 3:16–21, 33: 1–19. If a pastor did not do his job in warning his people appropriately, then God could judge the pastor.

31. Frederick Clifton Pierce, *History of Grafton, Worcester County, Massachusetts, From Its Early Settlement by the Indians in 1647 to the Present Time, 1879. Including the Genealogies of Seventy-Nine of the Older Families* (Worcester, MA: Press of C. Hamilton, 1879), 165–78.

32. Of course, the most famous fired pastor in colonial American history, Jonathan Edwards, learned this lesson as well when his Northampton Church fired him in 1750 for criticizing the Half-Way Covenant.

33. In an iconoclastic 1982 article, historian Jon Butler encouraged other historians to get rid of the term "Great Awakening," as it was an

"interpretative fiction." One reason was that the awakening was not "great." It did not occur all over the American colonies, mainly just in New England, New Jersey, and Pennsylvania. Also, no one used the term "Great Awakening" until Joseph Tracy in 1842, one hundred years after the supposed events. Finally, in criticism of Alan Heimert's *Religion and the American Mind: From the Great Awakening to the Revolution* (Cambridge, MA: Harvard Univ. Press, 1966), Butler declared that there was no significant link between revivals and political change around the time of the Revolution, except in Virginia. See "Enthusiasm Described and Decried: The Great Awakening as Interpretative Fiction," *Journal of American History* 69, no. 2 (October 1982): 305–25. Following Frank Lambert, the rest of my chapter assumes that the Great Awakening is an "invention," but one that its mid-eighteenth-century participants believed was real and were involved in constructing as they saw "the Work of God" unfolding around them. See Lambert's *Inventing the "Great Awakening"* (Princeton, NJ: Princeton Univ. Press, 1999), quote on 11.

34. Gardner, *Baptists of Early America*, 20–21.
35. According to John Corrigan, anti-revival Congregationalist ministers like Charles Chauncy and Jonathan Mayhew as well as the pro-revival Jonathan Edwards struggled to find "balance" between individual expression and social responsibilities to church and town in addition to trying to strike a balance between the use of reason and emotions because "religion in mid-eighteenth-century America was in a state of flux." See his *The Hidden Balance: Religion and the Social Theories of Charles Chauncy and Jonathan Mayhew* (Cambridge, UK: Cambridge Univ. Press, 1987), 54–58, quote on 58.
36. Harry S. Stout, *The Divine Dramatist: George Whitefield and the Rise of Modern Evangelicalism* (Grand Rapids, MI: William B. Eerdmans, 1991), 89.
37. Stout, *Divine Dramatist*, 89–90.
38. Timothy D. Hall, *Contested Boundaries: Itinerancy and the Reshaping of the Colonial American Religious World* (Durham, NC: Duke Univ. Press, 1994), 29–31, quotes on 30. See also the works of Hall's dissertation advisor, T. H. Breen, including "An Empire of Goods: The Anglicization of Colonial America, 1690–1776," *Journal of British Studies* 25, no.4 (October 1986): 467–99; and *The Marketplace of Revolution: How Consumer Politics Shaped American Independence* (New York: Oxford Univ. Press, 2004). Of course, Hall is using Benedict Anderson's phrase "print-capitalism." See Anderson's *Imagined Communities: Reflections*

on the Origin and Spread of Nationalism (London: Verso, 1991), 36–46, for his discussion of "print-capitalism."

39. Hall, *Contested Boundaries*, 31.
40. Calvinism was a religious movement that began in the sixteenth century under the leadership of Protestant Reformer John Calvin (1509–1564) in Geneva. As the movement developed in the sixteenth and seventeenth centuries, Calvinists became associated with five key beliefs as part of their doctrine of salvation, or soteriology: total depravity, irresistible grace, limited atonement, unconditional election, and perseverance of the saints. Foundational to those key beliefs is the priority of the sovereignty of God over the free will of human beings in matters relating to salvation. Calvinism is often used interchangeably, though somewhat imprecisely, with the terms "Reformed" and "Reformed Tradition."
41. Hall, *Contested Boundaries*, 7. Although Hall does not cite him, Hall's view of the metaphorical power of itinerancy is analogous to Certeau's contention that "walking" is "a space of enunciation." See Michel de Certeau, "Walking in the City," in *The Practice of Everyday Life*, trans. Stephen Rendall (Berkeley: Univ. of California Press, 1984), 98.
42. Hall, *Contested Boundaries*, 6.
43. Hall, *Contested Boundaries*, particularly chap. 2.
44. The classic text for preaching against unconverted ministers is Gilbert Tennent's *The Danger of an Unconverted Ministry, Considered in a Sermon on Mark VI. 34* (Boston: Rogers and Fowle, 1742). In this sermon, he poignantly asked, "Is a blind Man fit to be a Guide in a very dangerous Way? Is a dead Man fit to bring others to Life?" (8). People answering in the negative is what brought them out of churches that they perceived had unawakened (i.e., "blind" or "dead") ministers in charge.
45. Hall, *Contested Boundaries*, mainly chaps. 3 and 4; Lambert, *Inventing the "Great Awakening."*
46. Hall, *Contested Boundaries*, 15.
47. For another excellent source in examining Whitefield's ability to market religion like mid-eighteenth-century British Atlantic tradesmen marketed their goods, see Frank Lambert, *"Pedlar in Divinity": George Whitefield and the Transatlantic Revivals, 1737–1770* (Princeton, NJ: Princeton Univ. Press, 1994). In talking about peddlers of British goods, T. H. Breen noted how "peddlers operating with little overhead could easily undercut the established merchant's price." See Breen, "Empire of Goods," 494. Poor, uneducated itinerants who did not have to pay attention to parish boundaries undercut the ministry of the established church.

48. Stout, *Divine Dramatist*, chap. 7.
49. William L. Lumpkin, *Baptist History in the South: Tracing Through the Separates the Influence of the Great Awakening, 1754–1787* (St. John, IN: Larry Harrison, 1995), 8–9, quote on 8.
50. Goen, *Revivalism and Separatism in New England*, 37. Goen's book is the seminal book on the Separate movement in New England.
51. Goen, *Revivalism and Separatism in New England*, chap. 2.
52. Goen, *Revivalism and Separatism in New England*, 101–2.
53. Hannah Cory, "Relation," 1749, Sturbridge, MA, Separatist Congregational Church statements, 1745–1762, CLA. A printed version of the some of these relations can be found in Ola Elizabeth Winslow, *Meetinghouse Hill, 1630–1783* (New York: Macmillan, 1952), 232–36. Cory does not give the actual Bible verses for the three passages she cites, and she only paraphrases the passages. The first passage reads: "Wherefore come out from among them, and be ye separate." The second passage reads: "Can two walk together, except they be agreed?" The third one reads: "And (Jesus) said unto them, It is written, My house shall be called the house of prayer; but ye have made it a den of thieves." 2 Corinthians 6:17, "Be ye Separate," was the slogan of the Separate movement. Fellow Sturbridge Separate Hannah Callor cited this verse as her justification for leaving. See Hannah Callor, "Relation," April 6, 1749, Sturbridge, MA, Separatist Congregational Church statements, 1745–1762, CLA.
54. Hannah Cory, "Relation," 1749, Sturbridge, MA, Separatist Congregational Church statements, 1745–1762, CLA.
55. Sarah Marten (Morton), "Relation," n.d., Sturbridge, MA, Separatist Congregational Church statements, 1745–1762, CLA.
56. Jonathan Perry, "Relation," April 9?, 1749, Sturbridge, MA, Separatist Congregational Church statements, 1745–1762, CLA.
57. Naomy Ward, "Relation," January 10, 1762, Sturbridge, MA, Separatist Congregational Church statements, 1745–1762, CLA.
58. First Baptist Church of Sturbridge (also called Fiskdale) church records, 1747–1976 (Sturbridge, MA), ANTS.
59. Though William G. McLoughlin has contributed much to the scholarly study of Isaac Backus, Brandon J. O'Brien has recently written an excellent introduction to Isaac Backus's views on religious liberty for a popular audience. See his *Demanding Liberty: An Untold Story of American Religious Freedom* (Downers Grove, IL: IVP Books, 2018).
60. Isaac Backus, "Issac Backus His Writeing [sic] Containing Some Particular Account of My Conversion," August 16, 1751, in William G.

McLoughlin, ed., *The Diary of Isaac Backus* (Providence, RI: Brown Univ. Press, 1979), 3:1524–25, quotes on 1525.
61. Kidd and Hankins, *Baptists in America*, 31.
62. McLoughlin, *Diary of Isaac Backus*, 1:3.
63. McLoughlin, *Diary of Isaac Backus*, 1:6–7.
64. Isaac Backus, "The Confession of Faith and Church-Covenant, of the Church of Christ in the Joining Borders of Bridgwater and Middleborough," February 1748, in McLoughlin, *Diary of Isaac Backus*, 3:1529–31.
65. Kidd and Hankins, *Baptists in America*, 32–34.
66. Robert J. Dinkin, *Campaigning in America: A History of Election Practices* (New York: Greenwood Press, 1989), 1–3, quote on 2.
67. Dinkin, *Campaigning in America*, 5.
68. Dinkin, *Campaigning in America*, 7–8.
69. See Leland, "Events in the Life," 35, both quotes.
70. Leland, "Events in the Life," 19.
71. This scenario makes the most sense to me since the church started examining Wood right after they received him into their membership.
72. September 3, 1786, First Baptist Church of Medfield church records, 1771–1914 (Medfield, MA), ANTS.
73. September 3 and 10, 1786, First Baptist Church of Medfield church records, 1771–1914 (Medfield, MA), ANTS. For Baptists in the eighteenth century, licensing a minister was not the same as ordaining a minister. Francis Wayland (1796–1875), an extremely influential nineteenth-century New England Baptist, contended that a license was a temporary approval from a church for a man to preach whenever the preacher had the opportunity to do so. The license was also "renewable every year." In contrast, ordinations offered the chance to be a minister for life, and the church usually invited ministers and members of other churches nearby to assist in the ordination of the candidate. The church still voted on the fitness of the candidate for ordination, but the council of visiting ministers and members examined the candidate alone first and recommended to the church as a whole whether or not the candidate should be ordained. Also, according to Wayland, "the various services are assigned to the several brethren composing the council." See Francis Wayland, *Notes on the Principles and Practices of Baptist Churches* (New York: Sheldon, Blakeman & Co, 1857), 114. For example, for Thomas Gair's ordination (Gair was Wood's minister for Wood's licensing ten years later) in the First Baptist Church of Medfield, Elder Noah Alden of the First Baptist Church of Bellingham (Leland's pastor) was the ceremony's moderator,

gave the "right hand of fellowship," and said the last prayer; Samuel Stillman of the First Baptist Church of Boston was the clerk; and James Manning of the First Baptist Church of Providence gave the "charge," or a word of exhortation to be faithful in the ministry. See September 18, 1776, First Baptist Church of Medfield church records, 1771–1914 (Medfield, MA), ANTS. Another role not mentioned here is that it was someone's job to preach an ordination sermon, which outlined the responsibilities of ministers and sometimes the responsibilities of pastors and the congregation to one another. To finalize the ceremony, Wayland noted that the ministers, in a symbolic act of conferring authority to the ordination candidate, laid their hands upon him and prayed that the Holy Spirit would empower his ministry. Then, the candidate was officially ordained. See Wayland, *Notes*, 114.

74. Samuel Stillman, *A Good Minister of Jesus Christ: A Sermon, Preached in Boston, September 15, 1797. At the Ordination of the Rev. Mr. Stephen Smith Nelson* (Boston: Manning and Loring, 1797), 5.
75. Stillman, *A Good Minister of Jesus Christ*, 5–6.
76. William B. Sprague, *Annals of the American Pulpit: Or, Commemorative Notices of Distinguished American Clergymen of Various Denominations: from the Early Settlement of the Country to the Close of the Year Eighteen Hundred and Fifty-Five: with Historical Introductions*, vol. 6, *Baptists* (New York: Robert Carter & Bros., 1860), 71–72.
77. Sprague, *Annals of the American Pulpit*, 6:366.
78. Stillman, *A Good Minister of Jesus Christ*, 6, 8.
79. Stillman, *A Good Minister of Jesus Christ*, 8–9, quote on 9.
80. Stillman, *A Good Minister of Jesus Christ*, 10.
81. Stillman, *A Good Minister of Jesus Christ*, 10–11.
82. Wills, *Democratic Religion*, 18–19.
83. August 29, 1783, First Baptist Church of Norton church records, 1747–1835 (Norton, MA), ANTS.
84. December 11, 1783, First Baptist Church of Norton church records, 1747–1835 (Norton, MA), ANTS.
85. April 23, 1784; June 1, 1784, First Baptist Church of Norton church records, 1747–1835 (Norton, MA), ANTS.
86. Keith Harper, *A Mere Kentucky of a Place: The Elkhorn Association and the Commonwealth's First Baptists* (Knoxville, TN: Univ. of Tennessee Press, 2021), 42.
87. August 17, 1784, First Baptist Church of Norton church records, 1747–1835 (Norton, MA), ANTS. William G. McLoughlin identifies

Job Seamans as pastor of North Attleboro Baptist church. See his *New England Dissent*, 1:638. Seamans remained pastor there until he became the pastor of a Baptist church in New London, New Hampshire, in March 1788; see *New England Dissent*, 2:859–60.

88. September 24, 1784, First Baptist Church of Norton church records, 1747–1835 (Norton, MA), ANTS.
89. October 24, 1784, First Baptist Church of Norton church records, 1747–1835 (Norton, MA), ANTS.
90. Sydney E. Ahlstrom, *A Religious History of the American People*, 2nd ed. (New Haven, CT: Yale Univ. Press, 2004), 112 and chap. 13.
91. Kidd and Hankins, *Baptists in America*, 21.
92. Horatio G. Jones, preface to *Minutes of the Philadelphia Baptist Association, 1707–1807*, ed. A. D. Gillette (Philadelphia: American Baptist Publication Society, 1851), 4–5. I would like to thank Dr. Keith Harper, Senior Professor of Baptist Studies at Southeastern Baptist Theological Seminary, for bringing this source to my attention.
93. McBeth, *Baptist Heritage*, 242.
94. George Thomas Kurian and Mark A. Lamport, eds., *Encyclopedia of Christianity in the United States*, (Lanham, MD: Rowman & Littlefield, 2016), s.v. "Manning, James," 3:1047.
95. McLoughlin, *New England Dissent*, 1:503–5.
96. McLoughlin, *New England Dissent*, 1:503–5. Manning attempted to model the Warren Association after the PBA. From the PBA's outset in 1707, churches in the PBA agreed that the association would be the final arbiter in disputes between church members and their church: "If any difference shall happen between any member and the church he belongs unto, and they cannot agree, then the person so grieved may, at the general meeting, appeal to the brethren of the several congregations, and with such as they shall nominate, to decide the difference; that the church and the person so grieved do fully acquiesce in their determination." See Gillette, ed., *Minutes of the Philadelphia Baptist Association, 1707–1807*, 25.
97. McLoughlin, *New England Dissent*, 1:505. Also, see James F. Cooper, "Enthusiasts or Democrats? Separatism, Church Government, and the Great Awakening in Massachusetts," *New England Quarterly* 65, no. 2 (June 1992): 267–69.
98. [James Manning], *The Sentiments and Plan of the Warren Association* (Germantown, [Pa.]: Printed by Christopher Sower, 1769), 3.
99. McLoughlin, *New England Dissent*, 1:508.

CHAPTER 2

1. Elizabeth Backus to Isaac Backus, November 4, 1752, in Isaac Backus, *A History of New England with Particular Reference to the Denomination of Christians Called Baptists* (Newton, MA: Backus Historical Society, 1871), 2:98.
2. Frederic Denison, *Notes of the Baptists, and Their Principles, in Norwich, Conn., From the Settlement of the Town to 1850* (Norwich: Manning, 1857), 28.
3. E. Backus to I. Backus, in Backus, *A History of New England*, 2:99.
4. E. Backus to I. Backus, in Backus, *A History of New England*, 2:98–99.
5. Denison, *Notes of the Baptists*, 28.
6. William G. McLoughlin, introduction to *The Diary of Isaac Backus*, by Isaac Backus (Providence, RI: Brown Univ. Press, 1979), 1:xviii.
7. Denison, *Notes of the Baptists*, 27–28.
8. McLoughlin, *New England Dissent*, 1:556.
9. McLoughlin, *New England Dissent*, 1:457.
10. McLoughlin, *New England Dissent*, 1:454–56, 462–63.
11. Arminianism was the theological movement named after Dutch Calvinist theologian Jacobus Arminius (1560–1609). He disagreed with emerging Calvinist orthodoxy of his day regarding unconditional election, limited atonement, irresistible grace, and perseverance of the saints. Instead, he argued that human free will played a larger role in accepting or rejecting salvation than most of his contemporaries believed and that human free will worked in cooperation with the sovereignty of God.
12. McLoughlin, *New England Dissent*, 1:439–41, 455.
13. McLoughlin, *New England Dissent*, 1:462–63.
14. See Goen, *Revivalism and Separatism in New England*.
15. Certeau, *Practice of Everyday Life*, xix.
16. Certeau, *Practice of Everyday Life*, xix.
17. For "weak" and "strong" categories, see Certeau, *Practice of Everyday Life*, xvii. For McLoughlin quote, see his *New England Dissent*, 2:751, emphases original. John Corrigan notes that, in American history, religious groups sharing the same physical and social space have sought to "define themselves in relation to others. Specifically, groups define themselves by saying *what they are not* as much as by saying what they are." One way that Baptists defined themselves was that they were not, and could not be, part of the religious establishment and that, thus, they were not Congregationalists. See John Corrigan, *Emptiness: Feeling Christian in*

America (Chicago: Univ. of Chicago Press, 2015), 99–102, quote on 99, emphasis original. Baptists emphasized believer's baptism, a regenerate church membership, and a (mostly) unlearned ministry. These beliefs and their accompanying practices distinguished them from their Congregationalist and Separate neighbors.

18. McLoughlin, *New England Dissent*, 1:481–86, quote on 481.
19. McLoughlin, *New England Dissent*, 1:485–86, quote on 486.
20. McLoughlin, *New England Dissent*, 1:512–30.
21. McLoughlin, *New England Dissent*, 1:513.
22. McLoughlin, *New England Dissent*, 1:512–13, quote on 513.
23. Joseph Fish had been pastor of the North Stonington Church for thirty-five years before he published his sermons in 1767. See Joy Day Buel and Richard Buel Jr., *The Way of Duty: A Woman and Her Family in Revolutionary America* (New York: Norton, 1995), 4. Mary Fish is the subject of the authors' biography and is the daughter of Reverend Joseph Fish.
24. Local manifestations of the invisible or universal Church of Christ
25. Joseph Fish, *The Church of Christ a Firm and Durable House: Shown in a Number of Sermons on Matth. XVI. 18. Upon this Rock I Will Build My Church, and the Gates of Hell Shall Not Prevail against It.: The Substance of which was Delivered at Stonington, Anno Domini, 1765* (New London, [CT]: Printed and Sold by Timothy Green, 1767), iii–vii.
26. Fish, *Church of Christ*, iii. According to C. C. Goen, by 1765 two Separate Baptist churches and one Separate church existed in North Stonington. These churches drained church members from Fish's church. See Goen, *Revivalism and Separatism in New England*, 79.
27. Fish, *Church of Christ*, iv, emphasis original.
28. Fish, *Church of Christ*, iii–iv.
29. Fish, *Church of Christ*, iv.
30. Fish, *Church of Christ*.
31. Isaac Backus, *A Fish Caught in His Own Net* (1768), in *Isaac Backus on Church, State, and Calvinism; Pamphlets, 1754–1789*, ed. William G. McLoughlin (Cambridge, MA: Belknap Press of Harvard Univ. Press, 1968), 173.
32. William G. McLoughlin, introduction to *Isaac Backus on Church, State, and Calvinism; Pamphlets, 1754–1789*, ed. McLoughlin (Cambridge, MA: Belknap Press of Harvard Univ. Press, 1968), 25.
33. Carol Sue Humphrey, *The American Revolution and the Press: The Promise of Independence* (Evanston, IL: Northwestern Univ. Press, 2013), 25–26.
34. Humphrey, *American Revolution and the Press*, 33–34, quote on 33.

35. Humphrey, *American Revolution and the Press*, 36–37, quote on 36. Benedict Anderson also commented upon the importance of postmasters: "Since the main problem facing the printer-journalist was reaching readers, there developed an alliance with the post-master so intimate that often each became the other. Hence, the printer's office emerged as the key to North American communications and community intellectual life." See Anderson, *Imagined Communities*, 61.
36. Humphrey, *American Revolution and the Press*, 33.
37. Humphrey, *American Revolution and the Press*, 37.
38. Humphrey, *American Revolution and the Press*, 40–42.
39. Carol Sue Humphrey, *This Popular Engine: New England Newspapers during the American Revolution, 1775–1789* (Newark: Univ. of Delaware Press, 1992), 20–21, quote on 21. The New England cities that had at least one newspaper by 1765 were Hartford, New Haven, and New London in Connecticut; Providence and Newport in Rhode Island; Boston, Massachusetts; and Portsmouth, New Hampshire. See also Anderson, *Imagined Communities*, 61–62.
40. Humphrey, *American Revolution and the Press*, 42–45.
41. Humphrey, *This Popular Engine*, 144.
42. Humphrey, *American Revolution and the Press*, 45–51.
43. Anderson, *Imagined Communities*, 6–7, 61–64.
44. David A. Copeland, foreword to *The American Revolution and the Press: The Promise of Independence*, by Carol Sue Humphrey (Evanston, IL: Northwestern Univ. Press, 2013), xiii. Also, see Copeland's magisterial *Colonial American Newspapers: Character and Content* (Newark: Univ. of Delaware Press, 1997).
45. Bernard Bailyn, *Pamphlets of the American Revolution, 1750–1776* (Cambridge, MA: Belknap Press of Harvard Univ. Press, 1965), 3. Bailyn's much more well-known *The Ideological Origins of the American Revolution* (Cambridge, MA: Belknap Press of Harvard Univ. Press, 1967) is partially an expansion on the some of the themes and ideas prevalent in *Pamphlets*.
46. Bailyn, *Pamphlets of the American Revolution*, 5.
47. The following is the entire "chain-reacting personal polemics" of the Backus/Fish pamphlet war. Fish, *Church of Christ* (1767); Backus, *A Fish Caught in His Own Net* (1768); Fish, *The Examiner Examined: Remarks on a Piece Wrote by Mr. Isaac Backus, of Middleborough; Printed in 1768. (Called, "An Examination of Nine Sermons from Matth. 16. 18. Published Last Year, by Mr. Joseph Fish, of Stonington.") Wherein those Sermons are*

Vindicated, from the Exceptions Taken against Them by Mr. Backus—Many of his Errors Confuted, and his Mistakes Corrected (New-London, [CT]: Printed and sold by Timothy Green, 1771); Backus, *A Discourse, Concerning the Materials, the Manner of Building, and Power of Organizing of the Church of Christ;: with the True Difference and Exact Limits between Civil and Ecclesiastical Government; and Also What Are, and What Are Not Just Reasons for Separation.: Together with, an Address to Joseph Fish, A.M. Pastor of a Church in Stonington, Occasioned by his Late Piece Called The Examiner Examined* (Boston: Printed by John Boyles, in Marlborough-Street, 1773).

48. Bailyn, *Pamphlets of the American Revolution*, 6–7.
49. The work is Frothingham's *A Key, to Unlock the Door, that Leads in, to Take a Fair View of the Religious Constitution, Established by Law, in the Colony of Connecticut.: With a Short Remark upon Mr. Bartlet's Sermon, on Galations [sic] iii. 1.: Also, a Remark upon Mr. Ross, against the Separates and Others.: With a Short Observation upon the Explanation of Say-Brook-plan; and Mr. Hobart's Attempt to Establish the Same Plan* ([New Haven]: Printed [by Benjamin Mecom], 1767). See Advertisement, *Connecticut Journal, and New-Haven Post-Boy*, July 22, 1768.
50. Goen, *Revivalism and Separatism in New England*, 203–8, quote on 208.
51. For example, see Advertisement, *Connecticut Journal* (New Haven), November 9, 1780, and Advertisement, *Providence Gazette; and Country Journal*, June 29, 1782.
52. Advertisement, *Pennsylvania Herald, and General Advertiser* (Philadelphia), February 14, 1788.
53. Reuben Aldridge Guild, *Life, Times, and Correspondence of James Manning, and the Early History of Brown University* (Boston: Gould and Lincoln, 1864), 242–43, quote on 243.
54. Advertisement, *Providence Gazette; and Country Journal*, April 29, 1780.
55. Guild, *Life, Times, and Correspondence of James Manning*, 289.
56. For Manning's calls to the corporation for assistance with the "present deplorable situation of the college," see Advertisement, *Newport Mercury*, August 17, 1782; Advertisement, *Providence Gazette; and Country Journal*, August 17, 1782; Advertisement, *Providence Gazette; and Country Journal*, August 24, 1782; and Advertisement, *Newport Mercury*, August 30, 1782. For an account of the celebration of the college's September 1782 commencement, see Report, *Newport Mercury*, September 14, 1782. Concerning the Warren Association and the PBA voting to donate funds to Rhode Island College, see Warren Association,

Minutes of the Warren Association, Convened at Providence, the 10th of Sept. 1782 (Providence: John Carter, 1782), 5; and Gillette, ed., *Minutes of the Philadelphia Baptist Association, 1707–1807*, 181. The PBA just copied and voted on the Warren Association's motion.

57. Thomas Kidd, "'Becoming Important in the Eye of Civil Powers': New Light Baptists, Cultural Respectability, and the Founding of the College of Rhode Island," in *The Scholarly Vocation and the Baptist Academy: Essays on the Future of Baptist Higher Education*, ed. Roger A. Ward and David Gushee (Macon, GA: Mercer Univ. Press, 2008), 50, 57–60, 63–64.

58. Certeau, *The Practice of Everyday Life*, xix.

59. Sprague, *Annals of the American Pulpit*, 71–73.

60. Just a year after Stillman arrived at the First Baptist Church of Boston, he made a name for himself in Boston by preaching a sermon after the city heard that the Parliament had repealed the Stamp Act. Of course, like the rest of the city, Stillman rejoiced that the repeal "was a royal confirmation of [our] civil and religious liberties." But for most of the sermon, he linked the "good news from a far country" as relating to the gospel of salvation through Christ, not the repeal of the Stamp Act. Stillman did not expect the sermon to be so popular when he preached it, but he made the sermon available for publication because he received so many requests for copies of it. See Samuel Stillman, *Good News from a Far Country. A Sermon Preached at Boston, May 17. 1766. Upon the Arrival of the Important News of the Repeal of the Stamp-Act* (Boston: Printed by Kneeland and Adams, in Milk-Street, for Philip Freeman, in Union-Street., 1766), 31. His sermon text, Proverbs 25:25, was the inspiration for his sermon title.

61. For a few examples, see Advertisement, *Boston Gazette, and Country Journal*, November 22, 1773; Advertisement, *Massachusetts Gazette: and the Boston Weekly News-Letter Letter*, December 9, 1773; and Advertisement, *Massachusetts Gazette; and the Boston Post-Boy and Advertiser*, December 13, 1773.

62. Advertisement, *Newport Mercury*, January 17, 1774.

63. Advertisement, *Providence Gazette; and Country Journal*, February 12, 1763. The same ad appears six more times in the *Providence Gazette; and Country Journal*, almost every week from February 19 to April 9, 1763.

64. In this letter, Backus responded to his former minister in Norwich, the Congregationalist minister Benjamin Lord, who criticized his former church members in a 1762 ordination sermon that he preached. Backus's response is a precursor to some of the arguments that he later used against the Reverend Joseph Fish.

65. Advertisement, *Providence Gazette; and Country Journal*, May 5, 1764. A similarly worded advertisement appeared in the June 2, 1764, issue of the *Providence Gazette; and Country Journal*.
66. These four issues were July 7, 1764; July 14, 1764; July 28, 1764; and August 11, 1764, in the *Providence Gazette; and Country Journal*.
67. See the repeated advertisement in the four August 1766 issues of the *Newport Mercury* (August 4, 11, 18, and 25).
68. Three advertisements for Backus's *A Fish Caught in Its Own Net* appeared in 1768 alone. See the *Boston Gazette, and Country Journal*, August 8, 15, and 22, 1768.
69. Isaiah Thomas, *The History of Printing in America: With a Biography of Printers, and an Account of Newspapers: to Which Is Prefixed a Concise View of the Discovery and Progress of the Art in Other Parts of the World: in Two Volumes* (Worcester: From the Press of Isaiah Thomas, 1810), 2:409, 438.
70. Hugh Amory, "The New England Book Trade, 1713–1790," in *A History of the Book in America*, vol. 1, *The Colonial Book in the Atlantic World*, ed. Hugh Amory and David Hall (Cambridge, UK: Cambridge Univ. Press, 2000), 332, 586–87n47.
71. [Philip Freeman], "On Monday . . . will be offered . . . a Valuable Collection of Books . . . ," Broadside (Boston, September 30, 1766).
72. The years of *Minutes of the Warren Association* that explicitly name Philip Freeman as a member of the Grievance Committee are 1772 and 1775. Most of the time, the *Minutes* note that "the same agent here and committee for advice and counsel about the affairs of our churches were continued as we had last year." For an example, see Warren Association, *Minutes of the Proceedings of the Warren Association, in their Meeting at Medfield, September 7th to 9th, 1773* (Boston: Printed by Isaiah Thomas, at his Printing Office, near the Mill-Bridge, 1773), 5. The *Minutes* do not list the actual Grievance Committee members for every year. However, the 1772 *Minutes* do list Isaac Backus as the agent or head of the Grievance Committee and the following men, most of them well-known pastors, as the other members of the committee: Samuel Stillman, Hezekiah Smith, John Davis, Noah Alden, Nathan Plimpton, Philip Freeman, Richard Gridley, and Philip Freeman Jr. See Warren Association, *Minutes of the Proceedings of Warren Association, in their Meeting at Middleborough, in the County of Plymouth, September 8 & 9, 1772* (Boston: Kneeland for Freeman, 1772), 5. As best as I can determine, Philip Freeman served on the Grievance Committee from 1772 to 1781. For

the 1772 and 1774 annual meetings of the Warren Association, Freeman was also personally responsible for making sure that a printer in Boston published the association's minutes. See the publication information for the above 1772 *Minutes* specifying "Kneeland for Freeman," for instance. Kneeland was a Boston printer.

73. Although less is known about him, Philip Freeman Jr., like his father, appears to have engaged in the "importing bookseller" trade in Boston. Philip Freeman Jr.'s shop was located near the "Liberty Tree." He sold a lot of the same Baptist works as his father, including Backus's *A Fish Caught in Its Own Net* (1768). Advertisement, *Boston Gazette, and Country Journal*, August 15, 1768. The Warren Association's *Minutes* explicitly named Philip Freeman Jr. as a member of the Grievance Committee in 1772 and 1775. Overall, he served from 1772 to 1780. Much of what I have argued for Philip Freeman Sr. can be tentatively argued for his son as well.
74. Goen, *Revivalism and Separatism in New England*, 278.
75. Gillette, ed., *Minutes of the Philadelphia Baptist Association, 1707–1807*, 97.
76. Elders and Messengers of the Philadelphia Association to Elders and Messengers Meeting in Warren, Philadelphia, October 1766, in Appendix D of *A Memoir of the Life and Times of the Rev. Isaac Backus, A.M.*, by Alvah Hovey (Boston: Gould and Lincoln, 1858), 342–43, quotes on 343.
77. All verses quoted come from the King James Version.
78. Hovey, *Memoir of the Life and Times of the Rev. Isaac Backus*, 155.
79. *Minutes of the Warren Association* (1767), quoted in Hovey, *Memoir of the Life and Times of the Rev. Isaac Backus*, 155. The Warren Association did not publish the first three years of its minutes.
80. Gillette, ed., *Minutes of the Philadelphia Baptist Association, 1707–1807*, 60.
81. The passage describes how some Jewish Christians from Jerusalem came to Antioch in Syria and declared that the Gentiles who had been saved in that church should also become Jewish by undergoing circumcision and practicing the Mosaic Law. The Jewish Christians', or "Judaizers,'" words troubled the congregation, so they sent the Apostles Paul and Barnabas to the church at Jerusalem to receive some advice on how to solve the problem. In that church council in Jerusalem, the Apostles Peter and James argued that God provided for the salvation of the Gentiles by grace, as he had the Jews, and that it was unnecessary for Gentiles to become Jews to be saved. Peter and James convinced the rest of the apostles and the whole church with their arguments. Then, the church sent

a couple of representatives from Jerusalem to Antioch with Paul and Barnabas to bear witness to the decision of the council.

82. Benjamin Griffith, "On the Power and Duty of an Association of Churches," in Gillette, *Minutes of the Philadelphia Baptist Association, 1707–1807*, 62.
83. Goen, *Revivalism and Separatism in New England*, 292.
84. Hovey, *Memoir of the Life and Times of the Rev. Isaac Backus*, 155. In some unpublished records of the Warren Association from 1768, the Second Church in Coventry disagreed with Gano's (and Griffith's) interpretation of Acts 15 by saying "we are not convinced that that chapter, or any other sentence in the Bible, supports a classical government over the church or churches of Christ." They were "[grieved]" that a proposal to form an association even took place. See Second Church in Coventry (RI) to Warren Association, Coventry, 1768, quoted in Goen, *Revivalism and Separatism in New England*, 278.
85. Goen, *Revivalism and Separatism in New England*, 280.
86. [Manning], *The Sentiments and Plan of the Warren Association*, 3, emphasis original.
87. McLoughlin, *New England Dissent*, 1:507–508.
88. Also, the association's creation of the Grievance Committee fueled the growth of the association itself. The popular committee was a major factor in the "Association [growing] from four members in 1767 to thirty-eight in 1780." See McLoughlin, *New England Dissent*, 1:508.
89. Certeau, *Practice of Everyday Life*, xii, 37.
90. *Minutes of the Warren Association* (1769), quoted in McLoughlin, *New England Dissent*, 1:529. The first members of the Grievance Committee were Samuel Stillman, Hezekiah Smith, Isaac Backus, Richard Montague, Joseph Meacham, and Timothy Wightman.
91. I have found an excerpt of the 1770 *Minutes of the Warren Association* in a newspaper advertisement. See Advertisement, *Massachusetts Gazette: and the Boston Weekly News-Letter*, September 20, 1770. The Warren Association did not start publishing their minutes in pamphlet form until 1771.
92. McLoughlin, *New England Dissent*, 1:529
93. Advertisements, *Massachusetts Gazette: and Boston Weekly News-Letter*, August 2, 9, 16, 1770; Advertisements, *Boston Evening-Post*, August 6, 13, 20, 1770; Advertisement, *Providence Gazette; and Country Journal*, August 11, 1770; Advertisement, *Essex (MA) Gazette*, August 14, 1770; and Advertisements, *Boston Gazette, and Country Journal*, August 27, 1770, and September 3, 1770.

94. Advertisement, *Providence Gazette, and Country Journal*, August 11, 1770.
95. Richard D. Brown, *Revolutionary Politics in Massachusetts: The Boston Committee of Correspondence and the Towns, 1772–1774* (Cambridge, MA: Harvard Univ. Press, 1970), 43.
96. *A Report of the Record Commissioners of the City of Boston, Containing the Boston Town Records, 1770 through 1777* (Boston: Rockwell and Churchill, 1887), 92–93, quote on 93.
97. Brown, *Revolutionary Politics in Massachusetts*, 59.
98. Brown, *Revolutionary Politics in Massachusetts*, 62–64.
99. Brown, *Revolutionary Politics in Massachusetts*, 66–68, quote on 68.
100. Carl Bridenbaugh, *Mitre and Sceptre: Transatlantic Faiths, Ideas, Personalities, and Politics, 1689–1775* (New York: Oxford Univ. Press, 1962), 203–4, quote on 204.
101. Boston, Massachusetts, *The Votes and Proceedings of the Freeholders and Other Inhabitants of the Town of Boston in Town Meeting Assembled, According to Law* [Published by Order of the Town] (Boston: Edes and Gill and T. and J. Fleet, 1772), 3–4, 7–8.
102. Boston, Massachusetts, *Votes and Proceedings of the Freeholders*, 27–28.
103. Backus, *A History of New England*, 2:149–50.
104. Backus, *A History of New England*, 2:150–51; McLoughlin, *New England Dissent*, 1:533–35.
105. Backus, *A History of New England*, 2:151; McLoughlin, *New England Dissent*, 1:534–35.
106. Backus, *A History of New England*, 2:151–52.
107. Isaac Backus made this argument in his *An Appeal to the Public for Religious Liberty against the Oppressions of the Present Day* (Boston: Printed by John Boyle, 1773), 52–60. For another example of the same argument, see Warren Association, *Minutes of the Warren Association, in their Meeting at Middleborough, Sept. 9 & 10, 1777* (Boston: E. Draper in Newbury-Street, 1777), 5.
108. Backus, *A History of New England*, 2:153.
109. Warren Baptist Association Grievance Committee to [Thomas Hutchinson] and Mass. Council and House of Representatives, September 13, 1770, Backus Papers, ANTS. For a published copy of this letter, see Hovey, *Memoir of the Life and Times of the Rev. Isaac Backus*, 177–80.
110. McLoughlin, *New England Dissent*, 1:538–39.
111. James Manning, "Circular Letter of the Warren Association" (1770), quoted in Guild, *Life, Times, and Correspondence of James Manning*, 185.

112. Editorial, *Massachusetts Gazette: and the Boston Weekly News-Letter*, October 25, 1770. The editorial appeared in other newspapers as well. For two other examples, see Editorial, *Boston Evening-Post*, October 29, 1770; and Editorial, *Providence Gazette; and Country Journal*, November 17, 1770.
113. [Isaac Backus], *A Letter to a Gentlemen in the Massachusetts General Assembly, Concerning Taxes to Support Religious Worship* (Boston: n.p., 1771), 22.
114. [Backus], *Letter to a Gentleman*, 14–15, quote on 15.
115. [Backus], *Letter to a Gentleman*, 15–18.
116. McLoughlin, *New England Dissent*, 1:545–46.
117. McLoughlin, *New England Dissent*, 1:556.
118. Backus, *Diary*, 2:910–12.
119. Backus, *A History of New England*, 2:200.
120. The Quakers were generally proponents of religious tolerance or religious liberty and haters of Massachusetts Congregationalists, partly because the Congregationalists' ancestors, the Puritans, hung three Quakers in Boston Common in the late 1650s/early 1660s.
121. Backus, *Diary*, 2:915.
122. Backus, *Diary*, 2:916.
123. Ezra Stiles, *The Literary Diary of Ezra Stiles*, ed. F. B. Dexter (New York: C. Scribner's Sons, 1901), 1:472.
124. [Isaac Backus, James Manning, and Robert Strettle Jones], "Memorial," in Hovey, *Memoir of the Life and Times of the Rev. Isaac Backus*, 210. See 204–10 for the entire memorial.
125. *A Report of the Record Commissioners of the City of Boston*, 93.
126. Backus, *Diary*, 2:916–19.
127. McLoughlin, *New England Dissent*, 1:564–65.
128. John L. Brooke, *The Heart of the Commonwealth: Society and Political Culture in Worcester County, Massachusetts, 1713–1861* (Cambridge, UK: Cambridge Univ. Press, 1989), 158.
129. "The Charter of Massachusetts Bay-1691," The Avalon Project: Documents in Law, History, and Diplomacy, accessed April 20, 2014, http://avalon.law.yale.edu/17th_century/mass07.asp#b9.
130. Brooke, *The Heart of the Commonwealth*, 158; McLoughlin, *New England Dissent*, 1:594.
131. Brooke, *The Heart of the Commonwealth*, 172.
132. See Backus's trio of important pamphlets written during this time: *Government and Liberty Described and Ecclesiastical Tyranny Exposed*

(Boston: Printed by Powars and Willis, and sold by Philip Freeman, in Union Street, 1778); *Policy, as Well as Honesty, Forbids the Use of Secular Force in Religious Affairs* (Boston: Printed by Draper and Folsom, and sold by Phillip Freeman, in Union Street, 1779); and *An Appeal to the People of the Massachusetts State against Arbitrary Power* (Boston: Printed and sold by Benjamin Edes and Sons, in State Street: sold also by Philip Freeman, in Union-Street, 1780).

133. McLoughlin, *New England Dissent*, 1:599.
134. McLoughlin, *New England Dissent*, 1:602.
135. "Constitution of Massachusetts: 1780," *National Humanities Institute*, accessed April 19, 2014, http://www.nhinet.org/ccs/docs/ma-1780.htm.
136. "Constitution of Massachusetts: 1780."
137. "Constitution of Massachusetts: 1780."
138. Johann Neem, "The Elusive Common Good," *Journal of the Early Republic* 24, no. 3 (Fall 2004): 388.
139. See Backus's *An Appeal to the People*.
140. John Witte Jr. and Justin Latterell, "The Last American Establishment: Massachusetts, 1780–1833," in *Disestablishment and Religious Dissent: Church-State Relations in the New American States 1776–1833*, ed. Carl H. Esbeck and Jonathan J. Den Hartog (Columbia: Univ. of Missouri Press, 2019), 414. Witte and Latterell note that the adoption of Article III should not have succeeded because votes in favor of keeping Article III in the constitution stood at "8,865 to 6,225, or a little more than 58 percent." It did not reach the necessary two-thirds vote. They further add that "delegates to the convention—out of ignorance of the exact vote tally or perhaps indifference to the same given the political pressure to succeed—treated the Constitution as fully ratified." Witte and Latterell, 414.
141. Witte and Latterell, "Last American Establishment," 414.
142. McLoughlin, *New England Dissent*, 1:599.
143. McLoughlin, *New England Dissent*, 1:607.
144. McLoughlin, *New England Dissent*, 1:607–9.

CHAPTER 3

1. Richard D. Brown, *Knowledge Is Power: The Diffusion of Information in Early America, 1700–1865* (New York: Oxford Univ. Press, 1989), 197–203. I will soon discuss the outlook, background, and social status of a typical New England Federalist clergyman.

2. William Bentley, *Diary of William Bentley, D.D., Pastor of the East Church, Salem, Massachusetts*, ed. Joseph G. Waters and Marguerite Dalrymple (Salem: Essex Institute, 1905), 2:409.
3. Gaustad, Barlow, and Dishno, *New Historical Atlas of Religion in America*, 79.
4. Bentley, *Diary*, 2:409.
5. "To Thomas Jefferson from the Danbury Baptist Association, [after 7 October 1801]."
6. Denunciations and criticisms of Baptists pepper the pages of his diary. For example, Bentley visited Haverhill, another town in Essex County, on September 22, 1790. Once there, Bentley saw a Baptist church building where Hezekiah Smith was pastor and commented that the meetinghouse was "much out of repair, as are houses in general of that denomination," implying that Baptists' generally low socioeconomic status ensured that they had shoddy meetinghouses. See Bentley, *Diary*, 1:298. Years later, Bentley heard that there was an ordination service for a Baptist minister in his town of Salem. For him, "it was a dark day, because we were afraid of the uncharitableness of this Sect which has been the most illiterate in New England." The highly educated Bentley shared his Congregationalist colleagues' opinion that Baptist ministers were "illiterate" (i.e., not college educated) and thus unfit for ministry. That day, neither he nor any of his fellow ministers attended the Baptist proceedings. See Bentley, entry dated January 9, 1805, *Diary*, 3:134. One notable exception of a Baptist he liked was Dr. James Manning, Baptist minister and president of Rhode Island College. Upon hearing of Manning's death, Bentley wrote in an August 2, 1791, entry that Manning "possessed a fine person, & was entitled to the public esteem." See Bentley, *Diary*, 1:282.
7. Bentley, *Diary*, 2:409.
8. Bentley, *Diary*, 3:13–14.
9. Certeau, *Practice of Everyday Life*, xix. I realize that what I am describing as an aspect of Leland's and Baptists' strategy is what Certeau defines as a "tactic." The Congregationalists of Massachusetts, since they owned the social space of the state, engaged in a "strategy" of maintaining the religio-political status quo. However, by the beginning of the 1800s, Baptists' attempts to fight the establishment were a fairly well-defined counterstrategy. I am not aiming to use Certeau's categories in a static manner so that I can account for what is actually happening in early national Massachusetts between Congregationalists and Baptists.
10. I did not invent the term "political ecumenism." Although it is unclear to

me who first coined the term, the term is central to the thesis of Concordia University emeritus professor of history Geoffrey Adams's book *Political Ecumenism: Catholics, Jews, and Protestants in De Gaulle's Free France, 1940–1945* (Montreal: McGill-Queen's Univ. Press, 2006). In this book, Adams argues that French leader Charles de Gaulle united key members of the "three religious families" of France into a coalition that resisted Nazi Germany and Nazi puppet Vichy France after France fell to Hitler in June 1940. According to Adams, Catholics, Jews, and Protestants did not join forces in hopes of creating an "interconfessional communion: their ecumenism was strictly political; their motivation in joining de Gaulle, while strengthened in many cases by religious conviction, was primarily an act of patriotic republican commitment" (3). This alliance is surprising because, as Adams points out, for most of France's history since the French Revolution, there had been, in reality, "two Frances." The French Revolution was virulently anti-religion and specifically anti-Catholic, so there was often tension between Catholic France and "republican" France (8–21). But de Gaulle, himself a devout Catholic, was a pragmatist and needed political allies in the fight against fascism. He was willing to overlook religious differences if that meant the possibility of restoring freedom to France (32–49). Adams's book, and de Gaulle in particular, is a useful model and analogy for Leland's own form of political ecumenism. Leland, although a staunch Baptist theologically and practically, did not expect all of his allies to be Baptists and sought out anyone who would align in the Democratic-Republican Party to push for religious liberty in Massachusetts.

11. Leland, "Events in the Life," 19. Leland did not receive a "proper" ordination in Virginia until June 1787, when pastors Nathaniel Saunders, John Waller, and John Price laid their hands upon him. See Leland, "Events in the Life," 26.
12. Leland, "Events in the Life," 19.
13. Robert B. Semple, *A History of the Rise and Progress of the Baptists in Virginia*, rev. ed., ed. George William Beale (Philadelphia: American Baptist Publication Society, 1894), 206–7. Semple's original edition was published in 1810.
14. Semple, *History of the Rise and Progress*, 98.
15. Carl H. Esbeck, "Disestablishment in Virginia, 1776–1802," in *Disestablishment and Religious Dissent: Church-State Relations in the New American States 1776–1833*, ed. Carl H. Esbeck and Jonathan J. Den Hartog (Columbia: Univ. of Missouri Press, 2019), 140–41.

16. Esbeck, "Disestablishment in Virginia," 141.
17. Butterfield, *Elder John Leland, Jeffersonian Itinerant*, 174–75, quotes on 175.
18. John A. Ragosta, *Wellspring of Liberty: How Virginia's Religious Dissenters Helped Win the American Revolution and Secured Religious Liberty* (New York: Oxford Univ. Press, 2010), 9.
19. Semple, *History of the Rise and Progress*, 94–95.
20. Semple's account is found on pages 94–106 in his history.
21. Creed, "John Leland: American Prophet of Religious Individualism," 76.
22. Jefferson could not submit his bill in person because he was in Paris serving as the United States' ambassador to France from 1785 to 1789.
23. Mark S. Scarberry, "John Leland and James Madison: Religious Influence on the Ratification of the Constitution and on the Proposal of the Bill of Rights," *Penn State Law Review* 113, no. 3 (April 2009): 751–53, quote on 751; Butterfield, *Elder John Leland, Jeffersonian Itinerant*, 175–77. Scarberry concedes that no direct documentary evidence from the eighteenth century exists to prove that Leland himself urged Baptists to petition the legislature and/or partnered with James Madison to oppose Patrick Henry's general assessment bill (1784), yet Scarberry, L. H. Butterfield, American religious historian Edwin Gaustad, Baptist historian Robert Alley, and Madison historian Ralph Ketcham, among others, believe that Leland did. See Scarberry, 753–54n83.
24. John Leland, "The Virginia Chronicle," in *Writings*, 118. For a more detailed discussion on Leland's disapproval of laws that tax the populace to support Protestant teachers of religion in Massachusetts, see John Leland, "The Yankee Spy," in *Writings*, 220–27.
25. Semple, *History of the Rise and Progress*, 97–99, quote on 97.
26. Thomas E. Buckley, "Evangelicals Triumphant: The Baptists' Assault on the Virginia Glebes, 1786–1801," *William and Mary Quarterly* 45, no. 1 (January 1988): 35–38.
27. Semple, *History of the Rise and Progress*, 103–6. Leland did not complete the first three tasks before leaving for Massachusetts.
28. John Leland, "Address of the Committee of the United Baptist Churches of Virginia, assembled in the city of Richmond, 8th August, 1789, to the President of the United States of America," in *Writings*, 52–54. The actual date of Leland's letter is May 8, 9, or 10, 1789. See Editorial Note, "From George Washington to the United Baptist Churches of Virginia, May 1789," Founders Online, National Archives, accessed October 26, 2021, https://founders.archives.gov/documents/Washington/05-02-02-0309.
29. George Washington, "To the General Committee, representing the

United Baptist Churches in Virginia," [May 1789], in Leland, *Writings*, 54–55, quote on 55.
30. Semple, *History of the Rise and Progress*, 102.
31. Scarberry, "John Leland and James Madison," 759–60; Dinkin, *Campaigning in America: A History of Election Practices*, 2–3, 12–14.
32. James Madison Sr. to James Madison, January 30, 1788, in *The Papers of James Madison*, vol. 10, *27 May 1787–3 March 1788*, ed. Robert A. Rutland, Charles F. Hobson, William M. E. Rachal, and Frederika J. Teute (Chicago: Univ. of Chicago Press, 1977), 446, quoted in Scarberry, "John Leland and James Madison," 760.
33. James Gordon Jr. to James Madison, February 17, 1788, in *Papers of James Madison*, 10:515–16, quoted in Scarberry, "John Leland and James Madison," 761.
34. Scarberry, "John Leland and James Madison," 762–64; Butterfield, *Elder John Leland, Jeffersonian Itinerant*, 186.
35. A full text of Leland's objections exists in Butterfield, *Elder John Leland, Jeffersonian Itinerant*, 187–88. The quote is from 188. Not coincidentally, Thomas Jefferson expressed similar views to Leland's regarding the weaknesses of the Federal Constitution in a private letter to James Madison. After discussing with Madison some aspects of the Federal Constitution that he approved of, Jefferson "[added] what [he did] not like: First the omission of a bill of rights providing clearly and without the aid of sophisms for freedom of religion, freedom of the press . . ." See Thomas Jefferson to James Madison, Paris, December 20, 1787, in *The Portable Thomas Jefferson*, ed. Merrill D. Peterson (New York: Penguin Books, 1977), 429.
36. Joseph Spencer to James Madison, February 28, 1788, in *Papers of James Madison*, 10:540–42, quoted in Scarberry, "John Leland and James Madison," 764.
37. Scarberry devotes a significant portion of his article examining the evidence for and against whether a meeting between Leland and Madison occurred. See Scarberry, "John Leland and James Madison," 766–76.
38. Scarberry, "John Leland and James Madison," 765–66.
39. John Leland, "Address Delivered at Dalton, Massachusetts, January 8, 1831," in *Writings*, 605.
40. Scarberry, "John Leland and James Madison," 778–97.
41. Esbeck, "Disestablishment in Virginia," 149.
42. L. F. Greene, "Further Sketches of the Life of John Leland," in *Writings*, 55.
43. McLoughlin, *New England Dissent*, 2:924–28, quote on 926. Leland thus continued the New England Baptist leadership's strategy of using inex-

pensive newspapers and tracts to disseminate discussions of religious liberty to as many people as possible. See Smith, *John Leland*, 87.

44. Porterfield, *Conceived in Doubt*, 152. Porterfield further observes that the idea of "religious opinions" figures prominently in the complete and provocative title to Leland's "The Rights of Conscience Inalienable." The full title of the work is "The Rights of Conscience Inalienable, and, Therefore, Religious Opinions Not Cognizable by Law: or, The High-Flying Churchman, Stripped of His Legal Robe, Appears a Yaho." See Leland, *Writings*, 177.

45. John Leland, "The Rights of Conscience Inalienable," in *Writings*, 184, emphasis mine; Thomas Jefferson, *Notes on the State of Virginia*, in Peterson, *Portable Thomas Jefferson*, 210–12.

46. Leland, "The Rights of Conscience Inalienable," in *Writings*, 184–85, first quote on 184, second quote on 185; Jefferson, *Notes on the State of Virginia*, in Peterson, *Portable Thomas Jefferson*, 211–12.

47. Leland, "Events in the Life of John Leland," in *Writings*, 30.

48. Ellen M. Raynor and Emma L. Petitclerc, *History of the Town of Cheshire, Berkshire County, Mass* (Holyoke, MA: C. W. Bryan & Co., 1885), 10.

49. Goen, *Revivalism and Separatism in New England*, 255. Elder Peter Werden, a longtime minister in Warwick and Coventry, Rhode Island, moved to Cheshire (then called Lanesborough) and started the town's first Baptist church in 1770; he remained its pastor until his death in 1808. According to Leland, Werden "was a father to the Baptist churches in Berkshire and its environs, and in some sense an apostle to them all." See John Leland, "A Biographical Sketch of the Life and Character of the Rev. Peter Werden," in *Writings*, 319–20, quote on 320. Goen cites Leland's quote as coming from Baptist historian David Benedict. Benedict actually included Leland's entire biographical sketch of Werden in his own work. See David Benedict, *A General History of the Baptist Denomination in America, And Other Parts of the World* (Boston: Printed by Lincoln & Edmands, no. 53, Cornhill, for the author, 1813), 401–4. The quote Goen used appears on 402.

50. Greene, "Further Sketches of the Life of John Leland," in *Writings*, 56; March 24, 1792, Second Baptist Church in Cheshire, MA, Records 1789–1884, typed by Rollin Hillyer Cooke, 1903.

51. May 26, 1792, Second Baptist Church in Cheshire, MA, Records 1789–1884.

52. McLoughlin lists the beginning of the Shaftsbury Baptist Association as 1787 (McLoughlin, *New England Dissent*, 1:508), but this is probably

a typo. Associational minutes do not exist before 1786, but the 1786 minutes record that the Shaftsbury Baptist Association began in June 1781. See Shaftsbury Baptist Association, *Minutes of the Shaftsbury Association, at their Annuel* [sic] *Convention, Held at Elder Warden's Meeting-House, in Adams, 1786* (Albany, NY: Printed by Charles R. Webster, no 36, (north side of) State-Street, near the English church, Albany, 1786); 1.

53. McLoughlin, *New England Dissent*, 1:508–9, quote on 509.
54. Strange, "Baptists and Religious Liberty," 276, 276–77n87. Strange's lengthy footnote provides a sketch of all of Leland's associational activities from 1792 to 1808, which he gleaned from the *Minutes of the Shaftsbury Association, 1792–1817* (microfilm), Southern Baptist Theological Seminary, Louisville, KY. In 2017 one could also access all *Minutes of the Shaftsbury Association*, 1786–1819, minus the year 1787, from the Early American Imprints: Series I (Evans: 1639–1800) and Series II (Shaw-Shoemaker: 1801–1819) digital editions.
55. Ronald P. Formisano, *The Transformation of Political Culture: Massachusetts Parties, 1790s–1840s* (New York: Oxford Univ. Press, 1984), 156. Jonathan D. Sassi goes even further than Formisano's contention about at least 90 percent of Congregationalist ministers being Federalists by claiming that "probably not many more than a dozen [ministers] in Connecticut and Massachusetts" were Democratic-Republicans. See Sassi, *A Republic of Righteousness: The Public Christianity of the Post-Revolutionary New England Clergy* (Oxford: Oxford Univ. Press, 2001), 108. Sassi used the estimate of "not many more than a dozen" to be on the safe side. In his footnote, he cites that Paul Goodman "lists six Congregational ministers who were Republicans," and James M. Banner added two more to Goodman's list. See Sassi, *Republic of Righteousness*, 255–56n76. Here is Goodman's list: "Thomas Allen (Pittsfield), Joseph Barker (Middleboro), Ephraim Judson (Sheffield), Samuel Niles (Abington), David Sanford, Solomon Aiken (Dracut)." See Paul Goodman, *The Democratic-Republicans of Massachusetts: Politics in a Young Republic* (Cambridge, MA: Harvard Univ. Press, 1964), 277n43. Banner's additions are as follows: "Ebenezer Bradford of Rowley and John Giles of Newburyport." See Banner, *To the Hartford Convention: The Federalists and the Origins of Party Politics in Massachusetts, 1789–1815* (New York: Knopf, 1970), 152n2. To this total of eight Jeffersonian Congregationalist ministers, Sassi included William Bentley of Salem. See Sassi, *Republic of Righteousness*, 256n76.

56. Ronald P. Formisano, *Transformation of Political Culture*, 156.
57. James M. Banner, *To the Hartford Convention*, 168–69, 179–82, 202.
58. Leland, "An Oration, Delivered at Cheshire, July 5, 1802, on the Celebration of Independence: Containing Seventeen Sketches, and Seventeen Wishes," in *Writings*, 262–65, quotes on 262, emphasis original.
59. Porterfield, *Conceived in Doubt*, 13.
60. Porterfield, *Conceived in Doubt*, 13.
61. Den Hartog, *Patriotism & Piety*, 45–69, quotes on 46. Obbie Tyler Todd points out in his ground-breaking article that some notable Baptist leaders were dedicated Federalists, which bucks the tendency of historians to include all Baptists in Jefferson's camp. Some Baptist Federalist pastors in New England were Samuel Stillman, James Manning, and Jonathan Maxcy. See his "Baptist Federalism: Religious Liberty and Public Virtue in the Early Republic," *Journal of Church and State* 63, no. 3 (Summer 2021): 440–60. Just like the Congregationalist Federalist clergy, Stillman and Maxcy also strongly denounced the French Revolution, the rise of infidelity, and the dangers of Jeffersonianism. See Todd, 443–47.

    These three Baptist Federalist pastors had a lot in common with their Congregationalist pastoral colleagues. All three were well educated. Manning and Maxcy were even the first and second presidents of Rhode Island College, respectively. They all also had refined preaching skills, thus fitting in with their genteel Congregationalist colleagues on New England's east coast. For more on Stillman and Manning, see chaps. 1 and 2 of this book.
62. John Adams, "Proclamation 8—Recommending a National Day of Humiliation, Fasting, and Prayer," March 23, 1798, Gerhard Peters and John T. Woolley, eds., *The American Presidency Project*, accessed October 26, 2021, https://www.presidency.ucsb.edu/documents/proclamation-8-recommending-national-day-humiliation-fasting-and-prayer.
63. Constitutional Rights Foundation, "BRIA 19 4 b: The Alien and Sedition Acts: Defining American Freedom," accessed October 26, 2021, https://www.crf-usa.org/bill-of-rights-in-action/bria-19-4-b-the-alien-and-sedition-acts-defining-american-freedom.html.
64. "An Act in Addition to the Act, Entitled 'An Act for the Punishment of Certain Crimes Against the United States,'" The Avalon Project: Documents in Law, History, and Diplomacy, accessed October 26, 2021, http://avalon.law.yale.edu/18th_century/sedact.asp.
65. Jeffrey L. Pasley, *"The Tyranny of Printers": Newspaper Politics in the Early American Republic* (Charlottesville: Univ. Press of Virginia, 2001), 106, 118, quote on 106.

66. Pasley, *"Tyranny of Printers,"* 117–18.
67. Pasley, *"Tyranny of Printers,"* 124–31, quote on 126.
68. Pasley, *"Tyranny of Printers,"* 105.
69. Pasley, *"Tyranny of Printers,"* 7.
70. Pasley, *"Tyranny of Printers,"* 7–11, quote on 11.
71. Noble E. Cunningham Jr., *Jeffersonian Republicans: The Formation of Party Organization, 1789–1801* (Chapel Hill: Published for the Institute of Early American History and Culture at Williamsburg by the Univ. of North Carolina Press, 1957), 211.
72. Cunningham, *Jeffersonian Republicans*, 212–14.
73. The first "official" party platform for a presidential campaign did not exist until the Democrats crafted one during the 1840 election. See Dinkin, *Campaigning in America*, 52.
74. Thomas Jefferson to Elbridge Gerry, January 26, 1799, quoted in Cunningham, *Jeffersonian Republicans*, 211–12.
75. In a chapter that Robert J. Dinkin calls "The Golden Age of Parties" (years 1854–1888), national committees played an ever-increasing role in managing the electoral prospects of their presidential candidate and candidates in lower offices. One practice that they implemented was turning the "rather brief and vague" political platforms of past eras into statements "at least a few pages in length and fairly specific concerning the issues." See Dinkin, *Campaigning in America*, 70–71, quote on 71.
76. Ronald P. Formisano writes, "In Massachusetts Federalism as a statewide competitive force lasted longer than anywhere else in the country," until 1824. See Formisano, "Federalists and Republicans: Parties, Yes—System, No," in *The Evolution of American Electoral Systems*, ed. Paul Kleppner et al. (Westport, CT: Greenwood Press, 1981), 43–44, quote on 44.
77. Banner, *To the Hartford Convention*, 179–80.
78. Banner, *To the Hartford Convention*, 182–83, 193–94.
79. Formisano, *Transformation of Political Culture*, 158.
80. Reverend Billy Hibbard, quoted in J. E. A. Smith, *The History of Pittsfield (Berkshire County) Massachusetts: From the Year 1800 to the Year 1876* (Springfield, MA: C. W. Bryan & Co., 1876), 150.
81. Formisano, *Transformation of Political Culture*, 159.
82. Banner, *To the Hartford Convention*, 197.
83. McLoughlin, *New England Dissent*, 2:1158.
84. Banner, *To the Hartford Convention*, 198–99.
85. Richard D. Birdsall, *Berkshire County: A Cultural History* (New Haven: Yale Univ. Press, 1959), 1–4.

86. Butterfield, *Elder John Leland, Jeffersonian Itinerant*, 215–16, emphasis mine.
87. Butterfield, *Elder John Leland, Jeffersonian Itinerant*, 216. On the same page, Butterfield also reports that for the 1800 and 1808 presidential elections, Federalist politicians doctored the voting results to ensure they were reelected, so no reliable figures exist for Cheshire during those two presidential elections.
88. David Waldstreicher, *In the Midst of Perpetual Fetes: The Making of American Nationalism, 1776–1820* (Chapel Hill: Published for the Omohundro Institute of Early American History and Culture, Williamsburg, Virginia, by the Univ. of North Carolina Press, 1997), 2–3, and the book as a whole.
89. Jeffrey L. Pasley, "The Cheese and the Words: Popular Political Culture and Participatory Democracy in the Early American Republic," in *Beyond the Founders: New Approaches to the Political History of the Early American Republic*, ed. Jeffrey L. Pasley, Andrew W. Robertson, and David Waldstreicher (Chapel Hill: Univ. of North Carolina Press, 2004), 39. Ronald P. Formisano agrees that the political "parties" that existed before the 1840s "were more like factions or stable coalitions of limited duration than the highly articulated organizations of Democrats and Whigs." See Formisano, "Federalists and Republicans: Parties, Yes—System, No," 35.
90. Len Travers, *Celebrating the Fourth: Independence Day and the Rites of Nationalism in the Early Republic* (Amherst, MA: Univ. of Massachusetts Press, 1997), 4.
91. Travers, *Celebrating the Fourth*, 13.
92. Travers, *Celebrating the Fourth*, 48.
93. Before he gave the toasts for the ceremony, Leland commented that "As it is my custom, on our anniversaries, to retire from company as soon as the public exhibition is over . . . ," indicating that he and the town had an Independence Day celebration, and possibly other celebrations, frequently enough for him to develop a custom. See Leland, "An Oration, Delivered at Cheshire, July 5, 1802," in *Writings*, 269.
94. Leland, "An Oration, Delivered at Cheshire, July 5, 1802," 263.
95. Leland, "An Oration, Delivered at Cheshire, July 5, 1802," 267.
96. Leland, "An Oration, Delivered at Cheshire, July 5, 1802," 268–69.
97. Leland, "An Oration, Delivered at Cheshire, July 5, 1802," 262, 265.
98. Leland, "An Oration, Delivered at Cheshire, July 5, 1802," 263, 265
99. Leland, "An Oration, Delivered at Cheshire, July 5, 1802," 267.

100. Spencer W. McBride, *Pulpit and Nation: Clergymen and the Politics of Revolutionary America* (Charlottesville: Univ. of Virginia Press, 2018), 2.
101. Butterfield, *Elder John Leland, Jeffersonian Itinerant*, 169.
102. McBride, *Pulpit and Nation*, 142–43. Of course, the Federalists had their own "politicized clergymen" as well. Noteworthy pastors included Jedidiah Morse and Timothy Dwight. See McBride, chaps. 5 and 6, for his wider discussion of the involvement of the clergy in early national politics. Eric C. Smith further observes that "by wedding the office of preacher and politician, Leland helped establish an enduring pattern for American life." See Smith, *John Leland*, 189. Joseph Smith, Martin Luther King Jr., Pat Robertson, and Raphael Warnock are some key examples of preacher-politicians in American history.
103. Pasley, "The Cheese and the Words," 45.
104. Pasley, "The Cheese and the Words," 44.
105. I am guessing that, although most citizens in Cheshire seemed to be Baptists, it is unlikely that *everyone* in the town was a Baptist, sympathetic though they may have been to the Baptist churches in the town.
106. Dreisbach, "Mr. Jefferson, a Mammoth Cheese," 726.
107. Goodman, *Democratic-Republicans of Massachusetts*, 78.
108. Ronald Formisano records that 56.6 percent, 54.1 percent, and 59.7 percent of the citizens of Berkshire voted for a Republican candidate for governor in the years 1805, 1812, and 1824, respectively. See Formisano, *Transformation of Political Culture*, 151–52.
109. Goodman, *Democratic-Republicans of Massachusetts*, 79–80.
110. Goodman, *Democratic-Republicans of Massachusetts*, 81; Richard D. Birdsall, "The Reverend Thomas Allen: Jeffersonian Calvinist," *New England Quarterly* 30, no. 2 (June 1957): 151. For more on Thomas Allen, see Frank A. DeSorbo, "The Reverend Thomas Allen and Revolutionary Politics in Western Massachusetts," (PhD diss., New York University, 1995).
111. Birdsall, "Reverend Thomas Allen," 147.
112. Sassi, *Republic of Righteousness*, 110–11. For Thomas Allen's election sermon, see Allen, *A Sermon, Preached before His Excellency, James Sullivan, Esq., Governor; His Honor, Levi Lincoln, Esq., Lieutenant-Governor; the Honourable Council, and Both Branches of the Legislature of the Commonwealth of Massachusetts: On the Day of General Election, May 25th, 1808* (Boston: Printed by Adams and Rhoades, printers to the state, 1808). The year before, Sullivan asked fellow partisan William Bentley of Salem to give the election sermon. See Sassi, *Republic of Righteousness*, 110.
113. Birdsall, *Berkshire County*, 182–83, quote on 182.

114. Pasley, "The Tyranny of Printers," 165.
115. Birdsall, Berkshire County, 183.
116. Smith, John Leland, 180.
117. I tabulated these statistics using the online *America's Historical Newspapers, 1690–1922* database from the Florida State University Libraries online catalog in the years 2016–2017 and searching for key terms relating to Leland.
118. "Boston Post; Elder John Leland; Lt. Governor," Pittsfield *Sun*, August 22, 1839, 3.
119. Creed, "John Leland: American Prophet of Religious Individualism," 200.
120. Once again, these are my statistics using the online *America's Historical Newspapers, 1690–1922* database.
121. Phinehas Allen, "Death of the Rev. John Leland," Pittsfield *Sun*, January 21, 1841, 2.
122. McLoughlin, *New England Dissent*, 2:1084–86.
123. Johann Neem, "Elusive Common Good," 396–97, quote on 397.
124. Butterfield, *Elder John Leland: Jeffersonian Itinerant*, 212.
125. John Leland, "Speech Delivered in the House of Representatives of Massachusetts, on the Subject of Religious Freedom, 1811," in *Writings*, 354–55.
126. Leland, "Speech Delivered in the House of Representatives of Massachusetts," 355, emphasis original.
127. Leland, "Speech Delivered in the House of Representatives of Massachusetts," 355–56.
128. Commonwealth of Massachusetts, "An Act Respecting Public Worship and Religious Freedom," (Boston: Secretary of the Commonwealth, 1811), 1.
129. Commonwealth of Massachusetts, "An Act Respecting Public Worship and Religious Freedom," 1–2.

CHAPTER 4

1. The court case's official name was *Baker v. Fales*. Deacon Eliphalet Baker, who was a leader of the Unitarian group, sued Trinitarian Deacon Samuel Fales "for recovery of the church property—especially the sizable trust funds which had accumulated over the years by gifts for the support of the church (presumably made by Calvinists for the support of Calvinism) See McLoughlin, *New England Dissent*, 2:1190.
2. John D. Cushing, "Notes on Disestablishment in Massachusetts, 1780–1833," *William and Mary Quarterly*, 3rd series, 26, no. 2 (April 1969): 188–89.

3. McLoughlin, *New England Dissent*, 2:1190.
4. McLoughlin, *New England Dissent*, 1191–95.
5. McLoughlin, *New England Dissent*, 1196–97.
6. McLoughlin, *New England Dissent*, 1194.
7. Den Hartog, *Patriotism & Piety*, 7.
8. Den Hartog, *Patriotism & Piety*, 7–8. See also Hatch, *Democratization of American Christianity*, particularly 3–11. Conrad Edick Wright added that the Trinitarian Congregationalists' building a seminary, starting religious journals and magazines, and forming voluntary societies "introduced bureaucratic methods and values into ecclesiastical affairs. These are aspects of an institutional restructuring far more radical than anything taking place in the realm of doctrine." In contrast, theological debates about the unity or tri-unity of God and the divinity of Christ were well worn by that time. See Conrad Edick Wright, "Institutional Reconstruction in the Unitarian Controversy," in *American Unitarianism: 1805–1865*, ed. Conrad Edick Wright (Boston: Published Jointly by The Massachusetts Historical Society and Northeastern Univ. Press, 1989), 4–5, quote on 5.
9. Sassi, *Republic of Righteousness*, 179.
10. The phrase comes from the subtitle of Charles I. Foster's classic book *An Errand of Mercy: The Evangelical United Front, 1790–1837* (Chapel Hill: Univ. of North Carolina Press, 1960).
11. David Sehat, *The Myth of American Religious Freedom* (Oxford: Oxford Univ. Press, 2011), 58.
12. McLoughlin, *New England Dissent*, 2:1198.
13. Smith, *John Leland*, chap. 8.
14. Butterfield, *Elder John Leland, Jeffersonian Itinerant*, 159–60, 241; McLoughlin, *New England Dissent*, 2:932; Creed, "John Leland: American Prophet of Religious Individualism," 139–66, 176–97; Hatch, *The Democratization of American Christianity*, 93–101.
15. For a few sources that indicate Morse's and Dwight's preference for Federalist politics, see Den Hartog, *Patriotism & Piety*, 45–69; Jedidiah Morse, *A Sermon, Delivered at the New North Church in Boston, in the Morning, and in the Afternoon at Charlestown, May 9th, 1798,: Being the Day Recommended by John Adams, President of the United States of America, for Solemn Humiliation, Fasting and Prayer* (Boston: Printed by Samuel Hall, no. 53, Cornhill, 1798), 11–29; and Robert J. Imholt, "Timothy Dwight, Federalist Pope of Connecticut," *New England Quarterly* 73, no. 3 (September 2000): 386–411.

16. For two broader analyses on how American evangelical Protestants fought various forms of infidelity in the Early Republic, see Porterfield, *Conceived in Doubt*, and Schlereth, *An Age of Infidels*.
17. Shaftsbury Baptist Association, *Minutes of the Shaftsbury Association: Holden at Pittstown, June 5th and 6th, 1793.: Together with their Circular Letter* (Lansingburgh, [NY]: Printed by Silvester Tiffany, for the reverend Association, 1793), 7. Page 5 of these minutes identifies Leland as the author of the circular letter. See also John Leland, "Circular Letter of the Shaftsbury Association, 1793," in *Writings*, 196–99.
18. Shaftsbury Baptist Association, *Minutes of the Shaftsbury Association . . . 1793*, 7–11. William G. McLoughlin discussed how, after 1780, Baptists in New England had to worry about competition from other dissenting groups. For Baptists, Shakers and Universalists were clearly heretics. A minister influential in Leland's own conversion to Baptist Christianity, Elhanan Winchester, became a Universalist. He was a popular preacher in New England who eventually became pastor of the prestigious First Baptist Church of Philadelphia until he began openly promoting Universalism in 1781. Baptists' other major rivals, Methodists and Freewill Baptists, were Arminians, which the Calvinistic Baptists in New England viewed as heretical as well. McLoughlin further noted that "the Baptists never feared the inroads of deism or Unitarianism into their ranks. These were blatant anti-Christian heresies which found their foremost adherents among the upper classes, and which provided such perfect Satanic foils for orthodox Baptist preachers that they would have had to be invented had they not actually existed." Like Baptists, however, Shakers, Universalists, Freewill Baptists, and Methodists evangelized the middle and lower classes, which made those groups more troublesome competitors. See McLoughlin, *New England Dissent*, 2:709–50, quote on 709. The most detailed and helpful discussion of Shakers, Universalists, and Freewill Baptists in late eighteenth-century New England is Stephen A. Marini's *Radical Sects of Revolutionary New England* (Cambridge, MA: Harvard Univ. Press, 1982).
19. Warren Baptist Association, *Minutes of the Warren Association: Held at the Baptist Meeting-House in Bridgewater, September 8 and 9, 1795* (Boston: Printed by Manning and Loring, 1795), 7–12, quote on 8.
20. Warren Baptist Association, *Minutes of the Warren Association: Held at the First Baptist Meeting-House in Boston, September 12 and 13, 1797* (Boston: Printed by Manning and Loring, 1797), 7–11, quote on 10. For more examples on the Warren Association addressing infidelity in all of

its forms, see its *Minutes of the Warren Association: Held at the South Baptist Meeting-House in Middleborough, September 10 and 11, 1799* (Boston: Printed by Manning and Loring, 1799), 7–9; *Minutes of the Warren Association: Held at the Meeting House, belonging to the First Baptist Church in Sutton, September 8 & 9, 1801* (Boston: Printed by Manning & Loring, 1801), 7–10; and *Minutes of the Warren Association: Held at the Baptist Meeting-House in Wrentham, September 7 and 8, 1802* (Boston: Printed by E. Lincoln, Water Street, 1802), 10–11.

21. E. B. O'Callaghan, *A List of Editions of the Holy Scriptures and Parts Thereof Printed in America Previous to 1860: With Introduction and Bibliographical Notes* (Albany: Munsell & Rowland, 1861), v.

22. O'Callaghan, *A List of Editions of the Holy Scriptures*, xxxix.

23. Warren Baptist Association, *Minutes of the Warren Association: Held at the Baptist Meeting-House in Harvard, M,DCC,XC* (Boston: Printed by Samuel Hall, at no. 53, Cornhill, 1790), 6–7.

24. O'Callaghan, *A List of Editions of the Holy Scriptures*, xxxix–xli.

25. Keith Harper, "Thomas Jefferson, North American Baptists, and . . . *Home Missions*? Reflections on Unintended Consequences," (unpublished paper, in the author's possession, 2016), 1–2. Jefferson divided the territory into ten sections that had the ability to become states with rights equal to the original thirteen states. His plan laid the groundwork for the creation of the Northwest Ordinance in 1787. See Thomas Jefferson, "Report of the Committee, 1 March 1784," Founders Online, National Archives, accessed February 25, 2017, https://founders.archives.gov/documents/Jefferson/01-06-02-0420-0004. Of course, Jefferson also bought the Louisiana Territory from Napoleon in 1803. According to Keith Harper, "The Northwest Ordinance added approximately 260,000 square miles to America's land holdings while the Louisiana Purchase added 828,000 square miles to the nation's land holdings." See Harper, "Thomas Jefferson," 2n4.

26. Jedidiah Morse, *The American Geography, or, A view of the Present Situation of the United States of America Containing Astronomical Geography, Geographical Definitions, Discovery and General Description . . . to which Is Added a Concise Abridgment of the Geography of the British, Spanish, French and Dutch Dominions in America and the West Indies, of Europe, Asia and Africa* (Elizabeth Town: Printed by Shepard Kollock, for the author, 1789), 469.

27. Perry Miller, "Errand into the Wilderness," 1–15.

28. Margaret Lamberts Bendroth, *A School of the Church: Andover Newton Across Two Centuries* (Grand Rapids, MI: W. B. Eerdmans, 2008), 43–44.

For more on how the dramatic growth of religious works impacted antebellum America, see Candy Gunther Brown, *The Word in the World: Evangelical Writing, Publishing, and Reading in America, 1789–1880* (Chapel Hill: Univ. of North Carolina Press, 2004).

29. Bendroth, *School of the Church*, 2–7.
30. Bendroth, *School of the Church*, 16, 19; Holifield, *God's Ambassadors*, 116–17. Andover also started off on fortuitous financial footing. The wealthy Phillips family of Andover gave the school enough money to build two buildings that would house dormitories, a library, a public lecture hall, and a kitchen. Samuel Abbot, a businessman disaffected with the liberal theological drift of Harvard, gave $20,000 dollars to endow a chair of theology at Andover instead of Harvard. Newburyport merchants Moses Brown and William Bartlet, along with John Norris of Salem, gave a combined total of $40,000 as well. All of these donors were laity. See *The Constitution and Associate Statutes of the Theological Seminary in Andover* (Andover, MA: Printed by Flagg and Gould, 1817), 4–5, 26–27.
31. *Constitution and Associate Statutes*, 8–9. To further ensure the orthodoxy of the professors and the seminary itself, it had board of trustee members like Calvinist stalwart Jedidiah Morse. He served as trustee from Andover's beginning to his death in 1826. See Leonard Woods, *History of the Andover Theological Seminary* (Boston: James R. Osgood and Company, 1885), 231. Yale president and seminary supporter Timothy Dwight also preached a sermon on the first day of class, September 28, 1808. See Bendroth, *School of the Church*, 18.
32. *Constitution and Associate Statutes*, 5.
33. Bendroth, *School of the Church*, 32–33.
34. *Constitution and Associate Statutes*, 5–8, 12, quote on 5.
35. Bendroth, *School of the Church*, 18–19. E. Brooks Holifield adds that "by 1850, eight denominations had formed forty-four seminaries" total. See Holifield, *God's Ambassadors*, 116.
36. Bendroth, *School of the Church*, 6–7.
37. McLoughlin, *New England Dissent*, 2:707.
38. Warren Baptist Association, *Constitution of the Education Society of the Warren Baptist Association: And Circular Letter to the Ministers and Churches on the Importance of Education to Ministers of the Gospel* (Boston: Printed by James Loring, 1817), 3–4, 7–8.
39. Warren Baptist Association, *Minutes of the Warren Association, Held at the Baptist Meeting-House in Bridgewater, September 8 and 9, 1818* (Boston: Printed by James Loring, no. 2, Cornhill), 8–9.

40. Jonathan Going, "Outline of a Plan for Establishing a Baptist Literary and Theological Institution in a Central Situation in New-England. By a Friend to an Able Ministry," 1819, *Andover Newton Quarterly* 16 (January 1976): 187.
41. Despite Baptists and Congregationalists slowly uniting under the same types of causes in the first few decades of the 1800s, the subject and mode of baptism remained a point of contention. Second Baptist Church of Boston minister Thomas Baldwin and Samuel Worcester (1770–1821), Congregationalist minister of Salem Tabernacle Church, were both leaders in their respective denominations, especially in the areas of education and missions work. Despite their labors, however, they still found time to argue about baptism. See their following literary exchanges: Thomas Baldwin, *The Baptism of Believers Only and the Particular Communion of the Baptist Churches, Explained and Vindicated* (Boston: Printed and sold by Manning & Loring, 1806); Samuel Worcester, *Serious and Candid Letters to the Rev. Thomas Baldwin, D.D. On His Book, Entitled "The Baptism of Believers Only, and the Particular Communion of the Baptist Churches, Explained and Vindicated"* (Salem, MA: Printed by Haven Pool, for the author, 1807); Samuel Worcester, *Two Discourses on the Perpetuity and Provision of God's Gracious Covenant with Abraham and His Seed* (Salem, MA: Printed by Haven Pool, for the author, 1807); and Thomas Baldwin, *A Series of Letters. In which the Distinguishing Sentiments of the Baptists are Explained and Vindicated: in Answer to a Late Publication, by the Rev. Samuel Worcester, A.M. Addressed to the Author, Entitled "Serious and Candid Letters"* (Boston: Printed and sold by Manning and Loring, no. 2, Cornhill., 1810).
42. Going, "Outline of a Plan," 181.
43. Going, "Outline of a Plan," 181–82, quote on 181.
44. "Circular Respecting the Newton Theological Institution," *American Baptist Magazine* (July 1826): 219.
45. Bendroth, *School of the Church*, 30–31, quote on 31.
46. Bendroth, *School of the Church*, 32–34. Biblical theology's starting point is the scriptures themselves. For example, biblical theologians ask questions like, "What is the theology of the book of James?" Systematic theology starts with major topics like God, salvation, the Church, etc., and analyzes pertinent passages on those subjects.
47. Daniel G. Reid et al., eds., *Dictionary of Christianity in America* (Downer's Grove, IL: InterVarsity Press, 1990), s.v. "Beecher, Lyman," 123–24.
48. Lyman Beecher, *The Practicability of Suppressing Vice, By Means of*

Societies Instituted for That Purpose. A Sermon, Delivered before the Moral Society, in East-Hampton, (Long-Island.) September 21, 1803 (New London, CT: Printed by Samuel Green, 1804), 18.
49. Lyman Beecher, *A Reformation of Morals Practicable and Indispensable. A Sermon Delivered at New-Haven on the Evening of October 27, 1812*, 2nd ed. (Andover, MA: Flagg and Gould, 1814), 19–23.
50. Beecher, *A Reformation of Morals*, 18.
51. Beecher, *A Reformation of Morals*.
52. Beecher, *A Reformation of Morals*, 28–29.
53. McLoughlin, *New England Dissent*, 2:1029–33.
54. Nathan E. Wood, *The History of the First Baptist Church of Boston (1665–1899)* (Philadelphia: American Baptist Publication Society, 1899), 328. On January 31, 1830, Beecher's church building in Boston, the Hanover Street Congregational Meetinghouse, burned to the ground. The First Baptist Church of Boston offered its building for Beecher's congregation to use on Fridays. See Wood, 327.
55. "Sabbath School Meeting," *Christian Watchman* 10 (March 13, 1829): 42.
56. Brian Stanley, *The History of the Baptist Missionary Society, 1792–1992* (Edinburgh: T & T Clark, 1992), 5, 14, quote on 5.
57. Stanley, *History of the Baptist Missionary Society*, 1–23.
58. [London Missionary Society], *Introduction to Sermons, Preached in London, at the Formation of the Missionary Society, September 22, 23, 24, 1795: to which are Prefixed, Memorials Respecting the Establishment and First Attempts of that Society. By Order of the Directors. Published for the Benefit of the Society* (London: printed and sold by T. Chapman, Fleet-Street, 1795), iii–xi, xiv–xix. For the effect that the BMS and William Carey's Enquiry had on the creation of the London Missionary Society, see v and xvii specifically.
59. Walter B. Shurden, "Associationalism among Baptists in America, 1707–1814" (PhD diss., New Orleans Baptist Theological Seminary, 1967), 176–77.
60. Shurden, "Associationalism among Baptists in America," 177. For a few examples, see Warren Baptist Association, *Minutes of the Warren Association, Held at the Second Baptist Meeting-House in Newport, September 9 and 10, 1806* (Boston: Manning & Loring, No.2, Cornhill), 8, 11–12; *Minutes of the Warren Association, Held at the Baptist Meeting-House in Newton, September 13 and 14, 1808* (Boston: Manning & Loring, No.2, Cornhill), 13–16; *Minutes of the Warren Association, held at the Baptist Meeting-house in Haverhill, Sept. 12th and 13th, 1809* (Boston: Manning & Loring, No.2, Cornhill), 13–14.

61. Sassi, *Republic of Righteousness*, 136–37; See also Amy DeRogatis, *Moral Geography: Maps, Missionaries, and the American Frontier* (New York: Columbia Univ. Press, 2003).
62. Grafton, in addition to serving as one of the founding trustees of the Massachusetts Baptist Missionary Society, was the society's president from 1807–1825. See W. H. Eaton, *Historical Sketch of the Massachusetts Baptist Missionary Society and Convention, 1802–1902: With an Appendix and Other Related Matters* (Boston: Massachusetts Baptist Convention, 1903), 12, 235. Grafton was also Newton Theological Institution's first president of the board of trustees in 1826. See "Circular Respecting the Newton Theological Institution," 219.
63. Eaton, *Historical Sketch*, 7, 11–12.
64. Eaton, *Historical Sketch*, 8–9.
65. "Constitution of the Massachusetts Baptist Missionary Society," 1802, in Eaton, *Historical Sketch*, 9.
66. Eaton, *Historical Sketch*, 14–15.
67. Den Hartog, *Patriotism & Piety*, 7.
68. Their names were Samuel Mills, Harvey Loomis, James Richards, Francis Robbins, and Byram Green. See Bendroth, *School of the Church*, 50.
69. Bendroth, *School of the Church*, 50–51.
70. American Board of Commissioners for Foreign Missions, *First Ten Annual Reports of the American Board of Commissioners for Foreign Missions, With Other Documents of the Board* (Boston: Crocker and Brewster, 1834), 9–10, quote on 10.
71. American Board of Commissioners for Foreign Missions, *First Ten Annual Reports*, 11, 15.
72. Bendroth, *School of the Church*, 52.
73. James Langdon Hill, *The Immortal Seven: Judson and His Associates, Dr. and Mrs. Adoniram Judson, Samuel Newell, Harriet Newell, Gordon Hall, Samuel Nott, Luther Rice* (Philadelphia: American Baptist Publication Society, 1913). See also Joan Jacobs Brumberg, *Mission for Life: The Story of the Family of Adoniram Judson, the Dramatic Events of the First American Foreign Mission, and the Course of Evangelical Religion in the Nineteenth Century* (New York: Free Press, 1980). Standard histories of American Baptist and American Protestant missions have overlooked the first actual American missionary, George Liele (1750–1820). George Liele, sometimes known as George Sharp, was responsible for founding the First African Baptist Church in Savannah, Georgia, in the 1770s. He then became a missionary to Jamaica in 1782. His foreign missions work

predates both William Carey (1792) and Adoniram Judson (1812). Fortunately, scholars are beginning to focus on the life and work of Liele. For a prominent example, see David T. Shannon, Julia Frazier White, and Deborah Bingham Van Broekhoven, eds., *George Liele's Life and Legacy: An Unsung Hero* (Macon, GA: Mercer Univ. Press, 2012).

74. McBeth, *Baptist Heritage*, 344–45.
75. McBeth, *Baptist Heritage*, 345–46, 350–51, 354–56, quote on 346. Columbian College started in 1821, and Baptists relied on pledges to fund the fledgling college. However, not everyone paid their pledge money. Since the college was in a desperate financial state, the Triennial Convention gave up on the college in 1826. See McBeth, *Baptist Heritage*, 356. The college eventually became George Washington University.

    Of course, the biggest reason for the split between northern and southern Baptists was differences over slavery. See C. C. Goen, *Broken Churches, Broken Nation: Denominational Schisms and the Coming of the American Civil War* (Macon, GA: Mercer Univ. Press, 1985).

76. True to his principles, Leland turned down the MBMS appointing him as a missionary to the "Western Mission." See Eaton, *Historical Sketch*, 13–14. The MBMS probably tried to appoint him because of his fame among Baptists, and he already lived in Cheshire, near the western frontier.
77. John Leland, "Missionary Societies," in *Writings*, 471.
78. John Leland, "Extracts From a Letter to a Friend," in *Writings*, 530. The date of the letter is on page 532.
79. Leland's own association of which he was a part from 1792 to 1808, the Shaftsbury Baptist Association, had a more "biblical" model for conducting missions. Since 1802, the association, which encompassed western Massachusetts and parts of New York and Vermont, chose some of its own ministers to be missionaries to white settlers in frontier areas in western New York, Vermont, Upper Canada, and Lower Canada. They also sent missionaries to the Tuscarora Indians. See Stephen Wright, *History of the Shaftsbury Baptist Association, 1781–1853: With Some Account of the Association Formed from It, and a Tabular View of Their Annual Meeting: to Which Is Added an Appendix, Embracing Sketches of the Most Recent Churches in the Body, with Biographic Sketches of Some of the Older Ministers, and the Statistics of Most of the Churches Ever in the Association and Their Direct Branches to the Present Time* (Troy, NY: A. G. Johnson, 1853), 369–70. One of the missionaries that went to minister to the Tuscarora Indians, Lemuel Covell, was a co-pastor with Leland at the Second Baptist Church of Cheshire. See Wright, *History of*

the *Shaftsbury Baptist Association*, 369, 396. Covell died while ministering in Canada, and Leland praised him in a funerary poem. See John Leland, "Lines Introduced at the Conclusion of a Discourse Preached on the Occasion of the Death of Rev. Samuel Covell, 1806" in *Writings*, 315–17. "Samuel" is a misprint of Lemuel. Moreover, Sammie Pedlow Strange highlights how "Leland attended the Shaftsbury Association meeting in 1802, 1803, 1804, 1807, 1808 when it voted unanimously to support ministers who served as preaching missionaries in the West." See Strange, "Baptists and Religious Liberty," 279n97. Thus, Leland was a supporter of missions but not missionary societies. His long-term career as an itinerant minister showed his passion for evangelism as well.
80. John Leland, "Missionary Societies," in *Writings*, 472.
81. John Leland, "Extract of a Letter from J. L. To His Inquisitive Friend," in *Writings*, 497.
82. John Leland, "Missionary Societies," in *Writings*, 472.
83. John Leland, "Extracts from a Letter to Rev. John Taylor of Kentucky, Dated Dec. 10, 1830," in *Writings*, 601–2, emphases original. For just some of many examples of Leland's criticisms of Sabbatarianism, Sabbath societies, and vice societies, see his "On Sabbatical Laws," 440–46; "Catechism," 450–53; "Extracts from a Letter to a Friend," 530–31; "Extract of a Letter to Col. R. M. Johnson, Dated January 8, 1830," 561–63; "Transportation of the Mail," 564–66; and "Extracts from a Letter to Hon. R. M. Johnson, March 29, 1830," 567–69, all in *Writings*.
84. Keith Harper, "Downwind from the New England Rat: John Taylor, Organized Missions, and the Regionalization of Religious Identity on the American Frontier," *Ohio Valley History* 9, no. 3 (Fall 2009): 25–26. John Taylor's *Thoughts on Missions* was written in 1819 and published in 1820.
85. Harper, "Downwind from the New England Rat," 34–35, 38.
86. Harper, "Downwind from the New England Rat," 35.
87. John Leland, "Short Sayings on Times, Men, Measures and Religion, Exhibited in an Address, Delivered at Cheshire, July 5, 1830," in *Writings*, 580–81.
88. Harper, "Downwind from the New England Rat," 36–37.

CONCLUSION

1. 31 percent of Christians "definitely" agree, and 40 percent of Christians "somewhat" agree that a pastor is a trustworthy source of wisdom. See "Pastors' Credibility Is in Question—Even Among Pastors," Barna

Group, February 16, 2022, https://www.barna.com/research/pastors-trustworthy-reliable/.

APPENDIX

1. William Silverman, "The Exclusion of Clergy from Political Office in American States: An Oddity in Church-State Relations," *Sociology of Religion* 61, no. 2 (Summer 2000): 224.
2. Frederic S. Le Clercq, "Disqualification of Clergy for Civil Office," *Memphis State University Law Review* 7, no. 4 (Summer 1977): 557.
3. Le Clercq, "Disqualification of Clergy for Civil Office," 574.
4. Le Clercq, "Disqualification of Clergy for Civil Office," 568.
5. John Locke, "A Letter Concerning Toleration," in *The Works of John Locke in Nine Volumes*, vol. 5, 12th ed. (London: Rivington, 1824), 13, accessed Jun 2, 2021, https://oll.libertyfund.org/title/locke-the-works-vol-5-four-letters-concerning-toleration#Locke_0128-05_25.
6. Locke, "A Letter Concerning Toleration," 21.
7. The scripture cited is Acts 6:2. John Locke, "A Third Letter for Toleration," in *The Works of John Locke in Nine Volumes*, vol. 5, 12th ed. (London: Rivington, 1824), 179, accessed Jun 2, 2021, https://oll.libertyfund.org/title/locke-the-works-vol-5-four-letters-concerning-toleration#Locke_0128-05_25.
8. See Le Clercq, "Disqualification of Clergy for Civil Office." Those states were New York (572n98), South Carolina (572n99), Tennessee (573n101), and Mississippi (573n103).
9. John R. Vile, "John Witherspoon" (2009), in *The First Amendment Encyclopedia*, ed. John R. Vile, David L. Hudson Jr., and David Schultz, accessed May 19, 2021, https://mtsu.edu/first-amendment/article/1233/john-witherspoon.
10. Jeffry H. Morrison, *John Witherspoon and the Founding of the American Republic: Catholicism in American Culture* (Notre Dame, IN: Univ. of Notre Dame Press, 2003), 20. A Geneva collar or band consists of two white pieces of cloths that descend from the main collar. It was the characteristic garb of Reformed Protestant ministers. The center of Reformed Protestantism in the sixteenth century was Geneva, in what is now Switzerland.
11. John Witherspoon, "On the Georgia Constitution," in *The Works of John Witherspoon, D.D.*, vol. 9 (Edinburgh, UK: J. Ogle, Parliament-Square, 1815), 220.

12. Witherspoon, "On the Georgia Constitution," 221.
13. Witherspoon, "On the Georgia Constitution," 221–22.
14. In response to reading a copy of Thomas Jefferson's "Draft of a Constitution for Virginia" from 1783 at the request of John Brown, a friend who wanted his perspective on how Jefferson's draft could be implemented in Kentucky, which was planning to become a state, James Madison wrote down some observations and criticisms about Jefferson's draft. See Editorial Note, "Observations on Jefferson's Draft of a Constitution for Virginia, [ca. 15 October] 1788," Founders Online, National Archives, accessed June 6, 2021, https://founders.archives.gov/documents/Madison/01-11-02-0216.

    In his draft, Jefferson declared that "Ministers of the Gospel" could not serve in Virginia's General Assembly. He did not state his reasons why. See Thomas Jefferson, "Jefferson's Draft of a Constitution for Virginia, [May–June 1783]," Founders Online, National Archives, accessed June 6, 2021, https://founders.archives.gov/documents/Jefferson/01-06-02-0255-0004. Like Witherspoon did with the Georgia legislature, Madison took issue with Jefferson excluding clergy from the right to run for office: "Does not the exclusion of Ministers of the Gospel as such violate a fundamental principle of liberty by punishing a religious profession with the privation of a civil right? Does it not violate another article of the plan itself which exempts religion from the cognizance of Civil power? Does it not violate justice by at once taking away a right and prohibiting a compensation for it. And does it not in fine violate impartiality by shutting the door agst the Ministers of one religion and leaving it open for those of every other." See James Madison, "Observations on Jefferson's Draft of a Constitution for Virginia, [ca. 15 October] 1788," Founders Online, National Archives, accessed June 6, 2021, https://founders.archives.gov/documents/Madison/01-11-02-0216. Jefferson changed his mind on the issue by 1800. See Le Clercq, "Disqualification of Clergy for Civil Office," 578–79.
15. John Leland, "The Virginia Chronicle," in *Writings*, 122.
16. John Leland, "The Rights of Conscience Inalienable," in *Writings*, 188.

SELECTED BIBLIOGRAPHY

ABBREVIATIONS

ANTS   Trask Library, Andover Newton Theological School, Newton Centre, MA
CLA   Congregational Library and Archives, Boston, MA
Writings   John Leland, *The Writings of John Leland*. Edited by L. F. Greene. New York: Arno Press, 1969.

PRIMARY SOURCES

Sermons, Essays, Speeches, Letters, Books, etc.:

A Report of the Record Commissioners of the City of Boston, Containing the Boston Town Records, 1770 through 1777. Boston: Rockwell and Churchill, 1887.

Allen, Thomas. *A Sermon, Preached before His Excellency, James Sullivan, Esq., Governor; His Honor, Levi Lincoln, Esq., Lieutenant-Governor; the Honourable Council, and Both Branches of the Legislature of the Commonwealth of Massachusetts: On the Day of General Election, May 25th, 1808*. Boston: Printed by Adams and Rhoades, printers to the state, 1808.

American Board of Commissioners for Foreign Missions. *First Ten Annual Reports of the American Board of Commissioners for Foreign Missions, With Other Documents of the Board*. Boston: Crocker and Brewster, 1834.

Backus, Elizabeth. Elizabeth Backus to Isaac Backus, November 4, 1752. In *A History of New England with Particular Reference to the Denomination of Christians Called Baptists*, Vol. 2, by Isaac Backus. Newton, MA: Backus Historical Society, 1871.

Backus, Isaac. *An Appeal to the People of the Massachusetts State against Arbitrary Power*. Boston: Printed and sold by Benjamin Edes and Sons, in State-Street; sold also by Philip Freeman, in Union-Street, 1780.

———. *An Appeal to the Public for Religious Liberty against the Oppressions of the Present Day*. Boston: Printed by John Boyle, 1773.

———. "The Confession of Faith and Church-Covenant, of the Church of Christ in the Joining Borders of Bridgwater and Middleborough." In *The Diary of Isaac Backus*, Vol. 3, edited by William G. McLoughlin, 1529–32. Providence, RI: Brown Univ. Press, 1979.

———. *A Discourse, Concerning the Materials, the Manner of Building, and Power of Organizing of the Church of Christ; with the True Difference and Exact Limits between Civil and Ecclesiastical Government; and Also What Are, and What Are Not Just Reasons for Separation.: Together with, an Address to Joseph Fish, A.M. Pastor of a Church in Stonington, Occasioned by his Late Piece Called The Examiner Examined.* Boston: Printed by John Boyles, in Marlborough-Street, 1773.

———. *A Fish Caught in His Own Net* (1768). In *Isaac Backus on Church, State, and Calvinism; Pamphlets, 1754–1789*, edited by William G. McLoughlin, 167–288. Cambridge, MA: Belknap Press of Harvard University Press, 1968.

———. *Government and Liberty Described and Ecclesiastical Tyranny Exposed.* Boston: Printed by Powars and Willis, and sold by Philip Freeman, in Union-Street, 1778.

———. *A History of New England with Particular Reference to the Denomination of Christians Called Baptists.* 2 Vols. Newton, MA: Backus Historical Society, 1871.

———. "Issac Backus His Writeing [sic] Containing Some Particular Account of My Conversion." In *The Diary of Isaac Backus*, Vol. 3, edited by William G. McLoughlin, 1523–26. Providence, RI: Brown University Press, 1979.

[———]. *A Letter to a Gentleman in the Massachusetts General Assembly, Concerning Taxes to Support Religious Worship.* Boston: n.p., 1771.

———. *Policy, as Well as Honesty, Forbids the Use of Secular Force in Religious Affairs.* Boston: Printed by Draper and Folsom, and sold by Phillip Freeman, in Union-Street, 1779.

[Backus, Isaac, James Manning, and Robert Strettle Jones]. "Memorial." In Alvah Hovey, *A Memoir of the Life and Times of the Rev. Isaac Backus, A.M.* 204–10. Boston: Gould and Lincoln, 1858.

Baldwin, Thomas. *A Series of Letters. In which the Distinguishing Sentiments of the Baptists are Explained and Vindicated: in Answer to a Late Publication, by the Rev. Samuel Worcester, A.M. Addressed to the Author, Entitled "Serious and Candid Letters."* Boston: Printed and sold by Manning and Loring, no. 2, Cornhill., 1810.

———. *The Baptism of Believers Only and the Particular Communion of the Baptist Churches, Explained and Vindicated.* Boston: Printed and sold by Manning & Loring, 1806.

Beecher, Lyman. *A Reformation of Morals Practicable and Indispensable. A Sermon Delivered at New-Haven on the Evening of October 27, 1812,* 2nd ed. Andover, MA: Flagg and Gould, 1814.

———. *The Practicability of Suppressing Vice, By Means of Societies Instituted for That Purpose. A Sermon, Delivered before the Moral Society, in East-Hampton, (Long-Island.) September 21, 1803.* New London, CT: Printed by Samuel Green, 1804.

Benedict, David. *A General History of the Baptist Denomination in America, And Other Parts of the World.* Boston: Printed by Lincoln & Edmands, no. 53, Cornhill, for the author, 1813.

Bentley, William. *Diary of William Bentley, D.D., Pastor of the East Church, Salem, Massachusetts.* Edited by Joseph G. Waters and Marguerite Dalrymple. 4 Vols. Salem: Essex Institute, 1905.

Boston, Massachusetts. *The Votes and Proceedings of the Freeholders and Other Inhabitants of the Town of Boston in Town Meeting Assembled, According to Law.* [*Published by Order of the Town*]. Boston: Edes and Gill and T. and J. Fleet, 1772.

"Circular Respecting the Newton Theological Institution," *American Baptist Magazine* (July 1826): 217–19.

Commonwealth of Massachusetts. "An Act Respecting Public Worship and Religious Freedom." Boston: Secretary of the Commonwealth, 1811.

The Constitution and Associate Statutes of the Theological Seminary in Andover. Andover, MA: Printed by Flagg and Gould, 1817.

"Constitution of the Massachusetts Baptist Missionary Society." 1802. In *Historical Sketch of the Massachusetts Baptist Missionary Society and Convention, 1802–1902: With an Appendix and Other Related Matters,* by W. H. Eaton, 9–11. Boston: Massachusetts Baptist Convention, 1903.

Cutler, Manasseh. Manasseh Cutler to Dr. Joseph Torrey, January 4, 1802. In *Life, Journals and Correspondence of Rev Manasseh Cutler, LL D,* Vol. 2, edited by William Parker Cutler and Julia Perkins Cutler. Cincinnati, OH: Robert Clarke and Co., 1888.

Fish, Joseph. *The Church of Christ a Firm and Durable House: Shown in a Number of Sermons on Matth. XVI. 18. Upon this Rock I Will Build My Church, and the Gates of Hell Shall Not Prevail against It.: The Substance of which was Delivered at Stonington, Anno Domini, 1765.* New London, [CT]: Printed and Sold by Timothy Green, 1767.

———. *The Examiner Examined: Remarks on a Piece Wrote by Mr. Isaac Backus, of Middleborough; Printed in 1768. (Called, "An Examination of Nine Sermons from Matth. 16. 18. Published Last Year, by Mr. Joseph Fish, of Stonington.") Wherein those Sermons are Vindicated, from the Exceptions Taken against Them by Mr. Backus—Many of his Errors Confuted, and his Mistakes Corrected.* New-London, [CT]: Printed and sold by Timothy Green, 1771.

[Freeman, Philip]. "On Monday . . . will be offered . . . a Valuable Collection of Books . . ." Broadside. Boston, September 30, 1766.

Frothingham, Ebenezer. *A Key, to Unlock the Door, that Leads in, to Take a Fair View of the Religious Constitution, Established by Law, in the Colony of Connecticut.: With a Short Remark upon Mr. Bartlet's Sermon, on Galatians [sic] iii. 1.: Also, a Remark upon Mr. Ross, against the Separates and Others.: With a Short Observation upon the Explanation of Say-Brook-plan; and Mr. Hobart's Attempt to Establish the Same Plan.* [New Haven]: Printed [by Benjamin Mecom], in the year, 1767.

Going, Jonathan. "Outline of a Plan for Establishing a Baptist Literary and Theological Institution in a Central Situation in New-England. By a Friend to an Able Ministry." 1819. In *Andover Newton Quarterly* 16 (January 1976): 173–87.

Gordon, James, Jr. James Gordon Jr. to James Madison, February 17, 1788. In *The Papers of James Madison, Vol. 10, 27 May 1787–3 March 1788*, edited by Robert A. Rutland, Charles F. Hobson, William M. E. Rachal, and Frederika J. Teute, 515–16. Chicago: University of Chicago Press, 1977.

Griffith, Benjamin. "On the Power and Duty of an Association of Churches." In *Minutes of the Philadelphia Baptist Association, 1707–1807*, edited by A. D. Gillette, 60–63. Philadelphia: American Baptist Publication Society, 1851.

Helwys, Thomas. *A Shorte Declaration of the Mistery of Iniquity.* [Amsterdam?]: n.p., 1612.

Jefferson, Thomas. *Notes on the State of Virginia.* In *The Portable Thomas Jefferson*, edited by Merrill D. Peterson, 23–232. New York: Penguin Books, 1977.

———. Thomas Jefferson to Elbridge Gerry, January 26, 1799. Quoted in *Jeffersonian Republicans: The Formation of Party Organization, 1789–1801*, by Noble E. Cunningham, 211–12. Chapel Hill: Published for the Institute of Early American History and Culture at Williamsburg by the University of North Carolina Press, 1957.

———. Thomas Jefferson to James Madison, Paris, December 20, 1787. In *The Portable Thomas Jefferson*, edited by Merrill D. Peterson, 428–33. New York: Penguin Books, 1977.

Leland, John. "A Biographical Sketch of the Life and Character of the Rev. Peter Werden." In *Writings*, 319–21.

———. "Address Delivered at Dalton, Massachusetts, January 8, 1831." In *Writings*, 603–7.

———. "Address of the Committee of the United Baptist Churches of Virginia, assembled in the city of Richmond, 8th August, 1789, to the President of the United States of America." In *Writings*, 52–54.

———. "An Oration Delivered at Cheshire, July 5, 1802." In *Writings*, 257–70.

———. "Catechism." In *Writings*, 450–53.

———. "Circular Letter of the Shaftsbury Association, 1793." In *Writings*, 196–99.

———. "Events in the Life of John Leland: Written by Himself." In *Writings*, 9–40.

———. "Extracts from a Letter to a Friend." In *Writings*, 530–32.

———. "Extracts from a Letter to Hon. R. M. Johnson, March 29, 1830." In *Writings*, 567–69.

———. "Extracts from a Letter to Rev. John Taylor of Kentucky, Dated Dec. 10, 1830." In *Writings*, 600–602.

———. "Extract of a Letter from J. L. To His Inquisitive Friend." In *Writings*, 496–97.

———. "Extract of a Letter to Col. R.M. Johnson, Dated January 8, 1830." In *Writings*, 561–63.

———. "Lines Introduced at the Conclusion of a Discourse Preached on the Occasion of the Death of Rev. Samuel Covell, 1806." In *Writings*, 315–17.

———. "Missionary Societies." In *Writings*, 471–72.

———. "On Sabbatical Laws." In *Writings*, 440–46.

———. "The Rights of Conscience Inalienable, and, Therefore, Religious Opinions Not Cognizable by Law: or, the High-Flying Churchman, Stripped of His Legal Robe, Appears a Yaho." In *Writings*, 177–92.

———. "Short Sayings on Times, Men, Measures and Religion, Exhibited in an Address, Delivered at Cheshire, July 5, 1830." In *Writings*, 572–82.

———. "Speech Delivered in the House of Representatives of Massachusetts, on the Subject of Religious Freedom, 1811." In *Writings*, 353–58.

———. "Transportation of the Mail." In *Writings*, 564–66.

———. "The Virginia Chronicle." In *Writings*, 92–124.

———. "The Yankee Spy." In *Writings*, 213–29.

[London Missionary Society], introduction to *Sermons, Preached in London, at the Formation of the Missionary Society, September 22, 23, 24, 1795: to which are Prefixed, Memorials Respecting the Establishment and First Attempts of that Society. By Order of the Directors. Published for the Benefit of the Society*. London: printed and sold by T. Chapman, Fleet-Street, 1795.

Madison, James, Sr. James Madison Sr. to James Madison, January 30, 1788. In *The Papers of James Madison*, Vol. 10, *27 May 1787–3 March 1788*, edited by Robert A. Rutland, Charles F. Hobson, William M. E. Rachal, and Frederika J. Teute, 446–48. Chicago: University of Chicago Press, 1977.

Manning, James. "Circular Letter of the Warren Association" (1770). Quoted in Reuben Aldridge Guild, *Life, Times, and Correspondence of James Manning, and the Early History of Brown University*. Boston: Gould and Lincoln, 1864.

[———]. *The Sentiments and Plan of the Warren Association*. Germantown [Pa.]: Printed by Christopher Sower, 1769.

Morse, Jedidiah. *The American Geography, or, A view of the Present Situation of the United States of America Containing Astronomical Geography, Geographical Definitions, Discovery and General Description . . . to which Is Added a Concise Abridgment of the Geography of the British, Spanish, French and Dutch Dominions in America and the West Indies, of Europe, Asia and Africa*. Elizabeth Town: Printed by Shepard Kollock, for the author, 1789.

———. *A Sermon, Delivered at the New North Church in Boston, in the Morning, and in the Afternoon at Charlestown, May 9th, 1798,: Being the Day Recommended by John Adams, President of the United States of America, for Solemn Humiliation, Fasting and Prayer*. Boston: Printed by Samuel Hall, no. 53, Cornhill, 1798.

"Sabbath School Meeting," *Christian Watchman* 10 (March 13, 1829): 42.

Spencer, Joseph. Joseph Spencer to James Madison, February 28, 1788. In *The Papers of James Madison*, Vol. 10, *27 May 1787–3 March 1788*, edited by Robert A. Rutland, Charles F. Hobson, William M. E. Rachal, and Frederika J. Teute, 540–42. Chicago: University of Chicago Press, 1977.

Stiles, Ezra. *The Literary Diary of Ezra Stiles*, edited by F. B. Dexter. Vol. 1. New York: C. Scribner's Sons, 1901.

Stillman, Samuel. *A Good Minister of Jesus Christ: A Sermon, Preached in Boston, September 15, 1797. At the Ordination of the Rev. Mr. Stephen Smith Nelson*. Boston: Manning and Loring, 1797.

———. *Good News from a Far Country. A Sermon Preached at Boston, May 17, 1766. Upon the Arrival of the Important News of the Repeal of the Stamp-Act.* Boston: Printed by Kneeland and Adams, in Milk-Street, for Philip Freeman, in Union-Street., 1766.

Tennent, Gilbert. *The Danger of an Unconverted Ministry, Considered in a Sermon on Mark VI. 34.* Boston: Rogers and Fowle, 1742.

Thomas, Isaiah. *The History of Printing in America: With a Biography of Printers, and an Account of Newspapers: to Which Is Prefixed a Concise View of the Discovery and Progress of the Art in Other Parts of the World: in Two Volumes.* Worcester: From the Press of Isaiah Thomas, 1810.

"Warren Baptist Association Grievance Committee to [Thomas Hutchinson] and Mass. Council and House of Representatives," September 13, 1770. In Backus Papers, ANTS.

Washington, George. "To the General Committee, representing the United Baptist Churches in Virginia," [May 1789], in *Writings*, 54–55.

Wayland, Francis. *Notes on the Principles and Practices of Baptist Churches.* New York: Sheldon, Blakeman & Co, 1857.

Winthrop, John. Excerpt from "A Modell of Christian Charity." In *The American Intellectual Tradition*, Vol. 1, *1630–1685*, 6th ed., edited by David A. Hollinger and Charles Capper, 7–15. New York: Oxford University Press, 2011.

Witherspoon, John. "On the Georgia Constitution." In *The Works of John Witherspoon, D.D.*, Vol. 9. Edinburgh, UK: J. Ogle, Parliament-Square, 1815.

Woods, Leonard. *History of the Andover Theological Seminary.* Boston: James R. Osgood and Company, 1885.

Worcester, Samuel. *Serious and Candid Letters to the Rev. Thomas Baldwin, D.D. On His Book, Entitled "The Baptism of Believers Only, and the Particular Communion of the Baptist Churches, Explained and Vindicated."* Salem, MA: Printed by Haven Pool, for the author, 1807.

———. *Two Discourses on the Perpetuity and Provision of God's Gracious Covenant with Abraham and His Seed.* Salem, MA: Printed by Haven Pool, for the author, 1807.

Church Minute Books

First Baptist Church, Bellingham, MA. Records, 1737–1962. Book "A." ANTS.

First Baptist Church of Medfield, Medfield, MA. Church records, 1771–1914. ANTS.

First Baptist Church of Norton, Norton, MA. Church records, 1747–1835. ANTS.
First Baptist Church of Sturbridge (also called Fiskdale), Sturbridge, MA. Church records, 1747–1976. ANTS.
First Congregational Church, Georgetown, MA. Records, 1731–1866. CLA.
First Church Record Book, Hassanamisco, MA. 1731–1774. CLA.
Old South Church, Boston, MA. Records, 1669–2012. Reel 1. CLA.
Second Baptist Church in Cheshire, MA. Records, 1789–1884. Typed by Rollin Hillyer Cooke, 1903.
Separatist Congregational Church, Sturbridge, MA. Statements, 1745–1762, CLA.

Associational Minutes

Gillette, A. D., ed. *Minutes of the Philadelphia Baptist Association, 1707–1807.* Philadelphia: American Baptist Publication Society, 1851.
Minutes of the Shaftsbury Association, various years, 1786 to 1819, 1787 excepted. Early American Imprints: Series 1, Evans (1639–1800) and Series II, Shaw Shoemaker (1801–19). Online database.
Minutes of the Warren Association (1767). Quoted in Alvah Hovey, *Memoir of the Life and Times of the Rev. Isaac Backus, A.M.* Boston: Gould and Lincoln, 1858.
Minutes of the Warren Association (1769). Quoted in William G. McLoughlin, *New England Dissent, 1630–1833: The Baptists and the Separation of Church and State.* 2 vols. Cambridge, MA: Harvard University Press, 1971.
Minutes of the Warren Association, various years, 1771 to 1819. Early American Imprints: Series 1, Evans (1639–1800) and Series II, Shaw Shoemaker (1801–19). Online database.

Newspapers

America's Historical Newspapers, 1690–1922. Online database.
Boston Evening-Post, 1735–1775
Boston Gazette, and Country Journal, 1755–1793
Connecticut Journal (New Haven), 1775–1820
Connecticut Journal, and New-Haven Post-Boy, 1767–1775
Essex (MA) Gazette, 1768–1775
Massachusetts Gazette; And the Boston Post-Boy and Advertiser, 1769–1775

Massachusetts Gazette: and the Boston Weekly News-Letter, 1769–1776
Newport (RI) Mercury, 1759–1928
Pennsylvania Herald, and General Advertiser (Philadelphia), 1786–
Pittsfield (MA) Sun, 1800–1873
Providence (RI) Gazette; and Country Journal, 1762–1795

Web Sources

"An Act in Addition to the Act, Entitled 'An Act for the Punishment of Certain Crimes Against the United States.'" The Avalon Project: Documents in Law, History, and Diplomacy. Accessed October 26, 2021. http://avalon.law.yale.edu/18th_century/sedact.asp.

Adams, John. "Proclamation 8—Recommending a National Day of Humiliation, Fasting, and Prayer," March 23, 1798. Edited by Gerhard Peters and John T. Woolley, *The American Presidency Project*. Accessed October 26, 2021. http://www.presidency.ucsb.edu/ws/?pid=65661.

Barna Group. "Pastors' Credibility Is in Question—Even Among Pastors." February 16, 2022. https://www.barna.com/research/pastors-trustworthy-reliable/.

"The Charter of Massachusetts Bay-1691." The Avalon Project: Documents in Law, History, and Diplomacy. Accessed April 20, 2014. http://avalon.law.yale.edu/17th_century/mass07.asp#b9.

Committee of Cheshire, Massachusetts. "Committee of Cheshire, Massachusetts, [30 December 1801] to Thomas Jefferson." Founders Online. National Archives. Accessed January 13, 2017. https://founders.archives.gov/documents/Jefferson/01-36-02-0151-0002.

"Constitution of Massachusetts: 1780." National Humanities Institute. Accessed April 19, 2014. http://www.nhinet.org/ccs/docs/ma-1780.htm.

Constitutional Rights Foundation. "BRIA 19 4 b: The Alien and Sedition Acts: Defining American Freedom." Accessed October 26, 2021. https://www.crf-usa.org/bill-of-rights-in-action/bria-19-4-b-the-alien-and-sedition-acts-defining-american-freedom.html.

Danbury Baptist Association (CT). "To Thomas Jefferson from the Danbury Baptist Association, [after 7 October 1801]." Founders Online. National Archives. Accessed November 4, 2016. https://founders.archives.gov/documents/Jefferson/01-35-02-0331.

Editorial Note. "From George Washington to the United Baptist Churches of Virginia, May 1789." Founders Online. National Archives.

Accessed October 26, 2021. https://founders.archives.gov/documents/Washington/05-02-02-0309.

Editorial Note. "Observations on Jefferson's Draft of a Constitution for Virginia, [ca. 15 October] 1788." Founders Online. National Archives. Accessed June 6, 2021. https://founders.archives.gov/documents/Madison/01-11-02-0216.

Jefferson, Thomas. "Jefferson's Draft of a Constitution for Virginia, [May–June 1783]." Founders Online. National Archives. Accessed June 6, 2021. https://founders.archives.gov/documents/Jefferson/01-06-02-0255-0004.

———. "Report of the Committee, 1 March 1784." Founders Online. National Archives, Accessed February 25, 2017. https://founders.archives.gov/documents/Jefferson/01-06-02-0420-0004.

———. "To the Danbury Baptist Association, 1 January 1802," Founders Online. National Archives. Accessed March 14, 2017. https://founders.archives.gov/documents/Jefferson/01-36-02-0152-0006.

Locke, John. "A Letter Concerning Toleration." In *The Works of John Locke in Nine Volumes*, Vol. 5, 12th edition. London: Rivington, 1824. Accessed Jun 2, 2021. https://oll.libertyfund.org/title/locke-the-works-vol-5-four-letters-concerning-toleration#Locke_0128-05_25.

———. "A Third Letter for Toleration." In *The Works of John Locke in Nine Volumes*, Vol. 5, 12th edition. London: Rivington, 1824. Accessed June 2, 2021. https://oll.libertyfund.org/title/locke-the-works-vol-5-four-letters-concerning-toleration#Locke_0128-05_25.

Madison, James. "Observations on Jefferson's Draft of a Constitution for Virginia, [ca. 15 October] 1788." Founders Online. National Archives. Accessed June 6, 2021. https://founders.archives.gov/documents/Madison/01-11-02-0216.

Vile, John R. "John Witherspoon." In *The First Amendment Encyclopedia*, edited by John R. Vile, David L. Hudson Jr., and David Schultz. Originally published 2009. Accessed May 19, 2021. https://mtsu.edu/first-amendment/article/1233/john-witherspoon.

Watts, Duncan. "Whips." In *Dictionary of American Government and Politics*. Edinburgh, UK: Edinburgh University Press, 2010. https://lopes.idm.oclc.org/login?url=https://search.credoreference.com/content/entry/eupamgov/whips/0?institutionId=5865.

SECONDARY SOURCES

Books, Essays

Adams, Geoffrey. *Political Ecumenism: Catholics, Jews, and Protestants in De Gaulle's Free France, 1940–1945.* Montreal: McGill-Queen's University Press, 2006.

Ahlstrom, Sydney E. *A Religious History of the American People.* 2nd ed. New Haven, CT: Yale University Press, 2004.

Amory, Hugh. "The New England Book Trade, 1713–1790." In *The Colonial Book in the Atlantic World*, vol. 1 of *A History of the Book in America*, edited by Hugh Amory and David Hall, 314–46. Cambridge, UK: Cambridge University Press, 2000.

Anderson, Benedict R. O'G. *Imagined Communities: Reflections on the Origin and Spread of Nationalism.* Revised edition. London: Verso, 1991.

Bailyn, Bernard. *The Ideological Origins of the American Revolution.* Cambridge, MA: Belknap Press of Harvard University Press, 1967.

———. *Pamphlets of the American Revolution, 1750–1776.* Cambridge: MA: Belknap Press of Harvard University Press, 1965.

Banner, James M. *To the Hartford Convention: The Federalists and the Origins of Party Politics in Massachusetts, 1789–1815.* New York: Knopf, 1970.

Bendroth, Margaret Lamberts. *A School of the Church: Andover Newton Across Two Centuries.* Grand Rapids, MI: W. B. Eerdmans, 2008.

Birdsall, Richard D. *Berkshire County: A Cultural History.* New Haven, CT: Yale University Press, 1959.

Breen, T. H. *The Marketplace of Revolution: How Consumer Politics Shaped American Independence.* New York: Oxford University Press, 2004.

Brekus, Catherine A. *Strangers & Pilgrims: Female Preaching in America, 1740–1845.* Chapel Hill: University of North Carolina Press, 1998.

Bridenbaugh, Carl. *Mitre and Sceptre: Transatlantic Faiths, Ideas, Personalities, and Politics, 1689–1775.* New York: Oxford University Press, 1962.

Broadway, Mikael, "The Roots of Baptists in Community, and Therefore, Voluntary Membership not Individualism, or, the High-Flying Modernist, Stripped of his Ontological Assumptions, Appears to Hold the Ecclesiology of a Yaho." In *Recycling the Past or Researching History? Studies in Baptist Historiography and Myths*, vol. 11, edited by Philip E. Thompson and Anthony R. Cross, 67–83. Bletchley, Milton Keynes, UK: Paternoster, 2005.

Brooke, John L. *The Heart of the Commonwealth: Society and Political Culture in Worcester County, Massachusetts 1713–1861*. Cambridge, UK: Cambridge University Press, 1989.
Brown, Candy Gunther. *The Word in the World: Evangelical Writing, Publishing, and Reading in America, 1789–1880*. Chapel Hill: University of North Carolina Press, 2004.
Brown, Richard D. *Knowledge Is Power: The Diffusion of Information in Early America, 1700–1865*. New York: Oxford University Press, 1989.
———. *Revolutionary Politics in Massachusetts: The Boston Committee of Correspondence and the Towns, 1772–1774*. Cambridge, MA: Harvard University Press, 1970.
Brumberg, Joan Jacobs. *Mission for Life: The Story of the Family of Adoniram Judson, the Dramatic Events of the First American Foreign Mission, and the Course of Evangelical Religion in the Nineteenth Century*. New York: Free Press, 1980.
Buel, Joy Day, and Richard Buel Jr. *The Way of Duty: A Woman and Her Family in Revolutionary America*. New York: Norton, 1995.
Butler, Jon. *Awash in a Sea of Faith: Christianizing the American People*. Cambridge, MA: Harvard University Press, 1990.
Butterfield, L. H. *Elder John Leland, Jeffersonian Itinerant*. Worcester, MA: American Antiquarian Society, 1953.
Conforti, Joseph A. *Jonathan Edwards, Religious Tradition, & American Culture*. Chapel Hill: University of North Carolina Press, 1995.
Cooper, James F., Jr. *Tenacious of Their Liberties: The Congregationalists in Colonial Massachusetts*. New York: Oxford University Press, 1999.
Copeland, David A. Foreword to *The American Revolution and the Press: The Promise of Independence*, by Carol Sue Humphrey, ix–xvi. Evanston, IL: Northwestern University Press, 2013.
———. *Colonial American Newspapers: Character and Content*. Newark: University of Delaware Press, 1997.
Corrigan, John. *Emptiness: Feeling Christian in America*. Chicago: University of Chicago Press, 2015.
———. *The Hidden Balance: Religion and the Social Theories of Charles Chauncy and Jonathan Mayhew*. Cambridge, UK: Cambridge University Press, 1987.
Cunningham, Noble E., Jr. *Jeffersonian Republicans: The Formation of Party Organization, 1789–1801*. Chapel Hill: Published for the Institute of Early American History and Culture at Williamsburg by the University of North Carolina Press, 1957.

de Certeau, Michel. *The Practice of Everyday Life*. Translated by Steven Rendall. Berkeley: University of California Press, 1984.

Den Hartog, Jonathan J. *Patriotism & Piety: Federalist Politics and Religious Struggle in the New American Nation*. Charlottesville: University of Virginia Press, 2015.

Denison, Frederic. *Notes of the Baptists, and Their Principles, in Norwich, Conn., From the Settlement of the Town to 1850*. Norwich: Manning, 1857.

DeRogatis, Amy. *Moral Geography: Maps, Missionaries, and the American Frontier*. New York: Columbia University Press, 2003.

Deweese, Charles W. *Baptist Church Covenants*. Nashville, TN: Broadman Press, 1990.

Dinkin, Robert J. *Campaigning in America: A History of Election Practices*. New York: Greenwood Press, 1989.

Eaton, W. H. *Historical Sketch of the Massachusetts Baptist Missionary Society and Convention, 1802–1902: With an Appendix and Other Related Matters*. Boston: Massachusetts Baptist Convention, 1903.

Esbeck, Carl H. "Disestablishment in Virginia, 1776–1802." In *Disestablishment and Religious Dissent: Church-State Relations in the New American States 1776–1833*, edited by Carl H. Esbeck and Jonathan J. Den Hartog, 139–80. Columbia: University of Missouri Press, 2019.

Espinosa, Gastón. "Religion and the Presidency of William Jefferson Clinton." In *Religion and the American Presidency: George Washington to George W. Bush with Commentary and Primary Sources*, edited by Gastón Espinosa, 431–69. New York: Columbia University Press, 2009.

Formisano, Ronald P. "Federalists and Republicans: Parties, Yes—System, No." In *The Evolution of American Electoral Systems*, edited by Paul Kleppner et al., 33–76. Westport, CT: Greenwood Press, 1981.

———. *The Transformation of Political Culture: Massachusetts Parties, 1790s–1840s*. New York: Oxford University Press, 1984.

Foster, Charles I. *An Errand of Mercy: The Evangelical United Front, 1790–1837*. Chapel Hill: University of North Carolina Press, 1960.

Gardner, Robert G. *Baptists of Early America: A Statistical History, 1639–1790*. Atlanta: Georgia Baptist Historical Society, 1983.

Gaustad, Edwin S., Philip L. Barlow, and Richard W. Dishno. *New Historical Atlas of Religion in America*. New York: Oxford University Press, 2001.

Goen, C. C. *Broken Churches, Broken Nation: Denominational Schisms and the Coming of the American Civil War*. Macon, GA: Mercer University Press, 1985.

———. *Revivalism and Separatism in New England, 1740–1800: Strict Congregationalists and Separate Baptists in the Great Awakening.* Middletown, CT: Wesleyan University Press, 1987.

Goodman, Paul. *The Democratic-Republicans of Massachusetts: Politics in a Young Republic.* Cambridge, MA: Harvard University Press, 1964.

Greene, L. F. "Further Sketches of the Life of John Leland." In *The Writings of John Leland,* edited by L. F. Greene, 41–72. New York: Arno Press, 1969.

Guild, Reuben Aldridge. *Life, Times, and Correspondence of James Manning, and the Early History of Brown University.* Boston: Gould and Lincoln, 1864.

Hall, David D. *The Faithful Shepherd: A History of the New England Ministry in the Seventeenth Century.* Chapel Hill: Institute of Early American History and Culture, Williamsburg, VA, by the University of North Carolina Press, 1972.

Hall, Timothy D. *Contested Boundaries: Itinerancy and the Reshaping of the Colonial American Religious World.* Durham, NC: Duke University Press, 1994.

Hankins, Barry. *Uneasy in Babylon: Southern Baptist Conservatives and American Culture.* Tuscaloosa: University of Alabama Press, 2002.

Harper, Keith. *A Mere Kentucky of a Place: The Elkhorn Association and the Commonwealth's First Baptists.* Knoxville: University of Tennessee Press, 2021.

Hatch, Nathan O. *The Democratization of American Christianity.* New Haven, CT: Yale University Press, 1989.

Heimert, Alan. *Religion and the American Mind: from the Great Awakening to the Revolution.* Cambridge, MA: Harvard University Press, 1966.

Heyrman, Christine Leigh. *Southern Cross: The Beginnings of the Bible Belt.* Chapel Hill: University of North Carolina Press, 1997.

Hill, Hamilton Andrews. *History of the Old South Church (Third Church) Boston, 1669–1884.* 3rd ed. Boston and New York: Houghton, Mifflin and Co., 1890.

Hill, James Langdon. *The Immortal Seven: Judson and His Associates, Dr. and Mrs. Adoniram Judson, Samuel Newell, Harriet Newell, Gordon Hall, Samuel Nott, Luther Rice.* Philadelphia: American Baptist Publication Society, 1913.

Holifield, E. Brooks. *God's Ambassadors: A History of the Christian Clergy in America.* Grand Rapids, MI: Eerdmans, 2007.

———. *Theology in America: Christian Thought from the Age of the Puritans to the Civil War.* New Haven, CT: Yale University Press, 2003.

Hovey, Alvah. *A Memoir of the Life and Times of the Rev. Isaac Backus, A.M.* Boston: Gould and Lincoln, 1858.

Humphrey, Carol Sue. *The American Revolution and the Press: The Promise of Independence.* Evanston, IL: Northwestern University Press, 2013.

———. *This Popular Engine: New England Newspapers during the American Revolution, 1775–1789.* Newark: University of Delaware Press, 1992.

Jones, Horatio G. Preface to *Minutes of the Philadelphia Baptist Association, 1707–1807,* edited by A. D. Gillette, ix-xvi. Philadelphia: American Baptist Publication Society, 1851.

Juster, Susan. *Disorderly Women: Sexual Politics & Evangelicalism in Revolutionary New England.* Ithaca, NY: Cornell University Press, 1994.

Kidd, Thomas. "'Becoming Important in the Eye of Civil Powers': New Light Baptists, Cultural Respectability, and the Founding of the College of Rhode Island." In *The Scholarly Vocation and the Baptist Academy: Essays on the Future of Baptist Higher Education,* edited by Roger A. Ward and David Gushee, 50–67. Macon, GA: Mercer University Press.

Kidd, Thomas, and Barry Hankins. *Baptists in America: A History.* New York: Oxford University Press, 2015.

Kurian, George Thomas, and Mark A. Lamport, eds. *Encyclopedia of Christianity in the United States.* Vol. 3. Lanham, MD: Rowman & Littlefield, 2016.

Lambert, Frank. *Inventing the "Great Awakening."* Princeton, NJ: Princeton University Press, 1999.

———. *"Pedlar in Divinity": George Whitefield and the Transatlantic Revivals, 1737–1770.* Princeton, NJ: Princeton University Press, 1994.

Leonard, Bill. *Baptist Ways: A History.* Valley Forge, PA: Judson Press, 2003.

———. *Baptists in America.* New York: Columbia University Press, 2005.

———. *God's Last and Only Hope: The Fragmentation of the Southern Baptist Convention.* Grand Rapids, MI: W. B. Eerdmans, 1990.

Lumpkin, William L. *Baptist History in the South: Tracing Through the Separates the Influence of the Great Awakening, 1754–1787.* St. John, IN: Larry Harrison, 1995.

Marini, Stephen A. *Radical Sects of Revolutionary New England.* Cambridge, MA: Harvard University Press, 1982.

McBeth, H. Leon. *The Baptist Heritage: Four Centuries of Baptist Witness.* Nashville, TN: Broadman Press, 1987.

McBride, Spencer W. *Pulpit and Nation: Clergymen and the Politics of Revolutionary America.* Charlottesville: University of Virginia Press, 2018.

McLoughlin, William G. Introduction to *The Diary of Isaac Backus*, Vol. 1, by Isaac Backus. Providence, RI: Brown University Press, 1979.

———. Introduction to *Isaac Backus on Church, State, and Calvinism: Pamphlets, 1754–1789*, edited by William G. McLoughlin, 1-61. Cambridge, MA: Belknap Press of Harvard University Press, 1968.

———, ed. *The Diary of Isaac Backus*. 3 vols. Providence, RI: Brown University Press, 1979.

———. *New England Dissent, 1630–1833: The Baptists and the Separation of Church and State*. 2 vols. Cambridge, MA: Harvard University Press, 1971.

Miller, Perry. "Errand into the Wilderness." In *Errand into the Wilderness*, 1–15. Cambridge, MA: Belknap Press of Harvard University Press, 1956.

Morgan, Edmund S. *Visible Saints: The History of a Puritan Idea*. New York: New York University Press, 1963.

Morrison, Jeffry H. *John Witherspoon and the Founding of the American Republic: Catholicism in American Culture*. Notre Dame, IN: University of Notre Dame Press, 2003.

Najar, Monica. *Evangelizing the South: A Social History of Church and State in Early America*. New York: Oxford University Press, 2008.

Nettles, Thomas J., and Russell Moore, eds. *Why I Am a Baptist*. Nashville, TN: Broadman & Holman, 2001.

Noll, Mark A. *America's God: From Jonathan Edwards to Abraham Lincoln*. Oxford: Oxford University Press, 2002.

O'Brien, Brandon J. *Demanding Liberty: An Untold Story of American Religious Freedom*. Downers Grove, IL: IVP Books, 2018.

O'Callaghan, E. B. *A List of Editions of the Holy Scriptures and Parts Thereof Printed in America Previous to 1860: With Introduction and Bibliographical Notes*. Albany: Munsell & Rowland, 1861.

Pasley, Jeffrey L. "The Cheese and the Words: Popular Political Culture and Participatory Democracy in the Early American Republic." In *Beyond the Founders: New Approaches to the Political History of the Early American Republic*, edited by Jeffrey L. Pasley, Andrew W. Robertson, and David Waldstreicher, 31–56. Chapel Hill: University of North Carolina Press, 2004.

———. *"The Tyranny of Printers": Newspaper Politics in the Early American Republic*. Charlottesville: University Press of Virginia, 2001.

Patterson, Paige. *Anatomy of a Reformation: The Southern Baptist Convention, 1978–2004*. Fort Worth, TX: Southwestern Baptist Theological Seminary, 2004.

Pierce, Frederick Clifton. *History of Grafton, Worcester County, Massachusetts, From Its Early Settlement by the Indians in 1647 to the Present Time, 1879. Including the Genealogies of Seventy-Nine of the Older Families.* Worcester, MA: Press of C. Hamilton, 1879.

Pope, Robert G. *The Half-Way Covenant: Church Membership in Puritan New England.* Princeton, NJ: Princeton University Press, 1970.

Porterfield, Amanda. *Conceived in Doubt: Religion and Politics in the New American Nation.* Chicago: University of Chicago Press, 2012.

Ragosta, John A. *Wellspring of Liberty: How Virginia's Religious Dissenters Helped Win the American Revolution and Secured Religious Liberty.* New York: Oxford University Press, 2010.

Raynor, Ellen M., and Emma L. Petitclerc. *History of the Town of Cheshire, Berkshire County, Mass.* Holyoke, MA: C. W. Bryan & Co., 1885.

Reid, Daniel G., et al., eds. *Dictionary of Christianity in America.* Downers Grove, IL: InterVarsity Press, 1990.

Sassi, Jonathan D. *A Republic of Righteousness: The Public Christianity of the Post-Revolutionary New England Clergy.* Oxford: Oxford University Press, 2001.

Schlereth, Eric R. *An Age of Infidels: The Politics of Religious Controversy in the Early United States.* Philadelphia: University of Pennsylvania Press, 2013.

Sehat, David. *The Myth of American Religious Freedom.* Oxford: Oxford University Press, 2011.

Semple, Robert B. *A History of the Rise and Progress of the Baptists in Virginia.* Rev. ed. Edited by George William Beale. Philadelphia: American Baptist Publication Society, 1894.

Shain, Barry Alan. *The Myth of American Individualism: The Protestant Origins of American Political Thought.* Princeton, NJ: Princeton University Press, 1994.

Shannon, David T., Julia Frazier White, and Deborah Bingham Van Broekhoven, eds. *George Liele's Life and Legacy: An Unsung Hero.* Macon, GA: Mercer University Press, 2012.

Shurden, Walter B., and Randy Shepley, eds. *Going for the Jugular: A Documentary History of the SBC Holy War.* Macon, GA: Mercer University Press, 1999.

Smith, Eric C. *John Leland: A Jeffersonian Baptist in Early America.* New York: Oxford University Press, 2022.

Smith, J. E. A. *The History of Pittsfield (Berkshire County) Massachusetts: From the Year 1800 to the Year 1876.* Springfield, MA: C. W. Bryan & Co., 1876.

Sprague, William B. *Annals of the American Pulpit: Or, Commemorative Notices of Distinguished American Clergymen of Various Denominations: from the Early Settlement of the Country to the Close of the Year Eighteen Hundred and Fifty-Five: with Historical Introductions*, Vol. 6, *Baptists*. New York: Robert Carter & Bros., 1860.

Stanley, Brian. *The History of the Baptist Missionary Society, 1792–1992*. Edinburgh: T & T Clark, 1992.

Staton, Cecil P., Jr., ed. *Why I Am a Baptist: Reflections on Being Baptist in the 21st Century* Macon, GA: Smyth & Helwys, 1999.

Stout, Harry S. *The Divine Dramatist: George Whitefield and the Rise of Modern Evangelicalism*. Grand Rapids, MI: Eerdmans, 1991.

Sutton, Jerry Sutton. *The Baptist Reformation: The Conservative Resurgence in the Southern Baptist Convention*. Nashville, TN: Broadman & Holman, 2000.

Travers, Len. *Celebrating the Fourth: Independence Day and the Rites of Nationalism in the Early Republic*. Amherst: University of Massachusetts Press, 1997.

Waldstreicher, David. *In the Midst of Perpetual Fetes: The Making of American Nationalism, 1776–1820*. Chapel Hill: Published for the Omohundro Institute of Early American History and Culture, Williamsburg, VA, by the University of North Carolina Press, 1997.

Watson, Kevin M. *Pursuing Social Holiness: The Band Meeting in Wesley's Thought and Popular Methodist Practice*. Oxford: Oxford University Press, 2014.

Wills, Gregory A. *Democratic Religion: Freedom, Authority, and Church Discipline in the Baptist South, 1785–1900*. New York: Oxford University Press, 1997.

Winslow, Ola Elizabeth. *Meetinghouse Hill, 1630–1783*. New York: Macmillan, 1952.

Witte, John, Jr., and Justin Latterell. "The Last American Establishment: Massachusetts, 1780–1833." In *Disestablishment and Religious Dissent: Church-State Relations in the New American States 1776–1833*, edited by Carl H. Esbeck and Jonathan J. Den Hartog, 399–424. Columbia: University of Missouri Press, 2019.

Wood, Nathan E. *The History of the First Baptist Church of Boston (1665–1899)*. Philadelphia: American Baptist Publication Society, 1899.

Wright, Conrad Edick. "Institutional Reconstruction in the Unitarian Controversy." In *American Unitarianism: 1805–1865*, edited by Conrad

Edick Wright, 3–30. Boston: Published Jointly by the Massachusetts Historical Society and Northeastern University Press, 1989.

Wright, Stephen. *History of the Shaftsbury Baptist Association, 1781–1853: With Some Account of the Association Formed from It, and a Tabular View of Their Annual Meeting: to Which Is Added an Appendix, Embracing Sketches of the Most Recent Churches in the Body, with Biographic Sketches of Some of the Older Ministers, and the Statistics of Most of the Churches Ever in the Association and Their Direct Branches to the Present Time.* Troy, NY: A. G. Johnson, 1853.

Journal Articles

Birdsall, Richard D. "The Reverend Thomas Allen: Jeffersonian Calvinist." *New England Quarterly* 30, no. 2 (June 1957): 147–65.

Breen, T. H. "An Empire of Goods: The Anglicization of Colonial America, 1690–1776." *Journal of British Studies* 25, no.4 (October 1986): 467–99.

Buckley, Thomas E. "Evangelicals Triumphant: The Baptists' Assault on the Virginia Glebes, 1786–1801." *William and Mary Quarterly* 45, no. 1 (January 1988): 33–69.

Butler, Jon. "Enthusiasm Described and Decried: The Great Awakening as Interpretative Fiction." *Journal of American History* 69, no.2 (October 1982): 305–25.

Cooper, James F., Jr. "Enthusiasts or Democrats? Separatism, Church Government, and the Great Awakening in Massachusetts." *New England Quarterly* 65, no. 2 (June 1992): 265–83.

Cushing, John D. "Notes on Disestablishment in Massachusetts, 1780–1833." *William and Mary Quarterly*, 3rd series, 26, no.2 (April 1969): 169–90.

Dreisbach, Daniel L. "Mr. Jefferson, a Mammoth Cheese, and the 'Wall of Separation between Church and State': A Bicentennial Commemoration." *Journal of Church and State* 43, no. 4 (September 2001): 725–45.

Harper, Keith. "Downwind from the New England Rat: John Taylor, Organized Missions, and the Regionalization of Religious Identity on the American Frontier." *Ohio Valley History* 9, no. 3 (Fall 2009): 25–42.

Hicks, Jacob. "Baptist Churches as a Training Ground for Young Men's Political Activism in Late Colonial and Early National Massachusetts." *Baptist History and Heritage* 57, no. 1 (Spring 2022): 25–35.

Imholt, Robert J. "Timothy Dwight, Federalist Pope of Connecticut," *New England Quarterly* 73, no. 3 (September 2000): 386–411.

Le Clercq, Frederic S. "Disqualification of Clergy for Civil Office." *Memphis State University Law Review* 7, no. 4 (Summer 1977): 555–614.

Neem, Johann. "The Elusive Common Good: Religion and Civil Society in Massachusetts, 1780–1833." *Journal of the Early Republic* 24, no. 3 (Fall 2004): 381–417.

Scarberry, Mark S. "John Leland and James Madison: Religious Influence on the Ratification of the Constitution and on the Proposal of the Bill of Rights." *Penn State Law Review* 113, no. 3 (April 2009): 733–800.

Silverman, William. "The Exclusion of Clergy from Political Office in American States: An Oddity in Church-State Relations." *Sociology of Religion* 61, no. 2 (2000): 223–30.

Thomas, John L. "In Memoriam: William G. McLoughlin." *American Quarterly* 45, no. 3 (September 1993): 425–28.

Todd, Obbie Tyler. "Baptist Federalism: Religious Liberty and Public Virtue in the Early Republic." *Journal of Church and State* 63, no. 3 (Summer 2021): 440–60.

Dissertations

Broadway, Mikael. "The Ways of Zion Mourned: A Historicist Critique of the Discourses of Church-State Relations." PhD diss., Duke University, 1993.

Creed, John Bradley. "John Leland: American Prophet of Religious Individualism." PhD diss., Southwestern Baptist Theological Seminary, 1986.

DeSorbo, Frank A. "The Reverend Thomas Allen and Revolutionary Politics in Western Massachusetts." PhD diss., New York University, 1995.

Shurden, Walter B. "Associationalism among Baptists in America, 1707–1814." PhD diss., New Orleans Baptist Theological Seminary, 1967.

South, Dale R. "Saved for God's Possession: Recovering the Gospel Among Southern Baptists by Guarding against its Syncretization with Autonomous Individualism." PhD diss., Southeastern Baptist Theological Seminary, 2017.

Strange, Sammie Pedlow. "Baptists and Religious Liberty: 1700–1900." PhD diss., Southern Baptist Theological Seminary, 2006.

Miscellaneous

Harper, Keith. "Thomas Jefferson, North American Baptists, and . . . *Home Missions*? Reflections on Unintended Consequences." Unpublished paper. In the author's possession, 2016.

INDEX

Adams, John, 74–76, 96–99
Adams, Samuel, 67, 70, 74
Alden, Noah, 13, 15, 33, 54, 159–60n73
Allen, Thomas, 78, 106–7
American Board of Commissioners for Foreign Missions (ABCFM), 113, 131–33
Andover Theological Seminary, 120–24, 126, 131–32, 134, 187n30–31
Anglicanism. *See* Anglicans
Anglicans, 33, 68, 84–87, 114, 128
Antifederalism. *See* Antifederalists
Antifederalists, 88–90
Ashfield case, 69–73

Backus, Elizabeth, 39–40
Backus, Isaac, primarily chapters 1 and 2
Baldwin, Thomas, 114, 117, 129, 133, 188n41
Barnes v. Falmouth, 108–9
Beecher, Lyman, 125–27, 189n54
believer's baptism, 14, 16–17, 29, 53, 69, 123, 133, 162n17, 188n41
Bentley, William, 79–82, 173n6, 178n55, 182n112
Berkshire County (Massachusetts), 1, 101, 105–7, 177n49, 182n108
Bill of Rights, 89–90, 92, 176n35
Brady, Tom, 67

campaigns/campaigning, 29–30, 88, 97–98; 146, 154n15, 180n73
Carey, William, 128, 133, 189n58, 191n73
Cheshire, Massachusetts, 1–2, 7, 93, 95, 100–106, 108, 150n25, 177n49, 181n87, 191n76,79
church covenants, 18–20, 155n26
church discipline, 14, 18–19, 24, 34–35, 148n9
Clinton, Bill, 154n15
Committee of Cheshire, 1
communitarianism, 4, 8–9, 23, 151n30
Connecticut Missionary Society, 129
credobaptism. *See* believer's baptism

Danbury Baptist Association of Connecticut, 2, 80
Davenport, James, 21, 23, 27
De Certeau, Michel, 10, 43, 45, 82, 95, 157n41, 162n17, 173n9
Dedham case, 111–12
Democratic-Republicans, 1–2, 7, 81, 96, 99–100, 105–9, 113–15, 178n55, 181n89
Den Hartog, Jonathan, 12, 96, 112, 131
Dwight, Timothy, 96, 115, 125, 132, 182n102, 187n31

Edwards, Jonathan, 20, 33, 69, 74, 106, 121, 127, 151n30, 155n32, 156n35
"empire of goods," 59, 157n47

Federal Constitution, 88, 115, 176n35
Federalism. *See* Federalists
Federalists, 1–2, 12, 24, 79, 88–89, 94–103, 106–8, 112, 114–15, 131, 147–48n6, 172n1, 178n55, 179n61, 180n76, 181n87,89, 182n102, 184n15
First Baptist Church of Bellingham (Massachusetts), 13–14, 152n4, 159n73
First Baptist Church of Boston (Massachusetts), 114, 127, 160n73, 189n54
First Baptist Church of Haverhill (Massachusetts), 31, 37, 129, 173n6
First Baptist Church of Medfield (Massachusetts), 31, 44, 73, 159–60n73
First Baptist Church of Middleborough (Massachusetts), 29, 35
First Baptist Church of Norton (Massachusetts), 34–35
First Baptist Church of Providence (Rhode Island), 18, 160n73
First Church of Hassanamisco (Massachusetts), 19–20, 155n28
First Party Era, 41, 43, 79, 90–91, 94–95
Fish, Joseph, 46, 52, 58, 164n23, 166n64
Freeman, Philip, Jr., 56, 60, 167n72, 168n73
Freeman, Philip, Sr., 56, 59–60, 76, 167–68n72, 168n73
frontier, 11, 69, 71, 80, 101, 117–18, 127–28, 134, 137, 191n76, 191n79
Frothingham, Ebenezer, 53–54, 57, 169n49
Fuller, Andrew, 127–28

Going, Jonathan, 4, 11, 122–24, 139
Grafton, Joseph, 129, 190n62
Grafton (Massachusetts), 13, 19

Half-Way Covenant, the, 15, 24, 155n32
Hatch, Nathan, 6–7, 112, 114, 149n14, 149n17, 184n8
Helwys, Thomas, 16–17
Henry, Patrick, 30, 86, 89–90, 175n23
Holly, Israel, 54, 57

imagined community, 23–24, 41, 46, 61, 81, 140
individualism, 5–9, 148n9, 149n14, 150n25, 151n29
infant baptism, 14, 17, 29, 133
infidelity, 11, 96–97, 112, 115–16, 118, 122, 124, 126, 128, 134, 137, 140, 179n61, 185n16, 185–86n20
itinerancy/itinerant, 13, 20–24, 27–28, 30–31, 47, 83, 90, 117–18, 152n4, 157n41, 157n47, 192n79

James I (of England), 16–17
Jefferson, Thomas, 1, 9, 78–79, 81–82, 84, 90, 93–94, 96–98, 117, 140, 176n35, 194n14
Judson, Adoniram, 131–33, 136, 190–91n73

Leland, John, primarily introduction, chapters 1 and 3
Leonard, Bill, 9
Liele, George, 190–91n73
Locke, John, 144
London Missionary Society, 128, 189n58
Lord, Benjamin, 28, 40, 58, 166n64

Madison, James, 10, 78, 83–91, 94, 103–4, 140, 145–46, 175n23, 176n35, 176n37, 194n14
Mammoth Cheese, 1, 104, 147n1
Manning, James, 36–38, 41, 53–55, 57, 59, 61, 64, 71, 73–74, 82, 140, 160n73, 161n96, 165n66, 173n6
Massachusetts Baptist Missionary Society, 129–30, 192n62
Massachusetts Constitution of 1780, 41, 108, 140
Morse, Jedidiah, 96, 115–16, 118, 132, 134, 182n102, 184n15, 187n31

Narratives (conversion). *See* relations
Nelson, Stephen Smith, 32–33
Nelson, William, 34–35
New Lights, 20, 24, 27–28, 69
Newport (Rhode Island), 24, 55–56, 58, 74, 164n39
Newton Theological Institution, 120, 122, 124, 190n62
North Stonington Church (Connecticut), 46, 163n23, 26

Old South Church (Boston, Massachusetts), 19, 155n27

paedobaptism. *See* infant baptism
Paine, Solomon, 54–57
pamphlets, 10, 22, 41, 48, 51–52, 56, 59, 68, 76, 98, 119, 140, 164n45, 171–72n132
petitions, 44, 61, 65, 70–72, 75, 77, 84–86, 90, 116–17, 175n23
Philadelphia Baptist Association (PBA), 36–37, 55, 61–64, 73–75, 128, 161n92, 96, 165–66n56

political ecumenism, 83, 85, 90, 105, 114, 173–74n10
Pomeroy, Benjamin, 27
Porterfield, Amanda, 12, 92, 96, 177n44, 185n16
Preaching, 3, 13, 19–24, 26, 28, 30–33, 46, 53, 63, 83, 107, 122, 125, 146, 152n4, 153n14, 157n44, 166n60, 169n61, 192n79
"print-capitalism," 22–23, 156–57n38
printing, 2, 41, 45–46, 48–52, 58, 68, 81, 116, 119
Protestant Episcopal Church (PEC), 86–87
Providence (Rhode Island), 18, 55–56, 58, 62, 66, 160n73, 164n79
Puritans, 16–17, 19, 25, 33, 118, 171n120

Quakers, 4, 6, 18, 21, 36, 44, 73–74, 78, 152–53n5, 171n120

relations, 25–27, 158n53
Religious Freedom Act of 1811, 11, 109, 140
Republicans. *See* Democratic-Republicans
Rhode Island College, 37, 48, 53, 55, 58, 61, 122, 165–66n56, 173n6
Rice, Luther, 4, 11, 132–33, 135–36, 139

Seamans, Job, 35, 160–61n87
Second Baptist Church of Middleborough (Massachusetts), 37
Separates, 21, 23–27, 29, 33, 40–41, 43, 46–47, 53
Separatism. *See* Separatists

Separatists, 16–17
Shaftsbury Baptist Association
 (SBA), 93–94, 115, 150n25,
 177–78n52, 178n54, 185n17,18,
 191–92n79
Skinner Jr., Thompson J., 106–107
Smith, Chileab, 69
Smith, Ebenezer, 69, 71–72
Smith, Eric C., 7–8, 148n8, 182n102
Smith, Hezekiah, 54, 57, 129, 167n72,
 169n90, 173n6
Smyth, John, 16
Standing Order, 10, 40, 42–43, 51,
 53, 55, 63–65, 69, 71, 75–76, 78,
 80–81, 92, 100, 108, 117, 119, 140
Stillman, Samuel, 4, 10, 15, 32–33,
 41, 52–60, 82, 114, 116–17, 129,
 139–40, 160n73, 166n60, 167n72,
 169n90, 179n61

Taylor, John, 135–37
Triennial Convention, 113, 133, 136,
 191n75

Unitarianism. *See* Unitarians
Unitarians, 79, 81, 96, 111–12, 120,
 124, 127, 140, 183n1, 184n8,
 185n18
Universalism. *See* Universalists
Universalists, 96, 108, 115, 185n18

Virginia Baptist General Committee,
 84–87, 89, 94
Virginia Ratifying Convention,
 87–88, 90
Virginia Statute of Religious Freedom,
 86–87
voluntary societies, 11, 112, 114, 118,
 122, 124–26, 134–37, 184n8

Warnock, Raphael, 182n102
Warren Association, 10, 33, 35–37, 41,
 46, 52, 55, 59–68, 71, 73–77, 81,
 85, 93–94, 115–16, 122, 128–29,
 140, 161n96, 165–66n56, 167–
 68n72, 168n73, 79, 169n84, 91,
 185–86n20
Washington, George, 2, 82, 87, 90,
 96, 125
Wayland, Francis, 114, 151n29,
 159–60n73
Wetherel, James, 34–35
Whitefield, George, 20–25, 30, 33,
 157n47
Williams, Azubah, 34–35
Williams, Roger, 17–18, 93
Winchell, James, 122
Winchester, Elhanan, 13, 185n18
Winthrop, John, 17
Witherspoon, John, 144–146, 194n14
Worcester, Samuel, 132, 188n41